BANNED BY THE BBC!

BANNED BY THE BBC!

How I Became a Radio Pirate

Arnold M. D. Levine

McCaa Books • Santa Rosa, CA

McCaa Books
1604 Deer Run
Santa Rosa, CA 95405-7535

First published in 2021 by McCaa Books,
an imprint of McCaa Publications.

Library of Congress Control Number: 2020924311
ISBN 978-1-7358074-8-5

Printed in the United States of America
Set in Minion Pro
Book design by Waights Taylor Jr.

www.mccaabooks.com

Dedication

This book is dedicated to IssHaq Habib, my grandson,
who is here because of Pirate Radio

"I can't understand the Government's attitude over the pirates. Why don't they make the BBC illegal as well—it doesn't give the public the service it wants, otherwise the pirates wouldn't be here to fill the gap. The Government makes me sick. This is becoming a Police State. They should leave the pirates alone. At least they've had a go, which is more than the BBC has done..."

—George Harrison, in an interview with Ray Coleman in *Disc* August 6th 1966.

Contents

Foreword

ONCE UPON A TIME I was so desperate to hear rock'n'roll on the radio, I'd hide under the blankets in bed with a pair of ex-Army headphones, plugged into my parents' ancient wireless set and track down the only station playing music for youth at midnight.

At last! Over the airwaves came the thrilling sound of Gene Vincent and the Blue Caps, Buddy Holly, The Everley Brothers, Little Richard, Elvis, Bill Haley and Fats Domino. Their hit records were prone to fade in and out due to the strange effects of the atmosphere. But it was worth all the desperate Bakelite knob tuning. After all, the station was based miles away from our London home, in the Grand Duchy of Luxembourg.

It was 1957 when I first heard shows like *Rocking To Dreamland* on 208 Radio Luxembourg. It wasn't that I avoided the alternatives. BBC's radio shows like *Saturday Club* or TV's *6.5 Special* occasionally featured 'live' local rock'n'roll performers. But the nation's teenagers wanted more. Not just watered down, ersatz rock. We wanted the real thing.

Even 208 wasn't enough. Hallelujah! On Easter Saturday 1964 the sound of off-shore commercial radio smote Britain airwaves, much to the concern of the Government, the BBC and the Post Office.

A rebellious crew of pirate Radio DJs on board the good ship *Caroline* moored in the North Sea began broadcasting great music that boomed loud and clear, non-stop around the clock to eagerly receptive British fans.

More pirate stations followed and by 1967 a veritable fleet of ships were playing progressive pop tracks like Procol Harum's *A*

Whiter Shade Of Pale in heavy rotation. Amidst an Establishment outcry, The Marine Offences Act was brought in that put paid to the whole glorious Swinging Sixties broadcasting revolution.

But that wasn't the *end* of free, independent radio in the U.K. as Arnold Levine explains in this fascinating account of his extraordinary aerial adventures in London in the 1970s. Turn on, tune and listen, or in this case read how he co-founded *Radio Concord*, a land-based pirate radio station that dared to blast forth from secret locations in the heart of London.

No need to climb aboard a lurching motor vessel in freezing weather and turbulent seas to spin a few groovy 45s. It could all be done in the warmth and comfort of a bedroom or even a parked car, anywhere away from detector vans and officialdom.

What fun the new pirates had! Dancing naked at Stonehenge is just one story that must be told. Yet Arnold reveals a darker side to their antics, as he tells of a forceful, unrelenting campaign to thwart their perfectly reasonable desire to establish an alternative 'community radio' service.

I well remember when Brian Harrigan, a new reporter at Melody Maker, wrote his first story, all about *Radio Concord* in 1975. As the MM's Features Editor, it seemed to me a brilliant wheeze to spend a night at the station with the staff and give a fly on-the wall account of their goings-on.

Actually, I can't say it was my idea, but it was certainly a great scoop for Brian and caused a media sensation. It also boosted enthusiasm for a form of airwave piracy that the digital era has now revived, in perfectly legitimate form, we hasten to add.

Somehow there is nothing quite like listening to a seemingly private, secretive source of music and speech that defies tradition and convention. All power to its microphones. By the way, those ex-Army headphones of mine? Only one earpiece worked. Now that's what I call dedication.

Chris Welch, London, England 2019

Intro...

SOMETIMES A LARK CAN BECOME A CAUSE, and a cause can change the world.

In these days of packed radio dials and streaming Internet, it's hard to imagine how barren the electromagnetic spectrum of Great Britain was in the early 1970s. Although the taxpayer-funded British Broadcasting Corporation (the BBC) had been founded in 1922, successive governments had continued to severely limit its broadcast breadth and content.

For instance, when I was growing up in post-war London, the sixty million inhabitants of Britain had access to only one independent commercial TV channel, and just two ad-free BBC TV channels for our viewing pleasure. Radio was similarly constrained, with only three BBC Medium-Wave (MW) channels for the entire country, and no commercial radio stations, whatsoever. With such heavy-handed control, the concept of true media choice and free speech in the United Kingdom seemed a distant dream to the young working-class lad I was back then.

The first challenge to this institutional monopoly took place in March of 1964, when the legendary "pirate-radio" ships, led by a station called Radio Caroline, dropped anchor off of Britain's coast, broadcasting great pop music 24-hours a day. For the youth of the sea-locked radio realm, this was a revelation, a treasury of new music seldom, if ever, heard on the time-and programming-limited BBC. (The ship-pirate era was delightfully celebrated in a 2009 film called *The Boat That Rocked*, which was released as *Pirate Radio* in the US.) Despite their incredible popularity, the ships themselves were (figuratively) sunk after only three years, by harsh new maritime-radio laws rushed through by the Government.

By the early 1970s, this imposition of arbitrary controls had triggered a renewed attempt to break the BBC's stranglehold. Young, idealistic, radio pirates all over the country were drawn into the struggle to free the captive airwaves. Unlike the earlier ship-based DJs, whose main worries were rough seas and bad food, the land-based pirates had not only to cobble together their own equipment in secret, but also to face the possibility of capture and arrest with every broadcast. Bravely, if a bit sporadically, transmitting from bedrooms, fields, cars, and abandoned buildings, they began to provide an honest glimpse of what community radio could become in Britain if given the chance.

My role as co-founder of Radio Concord—one of the most notorious of the "land-pirate" radio stations operating amid the social turbulence of 1970s London—became a personal life-shaping experience. Having lived a fairly "normal" and well-behaved life until 1971, I careened wildly off-course when a phone call from a friend launched events that would take me deep into the radio-based world of music, politics, squatting, and creative counterculture undergrounds.

Looking back, I can only describe my years of pirate-radio experience as a bizarre mix of genres: the antics of the Keystone Kops; the altered-state comedy of Cheech and Chong; the surrealism of Monty Python; the tenets of Karl Marx; and the documented techs-ploits of *Revenge of the Nerds*. All of these characters/situations would have fit quite well into the amusing, absurd, revolutionary, and maladroit adventures encountered by the land-pirates in our quest for more community voices, alternative music/entertainment choices, and, most importantly, free speech, on the airwaves of Great Britain.

This addictive lark led me into one startling and improbable scenario after another: broadcasting from a squatted festival at the Queen's Windsor Castle Great Park; interviewing on-the-run revolutionaries; leaping from one secret broadcast location to the next, barely ahead of the arresting authorities; interviewing and befriending rock and pop idols ("Wait—you're changing your name to *Joe Strummer*?"); crashing the Royal Albert Hall; consorting with the King of the Hippies; dancing naked at Stonehenge; and, at nearly every broadcast, dangling from treetops, tall buildings, and even the balcony of Mick Jagger's Chelsea home in search of the perfect aerial placement.

These reckless actions of my youth, entertaining and fulfilling as they were, did come with a dark side. Why did I endure having my phone tapped, or being pursued by the police, Special Branch, crime reporters, and Post Office trackers? Why did I risk being brought into court, charged with, and fined for, the dastardly "criminal act" of talking and playing music on the radio? Free speech and privacy rights come at a steep price in any age, as I found out then, and as we now know in this post-Manning, Assange, Snowden, and "Fake News" world.

So, dear readers, close your curtains, climb under the covers, and tune in to my tale of broadcast infamy. Along the way, you'll meet pirates, squatters, eccentrics, Travellers, hippies, Yippies, rock stars, fugitives from justice, politicians, police, judges, spies—and yes, even Post-Office employees—as I present this previously untold tale of the valiant land-pirates of the British airwaves. *Aaarrrgh!*

Arnold 22

Jeffrey 22

1

Pirates?

IT WAS ALL JEFFREY'S FAULT, but then, it usually was.

One evening in the autumn of 1971, I was visiting my parents' council maisonette in Parliament Hill Fields, London, when a call came in from my old school friend Jeffrey Schwarz. To my family and friends, Jeffrey was notorious for somehow tracking me down wherever I was, at any hour of the day or night, in order to tell me some news, play me a song he'd written or heard, get me into mischief, or ask my advice about some totally doolally scheme he'd end up doing anyway, whatever I said. This call, however, would change my entire life.

When I picked up the handset of my parents' old Bakelite phone in the hallway, Jeffrey, without any preamble, blurted out: "Turn on a radio and go to 235 on the Medium Wave band!" Because it was Jeffrey, I didn't ask why. Returning to the living room, I waited impatiently for my parents' sleek walnut-veneered valve-radio/record player to warm up. Carefully, with my ear pressed against the gold-flecked fabric speaker cover, I tuned into Jeffrey's wavelength.

At first I heard nothing but static, but another slight twiddle of the dial produced the sound of a faint scratchy pop song, followed by some barely audible speaking. Picking up the phone again, I told Jeffrey what I'd heard. "From what I can tell," he gushed, "it's a clandestine pirate radio station called Odyssey! They're based in South London!"

It seemed that, while idly fiddling with the radio dial, looking for *anything* but the four boring BBC radio channels, Jeffrey had run across this elusive signal. Our animated phone conversation about the implications of this news continued episodically, with me running back and forth from the hallway phone to the living-room radio, listening in crackly bursts to my very first land-pirate broadcast.

Our discovery of illicit land-based pirate radio immediately transported us back to the heady days of late March 1964, with the launch of Radio Caroline and the infamous pirate radio ships and sea forts. Their greatly expanded pop-music playlists, and up to 24-hour broadcasting, had been a revelation for our entire generation. Since August 1967, we had mourned the ships' scuppering by arbitrary laws introduced by an entrenched system still insisting on tight control of radio content.

So this was the situation in 1971: Jeffrey and I thrilling to the discovery of Radio Odyssey; meanwhile, the government-controlled BBC Radio monopoly still ruled the British airwaves, and our generation's frustration with this condition, was welling up again. But this time around there was an important difference: it was no longer just a case of the usual lack of time allotted for "Top 40" music. The evolving rock-music scene had been splintering into many different sub-genres over the last four years—underground, progressive, art-rock, glam-rock, pub-rock, and folk-rock—all of which were largely and deliberately ignored by the BBC. Even the concept of an all-1950s-60s "oldies" show was not even considered—only a few of those inspirational gems ever got played, lost amidst a mush of new record company-generated pablum.

As Jeffrey and I talked that night, the fact that pirate radio was continuing, but on land this time, and under our very noses, or rather ears, began to register more deeply with us, and questions tumbled out one after another. What was the history of these pirates? How many were there? Where did they broadcast from? Did they build their own equipment? How did they elude capture on land? What would be their fates at the hands of the authorities?

Jeffrey and I were fascinated to learn much more about this surprising and swashbuckling venture we had tuned into.

The Next Step

AT THE FIRST OPPORTUNITY after our pirate radio discovery, I drove over to Jeffrey's house on my motorbike, and we picked up the hot topic the moment I walked through the door. Within a few minutes, we were discussing the delicious possibility of becoming pirates ourselves, of buying a transmitter and creating our own radio station to broadcast all of our beloved (but banned from the BBC) music.

The potential of going on-air, just like the old radio ship pirates in the North Sea, and broadcasting to a large part of London, with the added allure of a radio anonymity that suited my shy personality, was intoxicating. The negative ramifications of our decision didn't impinge on the excitement of the moment—they'd catch up with us later.

Our first step was to get in touch with Radio Odyssey, our initial scratchy introduction to that shadowy pirate world. A discreet inquiry to the mailing address given out openly on the air, set off a careful letter/phone-call vetting of us by the Odyssey crew. A couple of weeks later, we were invited to a secret radio station meeting; the address given was located on a quiet Victorian-era, upper-middle-class plane tree-lined street near Kew Gardens.

Life with Jeffrey

JEFFREY, WHO LOOMS LARGE AS THE INSTIGATOR of the events that led me to that first clandestine-radio meeting, was the perfect friend and social foil for me in my shy formative years. I clearly recall the two of us as nervous, skinny eleven-year-olds in short trousers, standing together outside the gates of the Jewish Free School in Camden Town, on the first day of "big" school. We were fast friends from that moment, and I watched in amazement as, with ever-more eccentric exploits, in which I willingly helped or tagged along, Jeffrey transformed himself into a celebrity at school.

His parents lived in Golders Green, a middle-class suburb of London. They had come to Britain from Cologne in Germany just before the outbreak of WWII, but most of their family had perished in concentration camps. Jeffrey's father was a toy and novelty importer, who had actually introduced the first wave of those ubiquitous Troll dolls into Britain.

Growing up, I had a very shy and self-effacing personality, and was loath to do anything that would put the focus on me, as my cheeks and ears tended to blaze with uncontrollable blushes any time I was singled out. I also found speaking in public very uncomfortable, so Jeffrey's audacity and *chutzpah* allowed and inspired me to join in on antics that I would never have perpetrated, or even thought of, on my own.

To balance our relationship, in me, he had a ready made co-conspirator and appreciative audience for his madcap adventures, as I allowed myself to become a willing victim/participant/co-dependent/enabler in ever more outrageous capers. From our teens to our early twenties, we went to concerts, dances, happenings, and parties, played music, made films, shared girlfriends, and traveled together through Europe by thumb, bicycle, motorbike, boat, and car.

Jeffrey's real passion was the Cinema, and Alfred Hitchcock was his hero. His life's highlight might well have been the time that he spoke by phone to The Master at the Dorchester Hotel when Hitch was filming *Topaz* in London. Indulged with good-quality filmmaking equipment by his parents, he made numerous 8mm and Super-8 one-reelers featuring school friends. *The Tramp*, a psycho-sadistic film that Jeffrey made at age twelve, won a national film competition, resulting in a long feature on him in the *Sunday Times Magazine* colour supplement, which dubbed him the "New Hitchcock." The article was accompanied by moody pictures (taken by Lord Snowdon, no less) of Jeffrey posing nerdishly in his school uniform. During his stint at the prestigious London Film School in the early 1970s, he made a documentary entitled *Sheila*, about a homeless, violin-busking, pram-pushing, Irish Transgender woman in London. Helping on it as a gofer, grip, and gaffer was quite a learning experience for me, especially as *Sheila* was shown to much acclaim on prime-time BBC-TV.

With all this shared history, I was still primed in 1971 to be sucked into any one of Jeffrey's escapades at a moment's notice. As usual, I dove in willingly, without much thought about where it would lead or the consequences thereof. On reflection, I realize now that our friendship was much too close for comfort to the comically dysfunctional relationship in *The Hitchhiker's Guide to the Galaxy*, with me channeling the ever-cautious Arthur Dent to Jeffrey's anarchic Ford Prefect.

The BBC, BBC, BBC, and ?

EXCUSE ME FOR AGAIN STRESSING THE PAUCITY of radio stations and programming in Britain in those years, but it is, after all, the main impetus and reason for this story. For those who don't know the history, or didn't live through those times, it's imperative that I explain why Jeffrey and I, and so many others, were desperately looking for something vaguely interesting to listen to on British radio in 1971.

On our wirelesses that year, we could tune into the BBC, the BBC, the BBC, and if you didn't like that, you could listen to...the BBC! All the official MW radio channels in Great Britain had been colonized by the British Broadcasting Corporation, and there were no FM stations yet in operation.

"The Beeb" as it was also known, had had a singular influence on the social, political and cultural lives of the residents in our green isle since its establishment in 1922. Through wars, depressions, triumphs, and tragedies, it determined what performers and records got played, whose shows were produced, and the tone of all the news that was broadcast.

It was only at their own peril that political parties messed with the provocative Fleet Street press, but the newer TV and radio technology was fair game for bureaucratic control and pressure. Giving ground, slightly, to allow a single commercial TV channel in 1956, the Beeb didn't add a second TV channel of their own until 1966.

As for radio, expanding the BBC's current offerings, or allowing *any* commercial radio, was not even a serious consideration, as detailed in the self-serving *Pilkington Report* of 1962. Any new local broadcasting, it declared, would be "entrusted" to the BBC; this action was specifically taken to head off the introduction of commercial radio in Britain. Ironically, the arbitrary policy decisions of this report helped to set in motion the pirate-radio revolution of 1964; because the Beeb was quashing the present and future development of any official commercial radio system, a unique entrepreneurial opportunity was created.

Yes, in the early 1970s, the British state still clung to the airwaves with an iron grip, as if London were caught in the midst of the Blitz, and the electromagnetic waves constituted a solid substance that needed to be locked up safely inside dark buildings with thick walls. The BBC-TV and radio channels were financed by the British government through annual TV and Radio license fees, where anyone who owned a radio and/or TV, were required by law to purchase. (This is still the case; as of 2020, the combined TV/radio license fee was £175.) The General Post Office (GPO) conducted the policing of all those precious airwaves in the name of the government.

Failing to obtain the official listening license for one's radio and/or TV could have horrific Big Brother repercussions. Detector vans roamed neighborhoods in search of homes with Radio Frequency (RF) signals emanating from within, but which had no license ascribed to their address. If not let in peacefully, they were authorized to break into the house in question, and thuggishly remove the TV or radio.

The BBC's own reach was vast. Utilizing long wave (LW), and the World Service shortwave (SW) broadcasting capacity, the network's signature sound of "Big Ben" chimed night and day out of radios around the world. For some overseas listeners, it was a source of rational news, and perhaps hope in their struggles in far-away lands, or provided a small window into our western culture.

Delights of BBC's Radio Monopoly and Luxembourg

PRE-1967, ON THE MW BAND, a sticky musical confection called *The Light Programme* aired what was then, to a broad range of the public, the "popular" music of the day. Because of so-called "needle time" restrictions imposed on recorded media by the strong Musicians' Unions, bland live teenage pop shows ran for a couple of hours a day at most. In 1967, *The Light Programme*, in a feeble effort to assuage public outrage at the government-orchestrated demise of the beloved radio ship pirates, was split up and repurposed as the "Radio 1 Pop Channel."

The Light's music shows were mostly hosted by DJs left over from the first British rock, trad jazz, and skiffle waves of the fifties. This modest nod to modernity was coupled with celebrity-based appearances by variety-show performers from the fading British-music-hall and end-of-the-pier traditions. (Many seaside resorts built ornate piers, on which tourists could walk to take the sea air, and play and gamble at funfair booths. These piers often had small theatres built at their ends to provide cheap, light entertainment, usually in the form of variety shows.)

Then there was *The Home Programme*, aimed at a family audience, with music from Bing to Boone, human-interest stories, game shows, and gems such as *Desert Island Discs*. Last, but not least, *The Third Programme* featured classical music, the outra-geous *Goon Show* and *Around the Horn* comedy shows, erudite game shows, kitchen-sink dramas, news and news-related stories. It was well known that Prince Charles listened to *The Third*.

The only fairly bright, and non-BBC spot on the dial, was Radio Luxembourg, at 208 m on the MW band, which broadcast in English at night from the tiny Duchy of that name in the center of Europe. Their DJ-led mix of popular American and British music, interspersed with lively jingles and commercials, provided a much wider selection of new music than did the BBC. The reception and sound quality of Radio Luxembourg, broadcast from such a distance, notoriously faded in and out, and was subject to sunspots and other atmospheric anomalies, but late at night, under the covers, in thousands of darkened bedrooms all over southern England, kids clasped transistor radios to their ears, experiencing the commonality of the music.

As we held our collective breaths, the sound would regularly fade into static, and then surge back with a hiss, setting all of us alight with the hope that it would fade back in before the end of the song. That phenomenon became known scientifically as the "Luxembourg Effect." (In case you're wondering, the Luxembourg Effect is defined as the fact that a long/medium-wave radio signal propagating through the ionosphere can be influenced by another strong long/medium-wave transmitter. A more scientific name for it is "ionospheric cross-modulation.")

Family Life and Music Tales

LOCATION, AND FAMILY FIGURED PROMINENTLY by determining my role in all of this cultural history. The earliest memory I have of radio and popular music was in the mid-1950s, listening to Mum sing "Que Sera, Sera" along with Doris Day on the BBC as she cooked supper in our home in Kentish Town. The five-story red brick council building where I was born on May 4th in 1950, was bracketed between a main railway line and the Highgate Road Baptist Chapel. On Sundays, if the English weather so permitted, we enjoyed the combined sound of church bells, hymns, and steam trains coming through our windows.

I was blessed with good parents. Billie, my indefatigable mother, was a Pitman-trained shorthand/typist who went back to work at an estate agent then bank after I reached nursery-school age. My father, Joe, a WWII veteran, was a gentlemen's barber and had a great sense of humour, which thankfully, I inherited. Curiously enough, he worked on Fleet Street for many years, just like the old Sweeney Todd, but I don't remember meat pies being on *our* menu! My three older siblings; Ralph, Deanna, and Alan, were born and raised during the earlier, tougher times of the Great Depression, World War II, and the London Blitz, during which they'd been evacuated to Northampton and then Newburgh, Scotland. Having experienced none of that family upheaval, I lived in the relatively peaceful, but slightly impoverished calm of nationalizing 1950s Britain.

In the mid-50s, my brothers Alan and Ralph got involved in the booming skiffle music scene. Alan played the tea-chest bass, and Ralph attempted to learn the sax. The discordant noises he produced prompted Mum to order him to practice in the small clothes cupboard, where the winter coats would further muffle the sound. It was not an inspiring location for this young closet Parker, so he hung up his sax in it and reluctantly became the band's manager. The ever-morphing group, finally a trio called "The Jeridales," with Alan, and friends Jerry and Dennis Fields as members, had one #50 single, and doggedly persisted until they were in a (non-fatal) car crash in 1964. Our family got vicarious thrills from listening to them on the radio, watching Alan performing on TV, at live performances with big stars like the Beatles, and seeing him meeting celebrities like Princess Margaret.

This musical immersion at home, along with my parents' Sinatra to Streisand tastes, gave me a broad appreciation of popular music at a young age. "The Breeze and I," by Caterina Valente, with its wild arrangement, probably had the deepest impact on my youthful music-appreciation genes. The radio at home was usually tuned into the BBC's *Home* or *Third* Channels. When my parents left the room, I would switch the dial to *The Light Programme*, with the hope of catching any newer music somewhere in its thin coverage. My own musical prowess, I should mention, was minimal, although I've tootled harmlessly on recorders, ocarinas and simple flutes since the age of ten, most probably to the annoyance of my neighbours and family.

In 1961, we moved a quarter of a mile up the road to St. Albans Villas, a newly constructed council building across from beautiful Parliament Hill Fields. Coincidentally, the new structure was built on a WWII bombsite that I'd played on during many previous trips to the park. The abandoned ruins across still war-scarred London were the favourite post-war playgrounds of kids like me. In our quest to discover buried treasures, and without a thought of potential unexploded bombs and cave-ins, we'd clear debris and scramble down into dark basements to uncover and explore rooms untouched since the war.

The Fall of the British Empire

As we're now six decades removed from most of those times, I should probably share my view of the larger social-history context for the English world in which Jeffrey and I grew up.

In the 1950s, 60s, and 70s, as we were reminded on the TV news every month, Great Britain was still financially crippled by its war debts to the USA. Nevertheless, the country still held on shakily to her far-flung colonies on all the continents, including Antarctica. In the 1950s, the pupils at my Burghley Road Primary School were kept persistently informed about Britain's proud, though now somewhat teetering, dominion over these lands. The geography teacher would spin the out-of-date desktop globe so that we could see the blood-red smear of the crumbling Empire and Commonwealth lands stretching in an unbroken blur around the multicoloured orb.

From the mid-1950s onwards, the dismal gray of a reconstructing but fading empire was broken up by the brightly dressed immigrants appearing on London streets from those far-flung red splotches on that spinning globe. Drawn by the severe shortage of manpower after the war, they made their home in England, and changed the white Christian homogeneous society forever. These ethnic and cultural changes had unsettled some of the white population of Britain, which began reacting negatively to this foreign influx with grim discrimination, leading to race riots in the late 50s.

Since I was Jewish, I must admit to being grateful that this situation did provide a little relief from the usual "You killed Jesus" beatings and chants, and all the other physical abuse and bullying I endured as a kid. (Jews were the only significant minority to oppress before that sudden influx from abroad.) I credit my youthful athleticism and school sports trophies, to the frequent desperate necessity of fleeing and performing what might be called an early form of Parkour, in order to escape from gangs who wanted to beat me up. Sometimes I didn't get away...

Through all these cultural changes, the new "youth generation" was also hearing tantalizing snippets of changing music from around the world, crackling out amid news of political and social upheavals from cheap, mass-produced-in-Hong Kong transistor radios and TVs. These imported dreams, music, and ideas filled the ears and minds of millions of teens, providing the perfect antidote to our scary atomic war-threatened present, where it could all end with a four-minute warning.

In spite of these technological innovations, the strictly controlled British broadcasting system of the early 1960s had not yet grokked that it would have to change its programming and content dramatically, nor that these changes would arise from any enlightened political or creative policy, but from a more primitive source—the loud drumbeats coming from Detroit, New York, Liverpool and London—the power of the music itself.

Beatles, Pacemakers and Dreamers, Oh My!

MANY PEOPLE WHO INHABIT SPECIAL ERAS aren't often aware of their significance, but for me, London in the early 1960s was a magical time and place in which to grow up (with the side benefit of being able to gloat about those days *ad nauseum* to all the next derivative generations). A pent-up creative wave was building quietly throughout Britain, soon to manifest itself to the world in nearly every artistic avenue. That surge meant that my life would change dramatically as a young teen, and by relative chance, I actually received fair warning of what was to come on the music front.

In the summer of 1961, my uncle and aunt, Rose and Jim McEntaggert, came down with my three young cousins from

Liverpool to visit us. One evening over tea, jam butties, and bikkies, our conversation turned to the music business—a topic of great interest, as my brother Alan was performing professionally with his music group at the time. They spoke of the many Liverpool bands they knew, and I vividly remember them telling us about the up-and-coming "Mersey Beat" (often abbreviated as simply "Beat") music scene up North. They reeled off some band names that I soon forgot, but I remember their friendly finger-wagging advice to: "Watch out for the Scouse groups one of these days!" Unimpressed, we took all this news with a pinch of salt, as Liverpool was not usually considered a place where *anyone* came from.

Soon after that visit, Alan's cabaret-style group began to appear on TV and radio shows, and they found themselves performing alongside these newer, rougher, Beat groups from unfashionable parts of England. Bands in this new genre blended an American rock & roll-type synergy, combining it with their own talents and British-Isles cultural background, with its unique echoes of folk, trad jazz, skiffle, and music hall.

I, like many others, claim that October 5th, 1962 was the starting day for the amazing changes to come. On this date, The Beatles released their first single, "Love Me Do." When my friends and I heard it on the radio and took in the punny name of the band, we knew it was something very different from the usual Tin Pan Alley pap. The Fab Four's funny brash edge and grittiness, had us roaring with delight. Heavens! British boys with outrageously long hair, playing a bluesy harmonica on TV! The Establishment shuddered.

The Cavern Club, we read, had become a musical shrine. Concerts were chaotic scream-fests. The ensuing "Beatlemania" craze was to utterly bowl over the Ameri-centric British music industry. With a shock, I realized that my relatives, the McEntaggerts', talk of a Mersey-music tidal wave, the prediction we'd arrogantly scoffed at nearly two years ago, was coming true. Group after group from Liverpool, Manchester and beyond, rattled south in their rusty Bedford vans, following the yellow-brick road of the newly opened M1 motorway to London. Many of these callow youths were already spinning out hit-after-catchy-hit songs, seemingly penned with ridiculous throwaway ease from those new homegrown songwriting demigods Lennon and McCartney, and by other kids like them. All these bands were, of course, hoping to be blessed by BBC Radio and TV with a place in those institutions' tight programming schedules.

With all eyes and ears on Liverpool, the Beat music craze also opened the doors for other creative forces to break through: acerbic playwright Alun Owen; feisty comedian Jimmy Tarbuck; an art-rock band called The Liverpool Scene; Scaffold, a comedy, poetry and music trio featuring Paul McCartney's younger brother Mike—all of these emerged into popular view. Goodness, even Harold Wilson—yes, "Mr. Taxman" Wilson—became the Labour Party Prime Minister!

The old British class system was being shaken to its calcified roots; *anyone* could be a rock & roll star! Walking down any street in London at that time, I was likely to hear emanating from at least one front parlour, the painful birth pangs of some hopeful band. Religious and political figures, when questioned about the possible effects of all this on the country's moral fiber, just sputtered. Parents began to mock the songs of their besotted children, especially taking glee in parodying the "Yeah, Yeah, Yeah" refrain in "She Loves You," as if to deride its vacuity. But that meant to us they were noticing, and it became a holy mission to defend our idols' integrity, hairstyle, hygiene, and musical prowess.

Schoolwork. Hah! I couldn't concentrate on anything else but this growing phenomenon. As I eagerly read all I could about the scene, music became my escape and the glue of my life. The dancing that accompanied the great sounds also brought me delightfully closer to the thrilling proximity of *girls*. Girding my loins with Carnaby Street's flamboyant and stylized "Mod" fashions, I was ready to follow this revolution anywhere.

Once the Southern R&B groups caught up with the northern Beat-music revolution, it seemed as if, on any given day in London, I could walk down a street and bump into a Kink, crash a party and see a Stone, go to a pub and see a Who, then dance in a club, and shake hands with a Beatle, because all those things happened!

Style Becomes Everything…Except at the BBC

BY 1962, BRITISH MUSIC WAS SWEEPING THE PLANET through the new space-communications satellites like Telstar, and the whole connected world was watching Britain in real time. This technological advance made the path clear for other creative geniuses to blossom under the fascinated attention newly re-focused on these ancient shores. Mary Quant's mini-skirt sales were rising along with their hemlines, reflecting the country's concurrent new sexual freedoms and growing demands for women's rights. Trendy British films with Julie Christie, Tom Courtney, and Rita Tushingham— all transplants from the newly vibrant British theater— excelled at the box office. Vidal Sassoon, in his West End salon, was snipping exciting new geometric styles that complemented those innovative Carnaby Street mod clothes.

The most startlingly simple revolutionary blow to the establishment and its fashion conformity, was the global reaction to the mop-top haircuts given to the Beatles by a young woman named Astrud Kirchherr in Hamburg. Somehow, four grown men sporting a kids' "puddin'-basin" hairdo managed to shake the status quo to its core. Hair length became a generational power struggle and rallying point for male youth at school or work. What if the Beatles had had regular haircuts? Would they have made the same waves in the world? (Since I was cursed with naturally frizzy hair, I was not fashionable when straight hair ruled the day. By the time the "Afro" came into style in the early 1970s, I had already lost a lot of my top hair and so was unable to embrace that contemporary extravagance.)

With all this wonderful art and craft emerging, and especially with Beat music leading the way, the British radio system would have been the obvious organ to celebrate this unique homegrown music phenomenon, and embrace its easy dissemination o'er land and sea. To our frustration, notwithstanding, the decrepit trolls at the BBC virtually ignored this huge generational shift, keeping to their strict "needle time" restrictions on popular music. Existing contracts with musicians' unions still required live union musicians on most shows, thus the airing of newly recorded pop music was squeezed into a couple of hours a day at best. Astonishingly, as most of the known world was lapping up the "British Invasion," listening to our beloved new music on their radio's day and night, yet in Britain, we couldn't hear the music on our own wirelesses!

Was there *anything* that was going to break or change this government-controlled impasse, and give the baby-boomer generation the music that it wanted? Despite the huge British commercial-music success washing around the world, the stodgy BBC refused to change their policies and programming. After all, the big mackerels must have reasoned amongst themselves, what power did kids have? Their parents, not those longhaired scruffs, were the ones who paid taxes and laid out for the annual TV and radio licenses. As a result, the cozy "old-boy" network at the BBC churned on as always, not yet realizing that this phenomenon was way bigger than their narrow view of the world. Something had to give.

Rescued by Pirates!

BE STILL, MY BEATING HEART! On March 28th, 1964, over a year after the onslaught of Beatlemania in Britain, when we thought the music scene had already reached its height, an entirely new phenomenon launched itself—thereby sealing my fate as a future outlaw. "*Aaarrgh!* Jim lad! Pirate-radio ships, me hearties!" Every school-kid's fantasy had come true, and it was way too much: genuine, sailing-on-the-high-seas, pop-music-playing radio pirates! Yesssss! The world was good, and anything was possible.

Up to that point, Pirate Radio Veronica had been broadcasting to Europe from a ship beaming from off Holland for a year or so, and the very first pirate ship, Radio Mercur, anchored off Copenhagen, still served Denmark without any significant governmental intervention.

Irishman Ronan O'Rahilly, who owned the proposed Radio Caroline, (named for JFK's daughter), was the first to comprehend the incredible potential of this form of mass communication for pop-radio-barren England. Buying a rust-bucket called *Fredericka*, he fixed it up for broadcasting on the high seas and recruited fresh British and American DJs.

Ronan, you see, had discovered a loophole in the regulations set out by the old British Wireless & Telegraphy Act of 1936, and, by old Father Thames, he was going to exploit it. His revolutionary plan was to moor the ship beyond the official three-mile-offshore international limit, at a place where the Thames Estuary meets the North Sea. The bow-to-stern antenna operating on 199 MW beamed its powerful frequency towards the crown-jewel listening audience of London and the Home Counties, and Radio Caroline began to broadcast in earnest.

"Emperor Rosko" (Mike Pasternak), an original Radio Caroline DJ, estimates that their audience ballooned from zero to twenty-three million listeners within a few weeks of that first broadcast. The BBC's stale format and time-limited programming was suddenly revealed as dry, stuffy and *old* in comparison to this vibrant upstart. Hearing about this new craze on the TV and in the newspapers, listeners avidly switched their loyalties. O'Rahilly had not only surfed successfully through the maritime laws, but he was able to exploit another vital financial and legal factor: beyond three miles out, the pirate ships were not liable to pay Britain's (or any government's) Broadcasting Rights and Royalty payments.

As soon as Radio Caroline's success became apparent, and by the time the torpedoed British government knew what was happening, many other entrepreneurs had taken note of this incredible potential. Within weeks, Radio London, Radio England, Radio Invicta, Radio Essex, Radio 390, Radio Atlanta, Radio North Sea International, and dozens more had sailed through this Bermuda Triangle in the law, although some (just figuratively) quickly sank without a trace, mainly from lack of ad revenue and poor equipment. These newer pirates moored their barnacled ships further up and down the coast, beaming strong MW signals into the Southeast-England radio market.

A few months after Caroline started, some daring entrepreneurs had the brilliant idea of taking up residence on the old tripod-like WWII sea forts built atop sandbanks out in the Thames Estuary, to defend Albion against invasion. One of those pirates was Reg Calvert, a successful rock-band manager, who set up wild rock singer Screaming Lord Sutch, (he was actually the Third Earl of Harrow) and serial parliamentary candidate, who ran against whoever was Prime Minister at the time, to reign over his own "Radio Sutch," for a short, but quite sublime gig. It wasn't long, however, until the outrageous peer got bored with his castle and huge moat, then fled to California, whereupon Calvert reconstituted the station and renamed it Radio City.

This move ultimately led to a dark chapter for pirate radio. When in the midst of nefarious pirate station mergers and intrigue, including a literally piratical boarding and take-over of his station, Calvert was shot and killed the next day, onshore, by Oliver Smedley, the former owner of a rival offshore station, Radio Atlanta. This lurid episode only gave the government another excuse for moving quickly to enact new broadcast laws.

During this on-air expansion, several pirate stations miscalculated and hijacked a sea fort within the three-mile limit. The British Navy were not amused, and, with an overblown show of strength against a few frightened DJs armed with nothing more lethal than some James Brown singles, the brave forces boarded the hulks and retook possession for the ruffled Queen.

For three thrilling years, the chilly seas bristled with MW antennas aiming their amplitude output, first at England, and then towards Holland, Belgium, and France. As the pirate MW band became more crowded, some ships started moving further up the coast into the North Sea, where they could serve Scotland and Northern England. Finally, there were even Irish Sea pirates beaming into the Liverpool, Manchester, Glasgow, Belfast, and Dublin conurbations. The new Labour government was embarrassed.

Questions were asked of the Prime Minister by MPs in Parliament, demanding action against this airborne anarchy that challenged the very foundation of the BBC and government censorship and control. This public pirating of the British airwaves could not go unchallenged, and official propellers began to churn by the River Thames.

Meanwhile, back on the boats, the pirates were delivering American-style DJ radio, the likes of which we had never heard before. This was definitely not the boring BBC or feeble Radio Luxembourg. The pirate DJs, with on-air styles ranging from amusingly manic to smoothly laid-back, played and said anything they liked. Dozens of new bands and singers that were debuted on the pirate ships began their climb up the British charts. Soul music that transcended the safe "Top 40" Motown hits also gained traction. Late at night, informed platter-spinners brought us excellent jazz, folk, and later, underground music, a cornucopia of delights. This format was mixed in with cute station-branding jingles to ensure our loyalty, and sprinkled with catchy commercials to make it all work. The pirates competed amongst themselves to develop the most popular radio personalities, thus gaining fan support to increase their ad revenue potential.

The music played by the ship-based pirates became the most important thing in the world to my friends and me. I made a hole in the inside of the side pocket in my school jacket, ran a small earphone wire up to my ear, and snuck my little transistor radio into classrooms. During any class, it looked like I was innocently leaning on my hand, but instead, just like many of my classmates, I was raptly listening to the pirates.

The BBC obviously didn't report much about this exciting but taboo challenge to their authority, but I scoured the newspapers daily and often checked the "Top 10" pop-music charts—now published three times a week because of the huge interest in them—for the latest tidings. My musician brother Alan usually had the weekly *Melody Maker* or *New Musical Express* lying around, so I could also keep up with their mounting coverage. The pirates' edgy cast of DJs played directly to us teenage baby boomers from expansive playlists; soul, funk, bluebeat, ska, folk, Beat and alternative rock filled the air. The pirates increased their success by stretching their broadcast times from 12 to 24 hours a day, *so* unlike creaky "Auntie Beeb," who still went to bed at 10 PM.

The government tried to convince the public that these broadcasts were interfering with legitimate critical maritime communications (they were not); told us it was a crime to listen to them; and even arrested a few people for that heinous action! Such feeble censorship attempts merely demonstrated how out of touch they were with this new generation. How could kids take their petty edicts seriously? The radio pirates' defiant stand (or float) bred in my generation of British teens a powerful sense of rebellion against the monolithic government machine, one that no straightforward party politics would ever quell. The pirates loved flaunting their newfound kid-power and massive popularity. Radio London and Caroline set up wildly successful weekly live shows at club venues in the center of London, bringing their rebellion to just a short walk from the BBC's Bush House headquarters and the Houses of Parliament.

After a couple of years, and with increasing government legal machinations to plug the gaps in its tattered laws, the Government had some success against the pirates by putting pressure on their domestic advertisers, or suppliers. Only the hardiest and better-funded pirate stations ultimately managed to build stable advertising and fan bases, yet still remain in action against those draconian odds. Despite this financial squeeze-play, the public's continuing and overwhelmingly positive response to this new form of entertainment kept the boats afloat and helped them play out their fate. With legal measures becoming increasingly disruptive, however, the pirates knew it was only a matter of time until their final demise.

Swinging London

THE SHIP RADIO PIRATES didn't invent the term "Swinging London," but they certainly helped promote and spread it across Britain, Northern Europe and the Americas. That ubiquitous phrase was coined by *Time* magazine in 1966 to encapsulate the creative and sexual renaissance that had made London the capital of the *cool* world in the 1960s. This was evidenced by the growing multicultural influx of expectant youth to these ancient shores.

The growth of the Beat music craze, and then the arrival of the ship pirates pumping out its great songs, led to an immediate increase of dance clubs to accommodate that interest, and clubs began staying open—day and night—seven days a week. Clubs like Tiles on Oxford Street were open every day at lunchtime for youths to dance, and perhaps catch a quick snog and knee-trembler. These dance clubs often openly accommodated a free sexuality by providing backrooms, dark corners, and/or mattresses for no-strings sexual contact of all kinds.

The club that had the fondest memories for me was called the "Country Club" (Please ignore the image evoked by the name, it being a World War II-leftover corrugated rusty-metal-arched Nissen [Quonset] hut located behind Belsize Park Tube Station). In 1963 I went there for the first time to see the Rolling Stones. Their first single, "Come On," had just been released and was getting a lot of London buzz, and although they were still playing small clubs, the Stones were clearly shaping up as the anti-Beatles. The management had squeezed way more than the legal limit of excited teens into the club, and when the show started, pandemonium began. I'd never had so much fun.

After that experience, I returned to the club nearly every Saturday and Sunday. The tame synagogue dances and spin-the-bottle house parties I could have been attending, paled in comparison with the excitement and energy at that Stones gig, and many later shows. If there was no live act at the club, or in between live sets, a DJ played great new music for dancing. This, of course, gave all of us hormone-laden teenage boys the opportunity to humiliate ourselves by asking girls to dance and getting rejected in front of our friends.

The very next time I went to the Country Club after seeing the Stones, I had my first "real" passionate kiss with an exotic gypsy princess with olive skin and long, curly raven hair. After we'd explored the chemistry of fast Beat-dancing together, I experienced my first achingly erotic slow-dance (accompanied by a simultaneous raging hard-on) as we kissed deeply on the darkened dance floor.

At fourteen, I met a girl called Beatrice, an experienced eighteen-year-old from the East End, who looked a bit like Sandy Shaw in the right light. After we'd danced and laughed a bit, I asked her to go "round the back." Nodding, she took my hand and led me through a red velvet curtained door. Inside the dark room, we tip-toed over engrossed couples to claim some space behind an unused drinks bar, where, on the floor, with soul music crashing through the curtains, I thrilled to my first complete sexual ecstasy.

Dancing was integral to the music, with "the Twist," a sensation around the world in the early 1960s, followed by gyrations like "the Locomotion," "the Frug," "the Hitchhiker," and "the Shake." The daring British entry was "the Philip," based on the penchant of Prince Philip, the Queen's husband, to walk around bent slightly forward from the waist with his hands clasped behind his back! Thankfully, this was a minor contributor to the *oeuvre*.

Mind-altering substances were also, it need hardly be said, *de rigueur*. It was fairly easy to get a pint in almost any pub in London if you were pubescent, dressed smartly, and behaved yourself. With no official photo IDs required in Britain, how old was anyone? Oddly enough, it was much more difficult getting into an 'A-' or 'X-'rated film at the local fleapit than down a beer!

Inevitably, this cultural revolution also had its dark side, with the introduction, in those early days of the Beat craze, of amphetamines, tranquilizers and other trendy pills on the scene. Uppers were taken to help dance and party all night, and downers at every other time. Pills called "Purple Hearts," and "Black Bombers" became part of the youth argot, and too many kids did a lot of damage to themselves and others with them. I tried some pills, but they didn't do much for me, as I had enough energy to dance all night anyway. There were also hints of the growing presence of marijuana in the community, with stories in local newspapers of persons arrested for possessing "sweet tobacco." It wasn't until I went to Paris in 1966 that I found myself sitting with a collection of other ne'er do-wells on the steps of the *Sacre Coeur*, gazing in fascination out over the "City of Lights" below, that I shared hash and kif.

Banned by the BBC!

Well! The stodgy government-funded BBC was certainly not going to compete for a place in the lurid side of Swinging London, with its outrageous social behavior. Talk about sex and drugs did become somewhat freer in British society, in part, I believe, because of the increased broadcast exposure from pirate radio ships. The freewheeling and less-censored playlists of music had apparently opened the minds of the previously stoic British public to some verbal and emotional freedom. Contemporaneously with these changes, members of Britain's money-strapped upper crust were reeling from lurid political and spying scandals, and, with the Labour party now in control, the time was ripe for all that emotional energy to emerge in British music.

Even with these new social mores sweeping the nation, most pop music still relied on traditional "moon-in-June" sentiments, though now wrapped up in a shiny rock & roll package. There were a few bands, nevertheless, that consciously or subconsciously pushed the boundaries of sexual or drug innuendo to reflect their life experiences or fantasies. If a song was deemed too risqué for the airwaves, the BBC's unilateral vision of public decency reigned, and the song would be banned from broadcast. Even though such bans were meant to be an admonishment, in fact, they mostly became a badge of honour for the censored musicians and their fans. Ironically, in response to the BBC's flaccid rulings, the publicity generated by a banned song usually translated into a monetary bonanza for its performers and/or record company.

Presumably, Auntie Beeb's censorship was intended to protect her youthful listening citizenry's fragile morality and stop the entire country from throwing off its collective clothes and rampaging wildly in the streets. Early proto-punk songs such as The Kinks' "All Day and All of the Night," that suggested sleeping together "all night," and The Troggs' "I Can't Control Myself," a sexual howl of a song, fell afoul of such arbitrary determinations. Even Carole King's "I'm Into Something Good," as rendered harmlessly by Herman's Hermits, was considered too suggestive to play! A few years later, similar exclusions banned (supposedly) drug-referencing songs such as the Byrds' "8 Miles High," and the Beatles' "I am the Walrus." Following a BBC song-ban, the ship pirates, in a two-fingered broadcast broadside, would play the song all the more, mocking the BBC for their fear of a youth culture they didn't understand. (This arbitrary content control by the BBC continues to the present day.)

The British Empire Strikes Back

ALL THROUGH THE PERIOD MARKING this sea change in cultural and social life, the British Government never ceased its attempts to stop the floating radio pirates from operating. They were not allowed to land in Britain for supplies or DJ rotations, and even tougher laws were passed forbidding the participation of British-based advertisers. As a result, those pirates who couldn't secure supplies or advertising revenue from European sources sank quickly into history, leaving only static on the dial to inform us of their fate. The legal process against the pirates culminated in August 1967, with the new Marine Wireless and Telegraphy Act that closed most of the loopholes in the old law. Broadcasters who defied the new law were subject to nasty fines; a few ship-owners even received short prison sentences as a warning to others.

The vast popularity of the pirates generated a massive upwelling of listener support during this extended battle. An excellent anthem-like pop song, "We Love the Pirate Stations," by a group called The Roaring 60s made the charts. The politicians' hearts, alas, were not moved by this unique musical plea, and the government didn't budge from its hard-nosed stance. Following the enactment of "The Act," the British military forcibly evicted all the sea-fort stations from their perches. Many of the boats sailed away towards other, more accommodating, West European or even Mediterranean waters. A few of the now-law-defying pirate broadcasters stayed on for a few months, but at last had to admit defeat.

This mass scuttling created a glut of now out-of-work, top-class, hot DJs seeking work in a very limited market, and the delighted Beeb welcomed them to its bosom with open arms. Many of the pirate DJs, not wanting to be classed as criminals who could never work in Britain again, allowed themselves to be hired (to great fanfare) by the BBC to stock their new Pop-music-only Radio 1. Created, as mentioned before, as a sop to fans of the pirates, and to show that the BBC had listened to their complaints, Radio 1 recruited favourite pirate personalities as Kenny Everett, Emperor Rosko, Tony Blackburn, Tom Lodge, Dave Lee Travis and Paul Raven. Even at the beginning of the second decade of this new millennium, some of those veteran pirate DJs can still be heard on the BBC and other stations, evident reminders of the deep love and affection still held by many British people for that special three-year period. After the legislative sinking of the pirate ships, the BBC once again had no legal competition on any radio band, and with this comfortable broadcast monopoly, it was relatively easy to get listeners to transfer their pirate loyalty back to the new and old BBC-radio channels.

By making the bold swashbuckling ship-pirates walk the plank, the BBC and the Government had reasserted their grip on the radio airwaves, but this unilateral action was not going to quell the renegades' devoted fans. Westminster's heavy-handedness left behind many radio listeners who were not content to sit back and be force-fed by the State-run and-controlled media system. Unknown to the Despots of Decency, the next broadside in the battle for the airwaves—and with it the hearts and minds of our generation—was yet to come, but this time the counterattack would not come from the sea.

The End of the '60s…Take a Little Piece of My Heart

IN 1966, I LEFT SCHOOL AND SIGNED a five-year indentured apprenticeship with a mechanical contractor in Willesden Green, starting at five pounds a week less tax. My routine over those seemingly never-ending years consisted of four days per week of work and training, then one full day and two further evenings at college, plus plenty of homework. In spite of that workload, I became a "weekend hippie," making the most of free evenings and weekends to explore new underground all-night clubs like the UFO, Middle Earth and The Roundhouse, with their psychedelic music and light shows. Sanctioned pop music still ruled the pages of the conventional press and the radio and TV airwaves, so I had to be creative in seeking out alternative music and art, hearing about it by word of mouth, in the underground press, or from a random poster on a wall.

As an apprentice with little money in my pocket, I bounced between cheap rentals and my parents' home. During those bleak radio years after the pirate ships sailed off into the sunset, I tried to live my life through the memory of the "Summer of Love" ethos I had embraced so wholeheartedly. Just before Christmas of 1968, I became a vegetarian, changing more than just my Carnaby-Street fashion style to more suit the new growing environmental and social movements. The desperate pleas for environmental awareness from the "tree-huggers" made a lot of sense to me as a budding engineer, and when I looked objectively at the way we were eating up the Earth's resources, it was not sustainable in any mathematical model.

For me, the tragic closing of that magical 1960s era began on 18th September 1970 in London, and was locked shut just a few weeks later, early on the evening of October 4th in Hollywood.

On October 5th, I passed the makeshift newspaper kiosk huddled against the entry steps of St. Pancras Railway Station and noticed large black headlines on the white *Evening Standard* teaser board: **FAMOUS WOMAN ROCK SINGER DIES**.

"Oh dear, who was it now?" I said to myself. So many icons had crashed and burned since the onset of the Beatle-led cultural revolution in 1962. Reluctantly, I walked over to the kiosk and looked down at the tabloid-size newspapers piled neatly on the counter. My heart sank down to my plimsolls. "Not her! No! Not Janis!" The bored newspaper seller ignored my outburst as I gave him sixpence for the dreadful news. That bad/great woman of rock, the singer whom many of us wanted to take in our arms and protect from the world that was eating her up, was dead, just another rockstar cliché in the end. Her immense talent and future wasted, her potential barely tapped, she almost seemed to embody the youth movement she helped shape and inspire. I played her vinyl albums hard to their scratchy end, just like Janis herself.

The End of the '60s…Cry for a Shadow

SIX WEEKS BEFORE JANIS'S DEATH, I'd set off on an absurdly shambolic road trip with Jeffrey, one that took us to Amsterdam, Hamburg, Fehmarn Island, Copenhagen and Sweden. Our transportation was a 1950s rusty green Morris Traveller van that we'd bought for £40. Its main problem centered on the whole upper part of the chassis, which had rusted entirely away from the lower part. (As you'll see later in the chapter, this fact actually saved our lives.) Gravity kept it all more or less in place, but the top part of the car always tended to go in a different direction from the wheels and engine—only a minor inconvenience for two determined travelers such as we. Onboard we carried sleeping bags, as one of the van's best features were seats we could lower forward, and thus sleep inside if need be, with a tent, some clothes, a little food, and primitive cooking equipment. Luckily the MW radio still worked, so we had entertainment on our travels.

After getting off to a late start out of London due to Jeffrey's usual dithering, we made a mad race to Harwich to catch the last late ferry. The man at the gate pointed out that the ferryboat was just leaving, and that we were too late to board it. The next ferry, he said, left at 6 AM the next day. Jeffrey would hear none of such nonsense, and immediately accelerated the car across the empty wet tarmac parking lot towards the upward-inclining boarding ramp. I nervously pointed out to Jeffrey all the people running after us, shouting and waving their arms frantically, but he just shrugged it off. "It's OK" he said.

As we zoomed up the metal dock ramp at some speed, I could see the ferry looming in front of us, but to my horror, there was a nasty-looking strip of open water roiling between us and the boat, now about thirty feet away from the dock and churning rapidly seaward. "Stop the van!" I yelled at Jeffrey, overcome with a sudden vision of him trying to make the leap to the boat. After a noticeably way-too-long, long moment of hesitation, he slammed the barely usable brakes to the floor.

Puzzled passengers on the stern of the departing ferry watched wide-eyed as our car raced to the brink. Thanks mostly to the ramp's upward incline, rather than to the van's braking capabilities, our front wheels stopped just two feet from the edge of the dock and our potential watery grave. The pursuing dock workers screamed at Jeffrey: "Are you a fucking madman!?" (No reply necessary.) Jeffrey backed up somewhat sheepishly; we slept in the car, and were the first to board the 6 AM ferry the next day.

Our first goal was to wallow in the mythical fleshpots of Amsterdam, which was then at the very centre of European hipness, and afterwards press on to Hamburg. As both of us were Beatle nuts, our goal was to walk down the storied *Reeperbahn*, stroll into The Star Club and Rathskeller to see for ourselves the very stages on which the Stu Sutcliffe Beatles had learned how to "mek show" night after night and hour after hour. The influence of the Fab Four on our lives was profound; their effect on our psyches was indeed bigger than that of any god we knew.

Staying in Amsterdam for a while was quite easy; we simply crashed in old warehouses that had been specifically set up for Europe's transient traveling youth. Amsterdam at that time maintained a very benevolent attitude towards the new youth culture, and even the psychedelic clubs were set up with approval of the authorities and flourished in old churches and warehouses with names like *Melkweg* and *Paradiso*.

Inside the clubs, we could openly buy and smoke grass, hash, hash oil, and opiated hash for the first time in our lives without fear of arrest. Psychedelic music, played by live underground groups, went on all night through a haze of smoke. Walking by policemen in Dam Square while smoking a joint and they'd just say cheerfully, "Good evening!" The exhilaration was intense: had we found Sixties heaven?

When we left Amsterdam and attempted to cross into Germany at a small border post located in a pine forest in the north of Holland, the coal-scuttle helmeted guard did *not* want to let us into his country. After inspecting the van, he pointed out animatedly that our tyres were too worn, and that the van was extremely dangerous, all of which was quite true. This was where Jeffrey's fluency in German came into play; he argued politely but insistently with the guard for some time and was not going to take "*Nein!*" for an answer. At last the official reluctantly agreed to raise the thin wooden barrier and let us through, with a stern warning to buy new tyres in Hamburg.

Apart from the Berlin and Frankfurt hippie scenes, men with long hair were still a very unusual sight in Germany. While driving through the town of Oldenburg, we stopped at a large warehouse supermarket to go to the toilet and clean up. Within seconds of our entry, the sound level began to diminish noticeably. We'd gotten about halfway to the toilets when the warehouse began to take on a Twilight-Zone aura. As we passed the checkout stands, I saw the cashiers literally frozen to their places, their fingers still on the buttons of the tills as they stared at us immobile and gapemouthed. Dozens of shoppers had stopped their carts, and blatantly looked at us with clear disgust. At least no one covered their children's eyes! As we completed our ablutions we could hear the noise level outside gradually rise to its previous level, but as we exited the very clean toilets, we experienced the same descending silence and indignant stares. Smiling to myself, I internalized, "Look out folks…pretty soon your children will all be looking like us!"

On our arrival in Hamburg, we discovered that cheap accommodation was in extremely short supply. In desperation, we took up residence on a scrap of linoleum hallway at a downtown hostel. From the window on the crowded sixth floor we could see the leaden and freighter-filled River Bremer flowing to the North Sea.

Our visits to the *Reeperbahn,* and the historic rock clubs and *Bierkellers* lining the seedy street, were of course disappointing. Hamburg's entertainment district was by then, many years removed from its days of Beatle glory. I knew from Beatle biographies and photos that the clubs weren't particularly well appointed even back in 1960, and these ten additional years had been hard on the decor. The current clientele consisted of the usual drunken sailors out for some fun, and a few tourist types like us. A mediocre rock band played to desultory applause in the Star Club, and strident accordion-driven polka music filled the gaps between sets. With this atmosphere, it appeared to us that there was absolutely no chance here of a future "Klaus" stumbling into the club and discovering a new social phenomenon that would change the world. (Klaus Voormann is an artist, musician and record producer who became a mentor to the group.)

The End of the '60s…and the Gods Made Love

BACK AT THE HOSTEL, WE HEARD ABOUT the upcoming three-day "Open Air Love and Peace Festival," starting September 4th on Fehmarn Island, a sparsely populated piece of greenery in the Baltic Sea off Germany's north coast. Jimi Hendrix, Canned Heat and dozens more bands were slated to perform, and we couldn't miss it for the world. Buying a few more supplies, we set off early the next morning, the day before the festival officially started.

A small car ferry from the German mainland to Fehmarn took us to a very flat, rural, wind-swept island. Perhaps we should have been forewarned about the chaos to come at the festival by the fact there were no discernable signs pointing the way to the grounds, and that no one at the small port knew anything about it. Eventually, we came to a large field, surrounded by thick hedges, which appeared to be serving as a parking lot. The field was located next to a stage and audience area, and we duly fell in behind a short queue of cars that waited at a break in the hedge to enter.

Guarding the entrance to the parking field were about a dozen very tough-looking German Hell's Angels, looking just like— German Hell's Angels! As we drew closer, we could see the gang gathering *en masse* around the cars in front of us, rocking them back and forth and banging on their windows and chasses. A man ran by from that direction, and stopped, wild-eyed, to gasp that they were extorting money from everyone coming to the concert. Jeffrey tried to turn out of the line, but the space between the waiting cars was too small, and we were trapped as the leather-and-chain clad group swaggered up to us. We locked all our doors and rolled up the windows.

The thugs gathered around our car, shouting and banging on the roof and windows, demanding money from us. Jeffrey shouted at them in German to leave us alone, and warned them that we were from the press, but that didn't stop their attack for one moment. Opening my window just a little, I shoved out some coins and bills, hoping they would scramble for them while we could skitter away in the melee, but they wanted more.

Intensifying the car-rocking, they rattled the door handles, and the blows inflicted on the roof were visibly denting the thin metal over our heads. They pushed in one of the rear windows, and a burly Angel tried to reach our possessions in the back. Jeffrey, seeing that the path into the parking field had cleared up, slammed the car into gear and slewed wildly away through the field on the wet grass.

This, alas, did not deter the marauders. Our defiance had infuriated them, and three climbed on the bonnet and roof of the van, with others running alongside, banging the vehicle with their fists and screaming at us. Jeffrey drove desperately, speeding over the bumpy terrain that eventually, to our great relief, tumbled our uninvited passengers off. They stopped their pursuit and went back to harass the next motorists in line, leaving us shaking at the close call and hoping they wouldn't come looking for us. Two days later these same Hell's Angels killed a man at the same gate, a horrible affirmation of our fears.

When we finally made it into the festival grounds, we weren't impressed with the camping sites in the outer farmlands reserved for the attendees. Jeffrey, who occasionally worked for the BBC at that time, had a press pass that he thought he could parlay into an entrée to the backstage area that was fenced off for the performers' trailers, cars, vans, and tents. His speaking the lingo and flashing the press card somehow convinced the gatekeepers that we were covering the concert for the BBC, and they waved us in.

Ironically, this was no protection from the Hell's Angels, who regularly wandered through the backstage area as if they owned it, provocatively threatening people and stealing random items. Despite that menace, we met some beautiful people there, like Uli, an older artist from Berlin who was camping in his VW van with two young hippie chicks. As the concert finally neared its late opening, we happily joined them in smoking throat-searing hash in *chillums*.

The concept of the festival was a good idea, as on the bright side, there was actually a performing stage, but unfortunately, there were a few minor details that the promoters (Helmut Ferdinand, Christian Berthold and Tim Sievers, with the sponsorship of German sex-shop pioneer Beate Uhse), had somehow overlooked. There was no real security in place, nor any decent form of food, fresh water, or toilets closer than a half-hour's drive for the 100,000 fans gathered. The dense woods nearby offered the only latrine relief for both performers and audience. We made friends with the stage crews and helpers, and everyone shared their food supplies.

Occasionally, someone from backstage would drive along a back entry through the woods, to avoid the Hell's Angels at the main gate, and go to the nearest village for some basic necessities. All through this, amazing music, now being continuously played up on the open stage, washed over our grubby heads. If a particularly good band was playing, we'd stroll around to the front of the stage to watch from the general audience.

The music smoothed over any other minor inconveniences, such as the frequent heavy rainstorms and mud. The promoters had touted a German Woodstock, and they certainly got the weather part right. The lineup announced was stellar for such an out-of-the-way/end-of-season concert: Embryo, Limbus 4, Fich de Cologne, Alexis Korner, Ginger Bakers Airforce, Cactus, Emerson, Lake and Palmer, Ten Years After, Taste, Canned Heat, and finally Jimi Hendrix, who was arriving directly from the Isle of Wight Concert, after playing on the bill with Bob Dylan.

Jimi was to perform during the evening of the second day, but because of the torrential rain they moved his set to the middle of the third. In the early afternoon, Jimi arrived backstage in a long black car. Looking really shaky on his feet in the now-bright sunshine, he walked, helped a little by his roadies and stumbling a few times, up the wooden stairs leading to the stage. Wasting no time, we went around to the front of the stage to watch the show. By this time, Jimi was not touring as the Jimi Hendrix Experience, but as his Band of Gypsies with Billy Cox on bass, and Buddy Miles on drums. One report on his set has fabled jazz trumpeter Don Cherry joining Jimi on stage, but I have no memory of that.

For me, I have to admit, Hendrix's music set was no more than mediocre. The sound equipment was of poor quality and his performance, after a long summer season of touring, not exactly a musical masterpiece. Though he appeared very frail, when he played it was just like my first time seeing him at the Brady's Boys' Club in the East End of London in 1967. Here, at Fehmarn, a strange event occurred, now impossible to imagine, considering the god-like reverence usually accorded to Jimi.

During his set some berks in the crowd began heckling him. Heckling Hendrix! In reply, he smiled wryly, gave the noisy boors the two-handed upraised finger, mouthing silently what I presume were florid epithets, and played on. That proved to me that not even the greatest rock guitarist ever could always feed the hungry crowd-beast and/or escape its revenge when it wasn't satisfied. My theory was that many in the crowd came to see the "Purple Haze" Hendrix, but that's not who he was now. Perhaps he didn't want to be doomed to still be playing "Hey Joe" more than sixty years later, as with Mick Jagger and "Satisfaction."

As we were cooking breakfast on the fourth and last day of the rain-extended festival, we got word that something big was afoot, resulting from the Hell's Angels' murder of a fan and other stabbings at the parking-gate the previous day. The performers and their teams were also extremely upset at the promoters' poor management, and the atmosphere was turning chaotic. A friendly roadie named Ulf ran up to us, panting, "You'd better get out while you can!" We threw our tent and belongings into the back of the van, leapt in, and reversed frantically out of the backstage area, dodging people who were dashing in every direction on their own wild flight. Even as we drove out of the back gate, a band was still playing obliviously up on the stage, to an increasingly puzzled audience that was just beginning to notice the backstage commotion.

Getting clear of the temporary scaffolded backstage structures, Jeffrey spun the car around, and I glanced over to the edge of the woods that had served as our mass latrine, to see about 100 machine-gun-toting helmeted police gathered in a menacing straight line facing one side of the stage and audience. "Bloody hell! Step on it!" I shouted to Jeffrey. As we lurched forward, I heard what sounded like gunshots and, looking back, saw that smoke and flames were erupting from somewhere behind the main amplifiers.

Within seconds, the loud rock music had crackled to a stop as the conflagration increased. All those on the stage and in the backstage area were now scattering from the flames; the uniformed storm troopers seemed to take this as a signal to march forward, adding to the growing panic and confusion. Speeding away across the rough grassy field, we watched in our rear-view mirrors as the entire stage and backstage area became engulfed in flames.

Ulf the roadie had told us to meet up with him at a motel near the ferry where the musicians were staying. As we waited in the motel parking area, we watched hundreds of dazed concert-leavers straggling in to queue up for the ferry back to Germany. When Ulf and his friends showed up, we hung out in the motel's café and pieced the whole story together. Not having washed for five days, we also took the opportunity to use Ulf's room to clean up.

We were joined in the café booth by Alexis Korner, and members of his band and other musicians. Alexis, a true giant and patriarch of the British Blues and R&B movement, was already a personal hero of mine, and to spend some time with him was a true pleasure. Now sporting a thick afro hairdo, (he was white), with bushy mutton-chop sideburns like Sly Stone's, Alexis held forth in his deep, dark chocolate voice, punctuated by his husky chuckle (both probably the result of his ever-present cigarette).

By general consensus, and from information at the scene, it was determined that the fire we had witnessed had been set by the promoters, who then sped off in the ensuing confusion with the concert proceeds, without paying most of the performers or stage workers. They had not been seen near the ferry, so it was generally presumed they were hiding out somewhere on the island, and we made plans to track them down. Cars were at a premium—most of the performers and their entourages had been delivered to the island by the ferry on foot—so we offered our trusty rust-bucket to the quest.

Before long, a small caravan of searchers had left the motel carpark and fanned out onto the few roads that crossed the island. Alexis Korner and one of his roadies had piled into the back of our van, and were sprawled on our sleeping bags, so it was hard to concentrate on our serious purpose as we careened around the island's narrow lanes, laughing and singing. At one point, we stopped at a small general store in a postage-stamp sized village, and the little old apron-clad lady behind the counter was happy to engage in general chat (in German) with Jeffrey.

She hadn't seen our prey, but as we were leaving, she asked Jeffrey if we would be interested in something she had been given. Reaching under the counter, she pulled out a wad of about sixty large-sized, wonderfully psychedelic, stylized-portrait posters of Jimi Hendrix with his multicolored hair coiling like snakes all over the rectangle. It appeared that the German magazine *Der Bild*, had had them printed to promote the festival, and they'd been delivered to her little shop along with their regular magazines.

The conservative inhabitants of this burg were obviously not into Hendrix posters, so I took charge, rolled them up and stashed the loot safely in the van. The promoters were not found that day (or at least not by us!). The next morning, after sleeping in our car in the parking area, we said our goodbyes, bought a ticket on a car ferry that went north to Denmark, and, in spite of the fact that we were nearly *Deutchmark*-less, rolled on board.

Copenhagen was a clean, unthreatening old city. The hostels were full, and hotels too expensive, so we slept in the van. The *Little Mermaid* statue and the famed Tivoli Gardens were wonderful, especially under the influence of opiated Kashmiri hash offered by a cool, be-fringed Danish hippie. The only other moment of interest was when we saw Charlie Watts of the Rolling Stones with his wife and three kids in tow. (The Stones were to perform in Copenhagen that week).

Denmark was expensive, and we were nearly out of money; we didn't even have enough money to pay for petrol and ferries back to England. Apart from our bodies, our only saleable commodity was the free posters given to us on Fehmarn. After the police quickly and politely dissuaded us from illegal attempts at street-selling, we noticed a poster and card shop on The Walking

Street, and miraculously skipped out five minutes later with a bunch of money—they'd bought the lot!

Gazing beyond Copenhagen Harbor, we could see the distant shore of Malmö in Sweden, and as we now had enough cash to continue our trip just a little bit further, we took the brand-new hydroplane ferry across the narrow channel for the day. Our hippie appearance almost guaranteed that we would be pulled over by customs officials at most borders, and Sweden was no exception. Finally, since we were really strung out for time and money, the invisible elastic band that attached us to England began to pull us inexorably back. Then we hit a snafu, or, more accurately, it hit us.

The End of the '60s...Won't You Buy Me a Mercedes-Benz?

AFTER CROSSING THE BORDER FROM DENMARK into northern Germany heading towards Hamburg, we had just stopped for a red light at the crossroads of a small village, when we heard the awful sound of a desperately screeching, braking car. An agonizing few seconds later, we were struck from behind at great speed and force. Shattered glass, luggage, and camping gear hit us and flew past our heads to end up on the front windshield. This was accompanied by the tortured sound of crumpling metal and a highly revving engine. The impact propelled us into the center of the intersection.

"Are you OK?" I called out to Jeffrey; He clutched my arm, and said, "I'm all right—I think!" Both of us shook our heads to dislodge the many pieces of window glass now embedded in our hair. Surprisingly, having been at the receiving end of such a hard impact, we were unhurt apart from a few minor cuts and scratches, but still stunned by the crash. Sitting there groggily, I suddenly realized I smelled leaking petrol, and yelled: "Get out of the car!" Both doors were jammed, so we scrambled out of our broken side windows, fell to the ground, and staggered away.

Safely out of the street, we gaped at the strange sight: a large new Mercedes-Benz saloon car had crashed into the back of our van. As previously mentioned, our vehicle's upper chassis was not actually metallically connected to the bottom half. The M-B had hit our unconnected rear end, then, without stopping, had ridden up onto the back of it, crumpling, bending, and concertina-ing the metal walls and roof to an alarming extent. The distinctive M-B front grille, now partially obscured by my dirty underwear, had stopped just behind our front seats. The rusty metal may have, in fact, saved our lives, as its disconnected state dissipated the high-speed impact. Villagers and shopkeepers, on hearing the crash, came running out of the surrounding buildings to see what had happened, and then to help us.

The M-B driver was moving erratically, struggling to open the door in his car that was now hitchhiking on top of ours. Because he didn't realize he was now three feet higher off the ground than before he got in, he stepped out, and comically fell the intervening distance, face-first onto the hard road. He got up and reeled around, appearing either dazed or drunk. Police cars slewed to a halt in the crossroads. During the ensuing interview the policeman's tone towards us changed, as the other driver was telling them that the lights had been green, and that we had suddenly stopped. From what Jeffrey could pick up from the other conversations going on around us, the driver was a local bigwig, so we began to realize that the chances for a couple of hippies getting a fair shake were not good.

Official information was exchanged by all parties, and there was no question that Jeffrey's fluent German kept the police from taking too much advantage of us. A tow-truck was called, and with much groaning of metal and tinkling of glass, the M-B was pulled slowly off of the back of our comically crumpled wreck, which was then pushed noisily to the side of the road.

So, there we were, in the remote German countryside, with a shattered car that was now nine feet wide. Unloading what remained of our battered belongings, we wondered what to do next. We'd been sitting morosely on our luggage weighing our options for about twenty minutes, when a strange clanking noise from down the street startled us from our self-pitying state; we stared unbelievingly as a camouflaged military tank thundered towards us, its long gun-barrel pointed purposefully forward.

Jeffrey and I gave each other a "What the hell now?" look. Transfixed, we didn't know whether we should run or wave some white underwear. As it thundered by, the tank suddenly slewed across the road and crashed to a stop about two feet away from our battered bags. A hatch opened on the side of the tank, and a fresh young face popped up and shouted, "Need sum 'elp mates?" Our eyes widened. It was, of all things, a British tank! It turned out that we'd been traveling in the British Occupational Zone, a left-over from a WWII treaty that split up Germany among the allies. Even in its futuristic Frank Gehry-like state, our car had helped us—the tank driver had seen the GB sticker on its rear-end and stopped to assist. More heads began popping out from the tanks' other hatches.

The Tommies offered to take us to the nearest town with a railway station, so we climbed into the cramped, uncomfortable, noisy interior, met the other soldiers, and had a great time inside the hot tin box, drinking strong tea as we clattered through the countryside. When the metal monster pulled up at a station, onlookers gaped to see two dusty hippies clambering out. Bidding our saviours farewell, we took the next train into Hamburg and booked passage on the ferry from Bremerhaven to Harwich. Back in old Blighty, now minus our car, we went back to our usual work and college routines.

Jimi Hendrix went back to London after the Open Air Peace and Love Festival, played a drop-in gig at Ronnie Scott's with Eric Burdon and War, and died in the Samarkand Hotel on September 18th, choking on his own vomit. I sat stunned for hours after watching the news on the TV the next day, finally realizing how my older brother had felt at the death of Buddy Holly.

Thus, by October 1970, I was feeling that the deaths of Joplin and Hendrix signaled the fractured end of "The Sixties." Our generation's greatest musician, and its greatest voice had been silenced within days of each other, leaving a gaping hole in our collective consciousness. The Beatles' acrimonious break-up around the same time compounded the losses. How could there not be new Beatle music released forever? From that point, the universe shifted, but not in the way I'd hoped. The stylized mod and psychedelic fashions I had worn in the late Sixties with such pleasure, gave way to a new look: second-hand, torn and tatty clothing, unruly hair, and the hangdog gait of the tough Seventies.

In quick succession, three more of my musical heroes were lost: Jim Morrison, Louis Armstrong and Gene Vincent. I mourned, but life went on, a bit too humdrum when compared with my Sixties adventures. I was adrift. Where would my future inspiration come from? How would the alternative ideas and artistry of the Sixties, manifestations that had meant so much to me, play out in the Seventies? Although I had my engineering work to anchor me, otherwise I had absolutely no clue; was there *anything* that could satisfy my soul and give some meaning to my rudderless life?

Wild Ones?

My indentured work apprenticeship and college ended in mid-1971, but I continued on at the same company as a junior mechanical engineer. My abysmal wages limited my budget for entertainment or travel. A car, with the costs of insurance and registration was out of the question, so I took London Transport, cycled or walked as needed.

As usual, Jeffrey provided the spark for me to change. I was sitting in my parents' living room one day, when I heard a loud motorbike drive up to our house and rev its engine. The doorbell ding-donged a few seconds later, and by the time I opened the door I saw Jeffrey, astride a dark-blue and black Norton 650cc motorbike, revving its engine and grinning at me impishly.

At this time Jeffrey had long, wiry, ginger hair that went with his fair, freckled complexion, fronted by John Lennon-style granny glasses. My attire was classic post-hippie deconstruction— bib overalls and a scruffy shirt or tee (or none at all if the weather was good). My long, wiry, dark-brown hair was receding rapidly from my formerly bushy "Jewfro," and I sported a scruffy beard and moustache, along with those ubiquitous Lennon specs.

Jeffrey obviously thought that our image needed improving, and, inspired by *Easy Rider*, he had bought the tastefully handle-bar-chopped bike. "Climb aboard, Arnold!" he shouted, which I tentatively did, barely settling onto the pillion seat before the machine lurched forward, almost sending me tumbling behind it. It was scary/thrilling/exhilarating as we roared around the narrow back streets. When he had delivered me back home, Jeffrey turned on his seat and said: "Get a bike Arnold! We could ride together!"

So, I bought for £50, a brightly coloured chopped BSA 1961 motorbike with a 1942 magneto-started 500cc engine, and we did our *Easy Rider* trip all the way to Italy and back that summer. Wearing my WWI leather flying helmet, goggles and a tatty fur jacket, I must have been quite a sight. That stylized motorbike gave me much more flexibility and freedom in my everyday life at a reasonable cost, and with that inspiration, I began to hatch a longer-range plan for my own future.

Radio Caroline—First Ship Pirates, March 1964

Jimi Hendrix
Fehmarn Poster
His Last Concert

The Jeridales
Arnold's Brother's
Band 1963

Arnold, Rhoda, and Jeffrey—Italy 1971

Jeffrey's House at 86 The Vale

Concord and Dynamite
Bumper Stickers

2

Aaarrgh!
How I Became a Pirate

So here we are, Jeffrey and I, back once more in the autumn of 1971, headed for our first clandestine Radio Odyssey meeting, our flatulent motorbikes making a discordant roar on the quiet street as we pulled up outside a tidy red brick house. We were greeted at the door not, disappointingly, by a suspicious-looking revolutionary, but by someone's prim middle-aged mum in a floral dress.

In the back of the well-appointed house, eight *Harry Potter*-ish-looking young lads were gathered in a wood-paneled ground-floor dining room that had been magically transformed into a radio-phonic workshop. Seating was scarce, with most horizontal surfaces covered in radio parts, electronics magazines, and mangled radio chasses, so we perched gingerly on top of a chest of drawers.

As the meeting progressed, we took in the rag-tag band of "pirates," with their unintelligible (to us) technical jargon interspersed with cavalier talk about their encounters with the GPO enforcement officers. The GPO (General Post Office) trackers, we learned, were the bad guys, charged with tracking, locating, and closing down pirate stations. The kids in this room were so familiar with the trackers that they knew their pursuers' names and ranks, and could identify their official cars on sight. During the meeting, they still had plenty of time for schoolboy fun and for dishing the dirt on absent friends or other pirate stations. Impressed with their knowledge, expertise, and passion, we were comforted to know that there were many who, like us, were inspired to make a difference. Our vetting contact introduced us, and we outlined for the Radio Odyssey group the still-forming plan for our station: play good music, cock a snoot at authority, and stir up a little notoriety.

After the meeting broke up, we spoke to a very young, bespectacled electronic whiz-kid named Richard Courtney, and he and his friend agreed to make us our very own transmitter. £15 in cash sealed the deal, and just a few days later we were the proud owners of an illegal sixteen-watt radio transmitter (also known as a Tx in tech shorthand). The young techies showed us how to use this minimalist glowing machine that would have made Dali and Duchamp envious, and which Escher could not have untangled. They'd written basic instructions and settings for its operation down on a small scrap of paper, and sold us a 500-foot reel of plastic-covered silver-coated copper wire to use as our first antenna.

These young landlubber pirates were taking advantage of the relative simplicity of the medium-wave radio technology, to make their own transmitters, usually from simple diagrams found in wireless magazines and military manuals. In London, there were still many used electronic-equipment suppliers and Army-surplus stores for the constructors to rummage through for their components. Recycled electronic equipment was dismantled carefully and scavenged for reuse; all the young techs needed to put the spaghetti together inexpensively, were a soldering iron, pliers, and an electrical meter.

The whole rig fit neatly under one arm and weighed about fifteen pounds, with most of the heft being in the transformer for the power supply. No case surrounded the inner workings, leaving the delicate glass valves and small transistors unnervingly exposed. We took the contraption home by public transport, not wanting to jar its delicate components with a motorbike ride. Back then, the sight of two wild-haired men carrying a suspicious bomb-like contraption and wire reels on the Underground back to Golders Green raised quite a few eyebrows; in today's security-conscious world, I'm sure we wouldn't have made it down to the first tube platform!

First Broadcast

LATER, ON THAT WARM AUTUMN DAY, with a tweak here, a bit of tree-climbing there, and an amplitude modulation somewhere else, we were ready to go on-air at Jeffrey's house. Our core piece of equipment (and door to the world) was the transmitter, though its sixteen-watts of power were not exactly competition for the BBC. Broadcast efficiency and range, we had been told by our young tech gurus, were dictated by optimally matching the antenna length, height, and placement to the surrounding environment. An FM antenna-system only requires a device a few feet long, like the tubing of a home TV antenna, but an MW antenna requires 200 feet or more of single insulated copper electrical wire, raised to a good height from the ground and connecting down to the transmitter.

Our efforts to achieve anywhere near ideal reception at this suburban house found me climbing to the top of a spindly 40-foot-tall tree about 120-feet down the garden, feeling quite Sir Edmund Hillary-like with the spool of wire slung over my shoulder and a pocket full of string. After attaching the wire to the tree with a spacer of about two-feet of doubled-up string between the tree and the wire for insulation, I threw the reel down to the ground. Carefully descending the shaky tree-trunk, I unreeled the wire back to the house and attached it to a string dangling from the bedroom. Jeffrey hoisted it up, knotted the wire above the second-floor window with another short string spacer, and dropped the wire-end down into his bedroom where the transmitter waited. With a piratical heave-ho, we hauled the slack out of the cable, and after the twanging of the line stopped, our singular antenna looked clear of obstructions, ascending in a gently sloping line upwards from house to treetop.

At the transmitter, I cleared back about a half inch of insulation from the end of the wire and wound it under the screw connection, tightened it down, then attached the earth wire from the transmitter chassis to the copper pipe on the central-heating radiator. The one strong warning the young boffins had given us was to *never* attach the earth-wire to a gas pipe, as the resulting catastrophic explosion would not be appreciated by the neighbourhood!

Jeffrey switched on the power for the first time. We held our breaths as a few scary crackles and pops erupted from within the Frankensteinian unit. The two simple VU output meters, built into the side of the transmitter to monitor over-modulation of the audio, jumped crazily, but then quickly settled down below the red line. The transmitter itself was an aluminium chassis about 15" long by 10" wide by 4" tall, with a mighty 5" tall "807" radio valve (tube) stubbing up further from the recycled metal. Inside this magical small glass vial was a metal grid, now flickering and glowing in silent reaction to our oscillating audio-test output. The 807-valve was the crucial output workhorse for most pirate stations, and ours had transistors, capacitors, crystals and power supplies crowding around it in a busy matrix.

Apart from the glowing tube, the most critical device on the transmitter was the crystal, literally a quartz crystal, which came wrapped in a small rectangular metal case the size of a shilling, about a quarter of an inch thick with two short metal connection prongs ready for soldering or plugging in. Depending on the size and shape of the quartz piece, the crystal, when activated, would resonate only on one very specific radio frequency for broadcasting.

The crystal supplied with our rig had been set for 225 on the MW. Checking the channel on a radio, we were pleased that it was quite a clear band for the North London area, (those young radio pirates knew their business). The crystals themselves were procured secretly and subtly by mail, since their tuned frequencies were not officially authorized by the British government or by the GPO. Excuses often used by the techs to obtain them were, for instance, to install them in a transmitter for a foreign country, or to be used in a piece of non-radio equipment. The crystal-making companies never let us down.

In order for us to communicate with the world, the other vital component to the broadcast was the audio equipment. For our first transmission, we set it up on Jeffrey's bedroom chest of drawers by the window to the back garden. As the transmitter quietly glowed with its dummy load on the floor nearby, we plugged together a cheap Radio Shack 4-port mixer, a turntable, a ¼" reel-to-reel tape recorder, a cassette player, Koss headphones, and a Radio Shack microphone.

All was finally ready for our first broadcast. We could hear the quiet hiss of the transistor radio, pre-set to 225 MHz, that I'd perched on the wall radiator to monitor our broadcast. Jeffrey lined up the first single on the record player, and slowly lowered the needle onto the spinning vinyl. Beautiful loud Beatle music, the fast version of "Revolution" with that wild John Lennon opening guitar line, blasted out of the radio from across the room.

We shrieked in unison and grinned ecstatically at each other; we were officially pirates!

Concord—Faster Than the Speed of Sound

WE SPENT THE REST OF THE AFTERNOON and evening blithely playing our music and blathering, in what we thought was a cool DJ-like manner into the cheap microphone. Since we were learning how to segue between our devices on the fly, we generated a lot of dead air, wrong speeds, stuck records, and ¼" recording tape unreeling across the room. Bad connections on the mixer also created random crackling on top of a constant nasty earth-hum. We called up a few friends during the test, and asked them to tune into us and report on how we were coming in. The surprising feedback was that we were broadcasting scarily well over a large part of northwest London.

But now that we had the transmitter and antenna, a sound set-up, and a place from which to broadcast, what were we going to do with this powerful device? Music was our first love, and both of us had a fair collection of LPs and singles, reel-to-reel tapes, and cassettes (no 8-tracks!). We decided that, in light of our bellyaching about the virtual non-existence of our kind of music on the radio, our purpose had to be grounded in indulging our sometimes quite eclectic tastes in the types of music rarely, if ever, played on BBC-controlled British radio.

A name and identity for the station was needed, something that was somewhat punchy, but not too corny. We batted some around for a while, then Jeffrey suddenly blurted out: "Concord!" The joint UK/French Concorde SST passenger jet was just starting service, and the allusion was perfect. "Faster than the Speed of Sound" was the motto we emblazoned on our first primitive black & white non-sticky-backed bumper stickers. I insisted that we drop the final 'e' of Concorde, since the Frenchification had been foisted on both the English and French SST fuselages by General de Gaulle over the weak objections of the lily-livered British Government. The other usages of the word such as harmony, formal agreement, and "of one mind," also greatly appealed to me.

For security's sake, we had to take some on-air personal precautions. The young radio whizzes had given us some basic information about fake names, broadcast-site security, and how to watch out for the GPO trackers. It was a given that our names and personae for our radio escapades had to be changed to protect the guilty, therefore we had quite a big decision to make for our first on-air aliases. Jeffrey went with "Matt Black." His surname was Schwarz, which means black in German, and Matt was for "matte black," a type of photographic paper. As he was rummaging through his singles, up popped "Outer Limits," by the Marquettes, which became his intro song—the eerie guitar riff was perfect for introducing his new persona.

Tommy, by the Who, was my most-played album at the time, so I went with the name "Tommy Arnold," and my first intro just *had* to be the 58-second "Tommy's Holiday Camp." Why did that name appeal to me? Well, "Tommy" is slang for a generic British soldier ("Tommy Atkins" was the British Army equivalent of the US' "John Doe"). After the war, many of the military bases by the

English seaside were converted into basic holiday-camp resorts—imagine a Club Med in pre-Communist-fall East Germany!

These camps were places where returning soldiers could go with their families and all get to know one another again after as much as six years apart. Parents could have some time to themselves, or participate in the numerous communal activities provided, and their children were well looked after in the same way. The intent for my show was to make it like those holiday camps, where listeners would never know what might happen next (because I know I sure didn't!).

I played a mix of my favourite classic "oldies," psychedelic rock, ska, blues, comedy, and the many contemporary folk/rock singer/songwriters that had fed my youthful angst, all selected from my collection of 45s, LPs and cassettes. Jeffrey played a mix of "oldies" with an emphasis on the Beatles, and some tasty contemporary pop music. For variety he also used his reel-to-reel to air a mix of classical and pop music, and would even occasionally grab his violin and scratch out some classical piece that came to mind.

That first official Radio Concord broadcast went on well into the wee hours, with the two of us switching over shows every hour with no real technical hitches on the equipment. Our adrenaline was flowing, and we loved being on the air, even if no one was listening except perhaps Jeffrey's Mum, Reggie the dog, some friends, and any poor soul desperately searching the radio dial as Jeffrey had done to find Radio Odyssey just a few weeks earlier. The transmitter turned out to be surprisingly well made and robust, and once we got a better earth connection, put out a good clean signal.

From that Sunday on, buoyed by our success, we began to broadcast regularly from Jeffrey's place, beginning at 11 AM, and going on until late into the night. Sometimes Jeffrey would go on by himself at random days and times, and I would roam around town on my motorbike and check the reception quality and the extent of the broadcast areas we were covering. From our amateur non-scientific methods, and my meanderings, we learned that Concord was being heard quite strongly over northwest London, with a potential listening population of perhaps three million people! The thought gave me the willies.

Through the very uncharacteristic (for me) action of starting a pirate radio station and putting myself behind the mic, I was surprised how easily I went from law-abiding citizen to outlaw, driven by this newfound passion. The shyness I'd experienced when speaking to live groups in the past was not a factor with this medium, that somehow enabled me to speak in front of an audience, imaginary or real, without embarrassment, literally finding my voice in this world, in a way I had never expected, allowing me to "transcend my stylistic boundaries*"

    * *Courtesy of a Flora Purim & Airto record sleeve note.*

With a Little Help from Our Friends

WE CONTINUED OUR BROADCASTING from Jeffrey's house without a hitch for a few exhilarating weeks, and came to the realization that, while this illegal romp was becoming quite important to us, we couldn't be on-air all night, all the time, by ourselves. As our next logical step in growing Radio Concord, we began recruiting friends to be DJs and help keep our extremely casual, at that point, lookout for the dreaded Post Office detector vans that supposedly roamed like radio-frequency zombies in the dead of night.

Rhoda Jaffe, my former girlfriend, who was always mod-styled and coiffed, got roped in first, and her radio name became Rhoda Orange (Jaffe is a brand of orange in England). I'd met Rhoda at a dance in the West End when I was eighteen; she was three years older than I, and it was my first serious romance, as it lasted some three or four months, rather than the usual one-night or fortnight stands. Rhoda liked pet names, and I was so dubbed "Arm'oles," and Jeffrey, "Jeffrey Boggles-Bon-Bon." She was a natural broadcaster, and played great soul music from her extensive vinyl collection.

For a while, Jeffrey brought in a film industry friend, whose "Uncles Festus' Time Tunnel" was a superb "oldies" show with wild sound effects, then three primary-school friends Robby Ryan, Jeff King & The Toffer came in; all of their shows were in the rotation for a couple of months. Sailor Sam and John (Sloopy)—(names in parentheses are broadcast aliases) hoisted their sails and floated around for a while.

My friend Mick Lewis came into the Concord mix as a blues-playing DJ called Rasputin, spontaneously named by us because of his physical similarity to photos of the infamous Russian, and for his deep resonant voice. Ultimately, he morphed into Joe Lung, self-named in reference to his prodigious smoking of cigarettes and hash.

Rose Lewis (nee Price) from Torquay, Mick's girlfriend and later wife, began appearing on a show as "Anne Nightingale Force 5." (Ann Nightingale was, from 1967 to 1972, the first and only female BBC Radio 1 DJ.) Rose, who flaunted bleached-blond wavy shoulder-length hair and wore elaborate make-up, played superb underground progressive music, pub-rock, glam-rock, and emerging American country-rock like the Eagles. She and Mick lived on the top two floors of a flat in Finsbury Park. Rose was a gracious and generous hostess, offering tea and sweet things to the many pirate visitors who came to the flat and hung out at all hours—this was a lifesaver, as we always seemed to be stoned from Mick's strong hash.

I'd met Mick in 1967 at a house party, and we discovered a mutual love for roots blues music. That love for me, started in 1964 when I'd seen John Lee Hooker, by chance, at a live BBC Radio show. Hooker's Delta blues music was nothing like the polished Detroit Soul, or the ersatz British blues bands I was used to. I felt somewhat humbled and unlearned in the face of Mick's fanatic obsession with the genre, and with chess. (His chess book collection almost rivaled his great blues-record collection.) After becoming friends, we'd listen to obscure blues and talk about music and chess all night, as his room in his parents' council flat slowly filled with hash smoke. That party where I met Mick, is also memorable to me because it was the first time I heard the Beatles' *Sgt. Pepper* LP. The host announced the new issue as he put it on the record player, and what excitement ran through me as I listened to those opening riffs! The sacred platter was kept on "repeat" for most of the evening.

Jeffrey's primary school friend Daniel Makeover, a seemingly straitlaced chap, came aboard, and was, in fact, crazier than the rest of us put together. For his show, he chose to turn himself into an oily radio-show personality called Louie Deeko, (named after the British Deeko paper serviette makers); it was an inspired move. Daniel worked in sales for his father's West End fabric company, and always wore a suit and tie for any occasion. In spite of his straight wardrobe, he ignored Sinatra and Dino, but adored to distraction Jimi Hendrix and all the heavier psychedelic-era music. He trusted me to get him through his first LSD trip when his parents were away, and I'm sure Daniel really did appreciate the additional help offered from his neighbours and police in his admirable goal of enlightenment, after he repeatedly cranked the music up to max at 3 AM! Totally obsessed with sex and women, Daniel talked nonstop about his failed and successful escapades. After broadcasting for a year, he went off to Sweden, and we all lost contact with him.

As we continued to broadcast untouched from Jeffrey's house, our weekly efforts, augmented by this fresh crew of friendly pirates, became a lot more fun as others became involved in our clandestine romp. The new DJs also brought their friends along to experience the tingle of an illicit broadcast; this added to the buzz and generated a party atmosphere during the shows. Some of these "tourists" enjoyed it so much they began to do their own shows.

My parents were quite puzzled by the whole thing but, having known Jeffrey for so long, they just shook their heads and let me get on with it. Jeffrey's eccentric night-owl mother didn't appear to have much say in the use of her house, and kept to her room through most of the broadcasts. She and her faithful companion Reggie the Pink-Butted Dog did occasionally provide amusement during the down times. (But that's a whole other story.)

Women on the Radio

AS I INDICATED EARLIER, ON BBC POP RADIO, and, somewhat embarrassingly, even with the old ship pirates and many of our newer land pirate ventures, there was one glaring omission: in that male-dominated technological age, there were virtually no women DJs or engineers at any level of the business. Jeffrey and I talked about this early on, and made a concerted effort to recruit women DJs from our pool of girlfriends, friends and casual acquaintances. We wanted Concord to be different from the beginning, and it seemed obvious to us that there was an untapped audience out there for half the population. As a result, within just a few weeks of operation we had many more women DJs than the BBC!

Testing Our Limits

THE FOUR-DAY WEEKEND OF THE 1971 Christmas holidays approached, and we decided to make full use of our resources and outdo our usual twelve-hour broadcast-programming limit. Obliviously assuming that the GPO detectors were home for the holidays instead of running around looking for the scruffy likes of us, we extended our usual programming, pulling in everyone we knew. The result was a bumper, all-long-weekend, all-day and night live show. Many DJs came and went, some doing a show and leaving, others staying to party and keep us company for a while. Mick and Rose Lewis, Rhoda Jaffe, and I stayed the entire course, along with Jeffrey and his long-suffering girlfriend Sue Bryan. Sue, a lovely woman, had stuck by Jeffrey for many years, I think for the same reasons I did: the fact that you never knew what would happen next.

We were joined, for the first time, at this holiday broadcast by Philip Bendall (Day), a young pirate radio aficionado who had heard our show from his home in nearby Hendon and called in, wanting to help out. A very friendly, lanky blond kid with a slight stutter, he became doubly invaluable to our collective enterprise when he allowed us to use his parents' home as our on-air mailing address. After broadcasting for over three months, we still knew our listeners only from live call-ins, but once we aired his mailing address, we began to receive letters from all over London and southern England. By the number of them, it appeared that we'd begun to gather quite a large listening audience.

In our bravado about never being raided, we had even begun giving out Jeffrey's home phone number to call for requests. (Note: The GPO also controlled telephone lines.) Jeffrey had the brilliant idea of taping the phone up to the mic and broadcasting live instant call-ins and requests, long before the BBC even thought of such a thing. Happy house-partyers called in all night through to request songs and send messages to friends as they danced to the music we played for them. Every station, pirate or public, had jingles extolling the station, and Concord was no exception. Our crew, whiling away time during that extended broadcast, produced classics such as "We're Just Mad About Concord," with Jeffrey playing the guitar and leading the chorus, or the "Come on Concord" segment from *Monty Python*.

Friends, Foes, Fields, and Phone Boxes

ALTHOUGH WE HAD SO FAR GOTTEN AWAY with the quite reckless number of occasions that we'd broadcast from Jeffrey's, we knew in the back of our minds that after this ridiculously successful outing, there were bound to be repercussions, and the high probability of a raid in the near future. "You've been lucky so far," said the radio pirates who had casually tracked us down during the holiday marathon and previous broadcasts. Deciding to take some precautions, we began to broadcast from a few other locations, hoping this would confuse the odious trackers.

Easier said than done. We discovered that the main problem with land-based pirate radio, when you do it seriously, not randomly from your bedroom, was the need to keep moving the location of the transmitter to avoid detection by the authorities, so the endless search for new broadcast locations began. Asking relatives, friends, friends of friends, and entire strangers if they would like to host a pirate radio broadcast at their place became one of our foremost activities. In spite of our misgivings, virtually everyone who entertained our proposition and took us up on it enjoyed the set-up process, the show, and even the titillating fear of a raid.

Explaining the legal ramifications of pirate radio to the location owners or renters, and assuring them that it was only a civil offence for them, was usually enough. Since we'd never heard of a case of a homeowner being charged, that made it a fairly easy sell. To our amazement, even when we did begin to get raided, literally all of our hosts seemed not to mind the police rampaging through their home. They apparently felt good that they were helping flout Britain's suffocating governmental media control (not to mention acquiring some great tales to tell their friends).

Leaving Home

FOR OUR FIRST FORAY OUTSIDE OF THE VALE (and to his parents' considerable consternation), Jeffrey's primary-school friend Marcus Haverstock let us use their elegant house on Exeter Road in Brondesbury Park a slew of times, with nary a raid. We'd place the equipment carefully on the highly polished dining room table, and I'd shimmy up a tree in the garden to put up the antenna. As with my family, it was an "Oh, it's just Jeffrey," experience for the Haverstock's.

At my friend Mick Dodd's upper floor flat on St. Charles Square near Ladbroke Grove, some nosy neighbours foiled our preferred antenna endpoint. Working around this inconvenience, we beamed out quite a few successful transmissions by simply dangling the wire out his window. Despite the short antenna length, adjacent metal-construction scaffolding, and the nearness of the wire to the building, our reception was still impressive, spilling strongly over West London. From these and other early excursions, we learned two maxims on the fly: always be adaptable, and never give up on a broadcast.

If our quest for an enclosed location failed, we'd fall back on one of two desperate alternatives: broadcasting from the back of a car, or sometimes even without that luxury, out in the open with just a couple of car batteries for power and a DC-to-AC alternator wired into the transmitter. This was a simple and viable option, as the site could be any convenient open park area, reservoir, or farmer's field. We'd climb a tree, drop the wire, hook up the antenna to the transmitter in the boot or on the dirt, ram an earthing rod into the ground and broadcast away. The downside of those mobile locations was that, without enough power or room for our audio equipment, we were limited to playing pre-recorded music tapes on a small battery-operated cassette recorder, with a single mic plugged directly into the transmitter for live announcements.

Nothing beats experience, and by operating from these many different sites all over London, we soon discovered the variables in how well and how far a signal could be heard. Even with our limited technical knowledge, we learned to adjust to each unique location and gain an inherent feel as to what extent the broadcast would be heard that week.

All of this effort, however, could be for naught if the human element broke down. This is where the glamourous undercover job of "lookout" came in. The spies that we enlisted seemed to enjoy the drama of conducting their covert duties in all weathers, patrolling the neighborhood, watching from a stationary or cruising car, and/or lurking in or on top of surrounding buildings. Sometimes we got lucky: the police and the GPO trackers were spotted in time, and our crew were alerted quickly enough to make a clean getaway. At other times, especially during the cold late-night winter shifts, one of our well-meaning lookouts would fall asleep at their post during the night, and miss the authorities gathering outside for a raid.

The second most glamourous task involved freezing to death in a classic British red phone box. In the days before cellphones, most homes from which we broadcast didn't have a telephone, mainly because it could take up to a year to get one installed by the only provider, the nationalized company. During that storied Clark Kent era, everyone involved in the broadcast took turns standing in a drafty cubicle (usually urine-soaked and broken-glass-littered) through icy nights and windy days, our minds and hands thankfully kept busy taking messages and listener requests. When our relief arrived, we'd get the circulation going in our extremities by walking the scribbled notes back to the DJs at the broadcast location.

This purposeful and organic expansion of our clandestine crew, coupled with our moves to multiple broadcast locations, was a major leap forward for Concord. From the "two-lads-in-a-bedroom" type of piracy, we had morphed into a fully-fledged pirate radio station operating regularly over many hours, with a diverse range of music and DJs.

The weekly effort Jeffrey and I expended to support this new-found passion took up a lot of our spare time and pocket money, often diverting us from our legitimate work and school schedules. As with any overriding passion, we managed to find the time to indulge it—it was way too much fun to stop now. The two of us developed an informal system of finding the broadcast location and checking out its neighbourhood and working phone boxes, scoping out the antenna-installation options, setting up the equipment, getting the crew to show up, and—usually—preparing for our own live shows at the last moment.

First Raid!

ON ONE BEAUTIFUL SUNNY SPRING SUNDAY, a new location had flunked out at the last moment, and, not wanting to cancel the broadcast, we decided to tempt fate and again base our operation at Jeffrey's house. A couple of hours into our transmission, we heard loud staccato knocking at the front door, accompanied by the sound of men shouting outside. Sad to say, our security and look-outs had been woefully inadequate that time around. Although our request-taker in the telephone box on Hendon Way didn't have a clear line of sight to the house, we had figured, because it was so early in the proceedings, there was no need to be worried yet. No one was even spying through the lace curtains, let alone sitting out in a car watching the street. On hearing the ruckus, I peeked out the front window, to see a bunch of official-looking men in suits, wearing well-polished shoes, gathered on the garden path, accompanied by a flurry of uniformed police officers.

Counting me, there were six pirate-crew members in the house at the time, and we all gathered in the front room wondering aloud what we should do. Since this was the first time that any of us had been on the receiving end of a massive police raid, our options appeared few, and our fears were many. At our very first broadcast we'd worked out an emergency getaway plan that fuzzily swam up into my memory, until with a jolt, I realized that I was it!

Because I was such a good runner and climber, it was my designated job to flee with the incriminating transmitter. Sprinting from the front window out to the back-garden patio as planned, I stood below Jeffrey's second-floor bedroom window and watched as the transmitter, tied to a thin string, descended with agonizing slowness. Meanwhile, Jeffrey's dear old hunched-over mother somehow held the GPO and police at bay at the slightly open front door all by herself, answering their insistent demands by muttering unintelligibly in her native German.

As the police waited politely to come in with their official search warrant, and despite the transmitter getting hopelessly tangled with the antenna and its string as Jeffrey lowered it, I somehow managed to cut it free and scarper off with the precious knobby box. My mission was to hightail it down to the end of the garden, climb over the solid wood fence, and hide out in the large public garden allotments directly behind all the houses on the block.

From what I heard later, my frantic sprint had me disappearing just as the police, growing weary of the frail gatekeeper's efforts to hold them back, had made an end run and leaped over the six-foot tall locked side gate into the back garden. Trembling from a huge adrenaline rush, I scrambled through the allotments and hid in an old potting shed for a couple of hours like Donovan's "Mad John," until I thought the coast might be clear. As I clambered back over the rickety garden fences in the dark, I managed to fall through and demolish one small shed and part of a wood fence, somehow without arousing the neighbours. I tapped on the back window of Jeffrey's place, and I and the now-cold transmitter were both greeted warmly by my fellow pirates.

Jeffrey told me that the police had finally brushed aside his mother, entered the house, and then teemed into the garden in force. Corralling the DJs in the front room, the Bobbies interrogated the crew about an "illegal radio broadcast," that everyone of course indignantly denied, while they searched the house in concert with the GPO officials. Naturally, no transmitter equaled no evidence. However much they'd have liked to, the desperate GPO officials couldn't charge us for illegally using a record deck, or having a very long "clothesline" in the back garden.

The GPO men were furious with our crew. The police were even more upset at the GPO for bringing so many of them out on a wild-goose chase on such a nice quiet Sunday. The GPO's supervisor would be incandescent with rage, we hoped, when they got the exorbitant overtime bill! Just for some perverse fun, as I was finishing a welcome cup of tea, we hooked up the transmitter again, and gleefully broadcast some music and announcements for about fifteen minutes, wishing the trackers were still listening. Nothing would have been sweeter at that point than to see their faces.

The exhilaration of my escape was quite intense, and, in a way, reminded me of being chased by, and evading, the anti-Semitic gangs of my past. The fact that we'd escaped by a hair was not lost on us, and coming up against the full weight of the law for the first time was quite sobering. It was now obvious to us that it was foolish to think of broadcasting from a location we'd used so many times. The trackers knew exactly where we were. Surprisingly, on discussing the future of the station, none of us were at all deterred by that overblown authoritarian display. On our subsequent transmissions, we accordingly ratcheted up our lookouts and area patrols, since we knew that, having thwarted their show-raid to the embarrassment of the perpetrators, we were now a marked station.

The Law

SINCE THE DAWN OF BROADCAST RADIO in the early 20th century, there had been many so-called "ham" stations in Britain, transmitting illegally from bedrooms, garden sheds, and attics while playing music and airing personal views. Wartime, obviously, had made all illegal stations suspect, and not a respectable hobby, unless you wanted to be taken for a Nazi spy.

As mentioned earlier, illegal land-based broadcasting had begun to ramp up in 1967 after the silencing of offshore radio by the new 1967 Marine Wireless and Telegraphy Act. These new pioneers were determined not to let the government get away with such arbitrary censorship. The difference this time around was that the pirates, instead of sticking to their previously solitary bedroom broadcasts, were banding together to create cooperative stations.

These new wave-radio types, not content to just broadcast for the sake of broadcasting, were demanding changes in the laws, with the aim of allowing and legalizing community radio stations and breaking the BBC's national monopoly. Brave land-based pirates were taking over the legacy of their inspirational offshore predecessors, but without the direct financial profit motive, and with a significantly increased risk of capture. This truly was an idealistic movement trying, with its passion, persistence, and belief in free speech, to influence a monolithic system.

Being a land-based radio pirate posed entirely different logistical and security problems from those encountered by the blatantly exposed, but out beyond the lawful limit, pirate ships. On land, there was no chance of legal stalling or appeals against marine and international laws. The regulations were clear. If they found you broadcasting illegally, "The GPO may use any reasonable means to enter the transmission site with or without police, and apprehend the people, and confiscate the equipment, records and paperwork found therein."

One of the regularly raided established pirates, Nick Catford (Price) of Radio Jackie, had been caught dozens of times. Finally, a judge got fed up at his law-flouting and threw him in the pokey for sixty days for contempt of court. Most of the raids only resulted in small fines and costs of less than a £100, coupled with a stern finger-wagging admonition from a judge to obey the law in future. At one infamous Radio Jackie broadcast from a country field, the GPO trackers went too far and actually assaulted the pirates while taking the equipment. The subsequent court cases upheld the charges, and Mr. Eric Gotz, the head of the GPO tracking unit, had to personally pay the hefty fine and costs.

Over the years and through many raids, busts, and court cases, the pirates had developed a list of the members of the GPO trackers unit, and the license plates and descriptions of the official vehicles they usually drove. This vital information was handed around and updated to enable lookouts to spot a suspicious car scouting out the area of a broadcast. I know for a fact, that precious list helped Concord and Dynamite avoid a raid on a number of occasions.

Our rights were often trampled underfoot, but having no money for legal help, we usually just let it go. Occasionally we managed to enlist a solicitor to take on a *pro bono* case, and sometimes the GPO lost a case on a technicality and were ordered to hand back the confiscated items. The condition of the returned equipment was not part of the deal however, and often the materials and records had been rendered unusable. Some of the confiscated gear and discs would end up in secondhand stores, and pirates might be able to buy some back if they acted quickly enough. Pirates also monitored the rubbish bins outside the GPO tracker offices, where sometimes confiscated and dumped equipment could be recovered with a bit of timely skip-diving.

The GPO trackers were kept busy with pirate activity. In 1971 and 1972 there were 152 prosecutions; 59 cases in 1973; and 86 in 1974. In the 1980s, with the availability of small cheap FM transmitters that didn't need the clumsy long antenna we'd had to deal with, there would be a huge surge in pirate radio. By 2002 there were about 1,000 raids per year.

The fines and court costs were bad enough, but the worst outcome of this raid-and-bust scenario for land pirates was permanent confiscation of our precious transmitters, electronic equipment, vinyl records and cassette tapes. It was a financial strain for us all to keep replenishing our hardware and record supplies from scratch; the only positive effect of the confiscation was the subsequent joy of spending days browsing through dusty used-record stores and damp street markets for a new record collection!

Last Broadcast? Off to Look for America

IN APRIL AND MAY OF 1972, WE BROADCAST a number of times from my girlfriend Sheila Macgregor's second-floor flat on Laurier Road. Sheila had come into the hardware shop where I was working one Saturday, and slipped on paint someone (not me) had just spilled next to the counter. I picked her up off the floor, cleaned off the paint as best I could, and we struck up a conversation. Ultimately, I volunteered to help with her flat redecorating, (ahem!), and we became lovers. There was an interesting pirate radio connection, in that her former boyfriend Harry Overnall, was the drummer for the Roaring Sixties, the group (which included bassist Rick Grech) that had recorded the protest single "We Love the Pirate Stations." This last desperate musical plea to the British Government to stop the incoming new laws banning pirate broadcasters in August 1967, had a great beat and chorus, but no discernible legal effect.

At the very beginning of our relationship, I made it clear to Sheila that my plan was to leave in late June for America, come hell or high water, and I had no idea when, if ever, I would return, and to my delight and surprise, she accepted this finite condition.

Buying that old motorbike the year before, had planted in me a yearning that, after my fun-filled ride with Jeffrey to Italy and my other solo trips around England, grew into a fully laid plan. I felt somehow that I had missed a lot of the Sixties, having been tied down for so long by my five-year work/school bondage. Now that was ended, and I wanted to break out of it with an adventure! Hearing about summer-camp jobs in the USA, I replied to some adverts in the BunaCamp student-exchange system and received a positive reply from a camp in the New York Catskills. The eight-week job paid for my round-trip flight, room and board, and included a one-time stipend of $170.

With a guaranteed job to start my sojourn, the final part of my American adventure required the appropriate transcontinental travel mode. As a Triumph was the brand of bike ridden by Marlon Brando in *The Wild Ones* (only recently released in England after a long ban because of greaser-gang riot fears), I was inspired to buy a lovely new Triumph Bonneville 650cc. Since I was removing the motorbike to America within six months, I didn't have to pay the onerous 25% Purchase Tax for so-called luxury items. Giddy with anticipation, I packed some appropriate tools and a few vital parts tightly into the black-plastic side panniers, and shipped the bike to New York.

This ambitious open-ended journey also meant that I would have to leave my newfound passion for Radio Concord. The weekly broadcast, along with the camaraderie of working with the crew towards a similar purpose, had grown to be an important part of my life. Even so, I realized that, although I was sad to be leaving it all just as we had established Concord as a "legitimate" pirate, I needed an escape more than anything else. As I wrapped up my broadcasts with Concord, I was happy that Jeffrey, Mick, Rose, Phillip, and the rest would be carrying on the fight for freedom of the airwaves. With the many supporters and listeners' we had accreted so far, there was a strong base for them to continue.

Having no idea what my future held in America, and perhaps beyond, I took a bit of comfort in knowing that my hard-earned engineering skills were there to fall back on if all else failed. After a boisterous goodbye party in a pub with my Radio crew, Sheila, and other friends, I left the life I'd known for twenty-two years, "Looking for adventure, and whatever comes my way." My parents came to Heathrow on the Tube with me to wave goodbye.

Exeter Road—Second Broadcast Location 1971

**Sheila MacGregor on My Motorbike
at Laurier Road Broadcast Location 1972**

COURT WIN FOR RADIO JACKIE

RADIO JACKIE, a pirate station, won a victory at Kingston Crown Court yesterday when Judge JOHN BAKER said the Post Office had no right to grab a transmitter from a field at Malden Manor, Surrey.

Post Office men in January last year raided the site from which Radio Jackie was broadcasting and a running battle took place, the court heard.

During the battle ERIC GOTTS, a Post Office employee, assaulted MICHAEL DUNKERTON, 23, a Radio Jackie engineer. Gotts was convicted of assault and appealed but yesterday his appeal was dismissed.

Order required

Judge Baker said the Post Office had no right under the 1949 Wireless Telegraphy Act to take equipment without a court order which in this case it did not possess.

Gotts' conviction — a conditional discharge for 12 months — was ordered to stand. He was also ordered to pay Mr Dunkerton's costs of £350.

Radio Jackie is a local community station in South-West London which is campaigning for such stations throughout Britain. It has been broadcasting since March, 1969.

Radio Jackie Court Case

MW Transmitter Example

St. Charles Sq. Ladbroke Grove Location

GPO Logo 1975

Arnold on Motorbike in Toronto

3

A Pirate Goes to America!

TURNING LEFT AT GREENLAND, I flew into Kennedy airport, and picked up my motorbike at a nearby warehouse. After spending a night in a hotel in Manhattan's theater district soaking up the dazzling array of TV and radio channels, I took an early-morning tour of the main New York landmarks, and then headed North to the Catskills. Camp Tahoe, near the legendary "Borscht-Belt" hotels like The Concord and Grossinger's, was a fat-farm for boys, run by members of the Bronfman family, owners of Seagram's Whiskey. Nearby was Camp Stanley, the equivalent for girls, which employed female counselors with whom we occasionally got to mingle socially. A few of us counselors also met up and partied with seasonal workers at the local hotels.

My experience at this dysfunctional summer camp, with a collection of 300-pound thirteen-year-old boys in my charge, certainly opened my eyes to the over-consumption of food, energy and material goods that had begun to characterize American society since WWII. Most of the boys had been returning for years, having regained even more weight than the year before. Their parents didn't help the process, sneaking junk food to their "starving" children on Visiting Day, halfway through their torture. A few times I was even called out in the middle of the night to go pick up unhappy campers trying to hitch their way to an all-night store!

Ten dollars was the highest eye-popping bribe the kids offered me for a peanut-butter-and-jelly sandwich (the counselors thankfully had access to this kind of food). That exorbitant, wasteful lifestyle hadn't spread to the rest of the world yet; Britain was still suffering its grim days of power outages and labour strikes and was not a dominant economic power anymore. The British would not truly experience "The American Way of Life," until capitulating completely during the Thatcher and Blair eras.

At the beginning of camp, I bought a small transistor radio, at a Five & Dime in the nearby town of Liberty, and in my off-hours in the counselor/camper bunkroom, was surprised to discover a plethora of truly local radio stations on the dial. Most of the AM (MW) stations broadcasting from nearby small towns were commercial and hokey, but they were *there*, and playing pop music and news along with the car-dealer ads. Checking out FM broadcasts was a whole new experience for me: better-quality sound coming from a few local ad-free community and college stations, that didn't just play pop music, but aired album cuts and lesser-known music genres. There didn't appear to be an American equivalent to the BBC's airwave exclusivity.

The summer-camp job served as a springboard for my primary reason to come to America. At the end of the season, I strapped my backpack to the pillion seat and straddled my new motorbike, planning to happily vibrate my kidneys on the endless roads from New York to the West Coast. After a few detours here and there for romantic, platonic, or familial visits, I set off into a vast, staggeringly scenic landscape that was utterly unlike my own cramped country.

Heaven was gas at only 25-35 cents a gallon, and the long straight roads inspired me to crank my bike up to a ton and scream at the wind. With its signature gold-and-black paint job and peardrop-shaped petrol tank, the bike was an unusual sight on American roads, and drew a lot of attention. Being pulled over by the cops every couple of hundred miles became routine, although it was never for traffic violations. Bemused by my unusual British license plates, they would put their flashing lights on behind me just to ask where I came from! One cop, on a South Dakota back road, when I told him I came from England, asked what state it was in! This, I would later learn, was an excellent example of American "geographobia."

By mid-October of my ambitious road trip, the country's mood had grown somber, with the Vietnam War on the mind of every young person I met. By all accounts, Nixon was about to be re-elected in a landslide and was at the height of his pre-Watergate powers. I watched with astonishment his vicious TV ads attacking George McGovern, a far cry from the polite and dry brand of British politicking I was used to. But still lost in my British-filtered Hollywoodesque dream of America, I went breezing through the real impacts of the war, untouched by the everyday draft-age Nephew Sam's nightmare, just wanting to be a freewheeling spirit like in *Easy Rider,* just hopefully, without the bad ending.

Alone in out-of-season campgrounds across the Plains and Rockies, I listened to the radio in my tent at night, with stations floating in and out from hundreds or perhaps thousands of miles away, just the way, I mused, that Concord, back in England, must be sounding to many of our continental listeners. That small radio provided a window for me into American culture, and assuaged my loneliness on those long autumn nights amidst beautiful rugged scenery.

I took a detour to see the famed Mt. Rushmore presidential heads, and their Chief Crazy Horse analog in the Black Hills of South Dakota. The rugged scenery was straight out of classic western films, and I decided to camp in the area for a while. As I'd not experienced Native American culture before, apart from Westerns, I took a short side trip to the Pine Ridge Indian Reservation. The open poverty on display near the trading post shocked me. The buildings were ramshackle, and the children who chased after my motorbike and then gathered around me were dressed in rags. They seemed to inhabit the worst of all worlds, living in such a harsh climate and terrain in the midst of such a rich country.

A Bike, a Brit, and Bison in the Badlands

MY PRIMITIVE CAMPSITE IN THE BADLANDS was many miles down a very bumpy, rutted dirt road that took me past spectacularly eroded scenery. After hiking around for a couple of days, I decided to head out, as the mountain winter was rapidly coming on, and was likely to make road conditions treacherous. Not wanting to return to the freeway, I charted a route through the depths of the Badlands, following a backcountry trail map supplied by a friendly park ranger. The next morning, as I packed my tent and belongings, snow began to fall lightly. My heavily laden motorbike, not built for these off-road conditions, made the going slow and tortuous along the pitiful excuse for a trail, and I found myself descending into small dry arroyos and surging up steep rocky banks for mile after jarring mile.

As I descended from the rocky hills, and began to skirt the edge of an expansive plain with shrubby vegetation, I rattled around a blind turn, and braked abruptly in a cloud of dust. It was only this sudden halt that kept me from barreling into a herd of about a dozen bison that were standing impassively, straddling the trail and embankments that ran atop a large concrete storm-flow culvert over a wide dry arroyo.

Gulp. There was no going back up that awful rocky road I had just barely navigated. The arroyo was deep and impressive, and I realized that even if I could get the bike down from the trail to the valley floor, there were too many fissures and obstacles for me to make it across in one piece. The only option appeared to be for-ward—through the bison.

Being an inner-city-London boy, I'd obviously had scant experience in herding bison. Hadn't I read somewhere they were almost extinct in the wild? Recalling all the wild-west films I had seen, I knew I hadn't packed the six-gun, lasso, and buckin' bronco necessary to wrangle the beasts. I *did*, though, have some experi-ence with recalcitrant Jersey cows in English country lanes, and so, based on that vast knowledge, I decided to believe that these mammoth creatures must be a little similar—after all, they also had four legs and horns, and liked to hang around together.

Plan A: Make some noise from a safe distance, and they would scatter to the wind to allow for my passage. I beeped my bike's horn, revved its engine, and shouted choice Cockney imprecations at them, denigrating their appearance and ancestry. The bison were not, it seemed, as impressionable as English bovines, who would have turned and scampered off the bridge at the first beep. Ignoring my desperate cacophony, the stoic beasts didn't even increase the beat of their regular tail-swishing.

On to Plan B: if I drove slowly towards them making a lot of noise, no matter how impassive they were, they must ultimately yield to my superior man-and-machine assault, and scatter. Aiming my bike towards them and rumbling up the gradual rise of the rocky span, I yelled and honked wildly at the herd, but as I careened ever closer to them, doubt assailed me. They weren't moving, although some of the hirsute, elephantine heads at least turned in my direction.

This was the point of no return: if I stopped, I wouldn't be able to turn around on the narrow road without a severe risk of falling over, or of the herd bolting and running over me. If I continued forward, and they still refused to move, a single nudge from one of these massive shaggy beasts would surely send me hurtling twenty feet down the steep, riprap-sided embankment to the hard arroyo floor. Neither was a cheerful thought, but I had no choice: gritting my teeth, I inched forward.

Although the bison occupied most of the dirt trail over the culvert, I suddenly noticed a gap open up between the edge of the herd and the unfenced drop-off on the right. Was it, I asked myself, large enough for me to possibly sidle by? I should perhaps mention that my cogitating brain had shut down at about this time, and the fanciful side came merrily forward, convincing me that just maybe, as the beasts apparently still hadn't noticed me, my luck would hold, and I'd be past them and on my way in a jiffy, without them even knowing I'd been there.

In my self-deluded state, it seemed a solid plan C at the time. As I neared the group, they remained unmoving, appearing almost as inert as the four stone presidents I had just seen. So far, so good. I gripped my handlebars tightly and wobbled toward the skinny gap. As I approached them, I realized for the first time just how *big* these behemoths were. They were magnificent primitive beasts— but I had no more time to admire their many attributes. The precious gap remained open, and I plunged into their midst.

To my horror, as I drew side by side with the bison nearest to my escape route, it suddenly wheeled around, and a moment later the whole herd had rotated clockwise, in formation, like a flock of one-ton murmurating starlings, stampeding beside, ahead of, and most terrifyingly, behind me. I had no choice now but to continue in a wild career over the bridge with the buffalo herd rumbling in unison with me.

For a moment, all I could hear was the steam-engine snorting of their nostrils. Who knew my harebrained plan would take such an unexpected twist? I was running with, not past, a herd of *Bison bison*. My fate was entirely entangled with the moment, caught up in the direction of their pounding hooves. Reluctantly, but inexorably drawn, I dared to turn my head to the left. Just two feet from my horrified eyes were the sharp pointy horn, large liquid eye, matted fleecy side, and bobbing head of a galloping bison. For a moment, my gaze became helplessly fixed on the eye watching me, its white showing thinly around the dark center, as the majestic animal kept pace with me.

Jolted away from our hypnotic communion by the rough ride, I was brought back to the moment: teetering on the edge of the steep embankment on the right, so I adjusted my forward trajectory just in time to avoid disaster. But then another strange thing happened: as I returned my attention to my fellow dusty travelers, an unexpected calm came over me, and I began savouring this incredible moment. It was one of those rare occasions on which an innocuous random snippet of life suddenly becomes sharp and defined in an extraordinary way. With this clarity, all other senses, including that of time, became distorted, inducing what I'd best call an out-of-body experience. In this slowed-down perceptive state I could see all the bison jostling each other for position on the bridge, yet never touching me as we continued our joint exercise. In our shared journey, they hadn't barged into me yet, and I began to feel they didn't intend to.

As we galloped together down the other side of the bridge, the beasts' heavy breathing drowned out the noise of my motorbike, and the thunderous hooves kicked up a dust cloud that filled my vision. When the trail eventually met the arroyo floor, the bison herd peeled away to the left and slowed to gather a short distance away on the plain. Shaking, I braked to a stop.

Coming back into my body as the incredible rush of adrenalin ebbed, I found myself sitting on my idling motorbike, watching my erstwhile fellow travelers peacefully munching on the sparse vegetation of the range. I realized that I had just survived an extraordinary adventure, one of my own stupid making, surely, but one I'd remember for the rest of my life.

As I watched and reflected, my American journey's jigsaw parts seemed to come together as a whole in my mind. First, I realized the connection between the near extinction of this proud animal species, the accompanying removal of their native environment, and the impact of these changes on the indigenous human cultures that had relied on them for millennia. That thought then blended with the dysfunctional effects of consumerism I had experienced in the kids' camp, and so far, on my journey across America. Through this lens I could see how directly all our entitled cultural actions, responsibilities and fates were linked.

This trip, travelling on my own in such a foreign, yet familiar land, had already taught me a lot. In Europe, there was only so deep I could go into a society because of the language and cultural barriers, but this was different. Americans, I found, were very friendly, and their hospitality to strangers like me was truly genuine and selfless. I realized that going to a new place, getting out of my comfort zone, had created for me a clearer perspective in the human condition, one I'd missed in my everyday insular London life.

Even though it had been snowing when I left the campsite, the day had warmed on the plain, and I stripped off my military-surplus jacket to cool off. I took some pictures of the herd—they were in no hurry to wander off yet—had a swig of water, then, waving goodbye to my shaggy friends, drove out of the Badlands at Scenic, heading for the coast.

By taking the northern route into the San Francisco Bay Area, I could also accomplish another dream, to ride my namesake Bonneville bike on the legendary Bonneville Salt Flats in Utah. Once at that hallowed spot, I cranked the accelerator as far as I could, and the bike rumbled up well beyond 100 mph, until the force of the wind blurring my eyes and threatening my hold on the handlebars, made me decide to throttle back and just enjoy the dazzling flats and the spectacular mountains surrounding them.

Autumn of Love? Minnie Mouse to the Rescue!

PERSONAL SACRED PLACES CAN COME in all shapes and sizes; for me, one of these was San Francisco, even though I would be arriving in October 1972, a bit late for the fabled "Summer of Love." The City was still the Holy Grail for the transformational era that had so profoundly affected my life from afar, but San Francisco was *not* as I had fantasized from across the ocean. When I arrived in late October, Haight Street was a scary boarded-up strip, with no hippies in sight. Market Street and downtown were ripped up for the new BART train-system construction. The Transamerica Pyramid had just opened and was still the object of much architectural scorn. There were no love-ins in Golden Gate Park.

Staying at a fellow camp counselor's flat in Pacifica near the beach, I roamed the area for a few weeks on my motorbike; although the weather was mainly cold and wet, shockingly unlike the California I had seen on the silver screen. The sheer beauty of driving up the coast on curvaceous Highway 1, and across the

Golden Gate Bridge into Marin and Sonoma Counties, made these rides one of the most enjoyable parts of my entire trip.

Although the Haight was no longer the center of the hippie world, its ethos had filtered out and left its mark on the San Francisco Bay Area as a whole, and especially, I was glad to see, on its youth. The energy and positive outlook of the people I met made such a contrast from the general apathy of 1970s England, fraught with labour strikes, unemployment and enforced power-cuts.

Despite the cool weather, one bright and sunny area of my stay was the discovery of the Bay Area's AM and FM radio stations, including a whole dial full of FM! Groundbreaking stations such as KSAN, KPIG and KPFA took my radio experience to another level. The laid-back DJs were allowed to play entire albums of obscure music, and this, with a deep knowledge of the scene, gave them the freedom to tap into the gestalt of their enlightened listeners. Back in London, precious cassette tapes of shows on these very stations were passed hand-to-hand, embodying for us the wished-for future of radio. It felt so good to me to note that Radio Concord's free-form programming had been intuitively following this genre of radio, rather than the BBC's formatted stodge.

Slipping into the beauty and lifestyle of the Bay Area was so easy that I was tempted to stay longer, but after a few weeks I had the urge to head south to warmer weather. L.A. was pretty much as I'd imagined, with all the celluloid sights I'd taken in from films and TV. Although not much of an amusement-park-ride person, I still *had* to go to Disneyland, for the American experience like no other. I parked my motorbike near the main entrance, and lined up at a booth to buy my "E ticket."

As I was purchasing my ducat, I heard someone say in a deep voice, "Excuse me sir, can I speak with you?"

Turning in the direction of the voice, I saw a burly man in a light-gray suit, with mirrored sunglasses and a label on his breast pocket distinguishing him as Disneyland Security.

"What for?" I asked.

"Please sir, step to one side with me and let the line continue."

Obligingly, I walked with him a short way from the line. After identifying himself, he said, "I'm sorry sir, I can't let you in Disneyland dressed like that."

Admittedly, I was not expecting that comment. I was dressed in a clean T-shirt with no offensive words or insignia, and a pair of innocuous trousers; my hair was not particularly long or ungroomed.

"What do you mean?" I replied, " I think I'm dressed quite appropriately!" I replied. He then repeated his warning, but this time pointed at the side of my trouser leg, where I had sewn a two-inch round patch to cover up a small hole.

"What's wrong with a patch?" I asked incredulously.

"It's not the patch sir, it's what's on the patch; the number 13."

Defensively, I replied "What's wrong with that? It's my lucky number!"

"Sir, Disneyland has rules concerning drug issues, so we can't let you in dressed like that."

"What the hell do you mean!" I asked with growing puzzlement.

"Well sir," he gruffly replied, "the thirteenth letter of the alphabet is M, and M is used to signify marijuana in this area, so we cannot encourage or allow that sort of message inside Disneyland."

"You have to be kidding me!" was all I could say.

After a pause he said, "Sir, I notice you're not from America and I don't want to spoil your Disneyland experience, so please come with me."

Perplexed, I followed him over to the gift shop next to the entrance. With a nod to the shop worker, he reached over the counter and picked up a large Minnie Mouse sticker. Unpeeling the adhesive backing, he crouched down to slap the patch over my #13 abomination, stood up, and said, "You can go in now sir." As I shook my head bemusedly, he led me through the entry to the park, and when he was out of sight, I ripped the sticker off.

My journey back east was going to be through the winter months, so I decided to trade my bike in for a beige VW Beetle. I travelled through the southwest and south, the car radio my main communication with the world, as I passed through incredible scenery and mind-boggling natural formations: Death Valley, the Painted Desert, the Grand Canyon, Indian cliff dwellings, meteor craters, Carlsbad Caverns and Texas!

The Big Easy, and a Big Launch

New Orleans was my next destination. June Weisheit, a nurse at the kids' camp, had invited me to visit. The Big Easy was a revelation, so unlike the rest of America I had seen on my journey. My archetypally hospitable Louisianan hostess gave me incredible exposure to its wonders, which ranged from the incredible food to the music scene and humid tours of exotic Mississippi-Delta locations. Meeting the charismatic Moon Landrieu, then the Mayor of New Orleans, his young children (all future politicians), and other Louisiana bigwigs, through June's connected friend Henry Lambert was eye-opening. My first Thanksgiving meal, held in the back of June's parents' store, "Ed's Superette," in Houma, deep in the fecund Cajun bayous, was a sumptuous feast of new tastes, and an introduction to the delights of pumpkin, pecan, and sweet-potato pies.

June was happy for me to stay at her house, which was located not far from the French Quarter, and the hedonistic delights of Louisiana were very distracting. One of the reasons, apart from the food, to go to New Orleans is the music, and we explored the scene, from Preservation Hall, where the cost for a request was only $1, but became $5 if "When the Saints Go Marching In" was called for, to Tipitina's, and the nameless dark bars scattered along Bourbon Street and across the city.

A B.B. King concert at the old Tulane basketball arena became a scary situation for us after it was announced, following a long delay, that B.B. would not appear. Hundreds of riot police poured in and subdued the whole arena, and I'm still thankful to Curtis Mayfield, who stood courageously on the missile-littered stage, calming the crowd, and perhaps saving our lives.

Listening to the radio news over breakfast beignets one morning, when it registered on me that Apollo 17 was going to blast off to the moon at Cape Canaveral in Florida just before Christmas; it was to be the first nighttime launch, of what was to be the (ultimately) last Apollo moon rocket. As I was so comparatively close, I couldn't miss the chance to see this epic event. While staying at a campground on Cocoa Beach, the closest the public could get to the launch, I had a splendid time with the other people who'd come to watch the spectacle, and communal cooking brought a great camaraderie to the mostly young crowd. Attempting to surf was another new experience for me, but even after I was coached by some pros, the less said about that debacle the better!

How can I ever forget standing on the warm sand that night, as Apollo 17 took off? A low rumbling and flash near the ground, then the rocket working its way up into the clear night air on top of a bright squat yellow body that elongated into a red tail. The sound was perhaps the most impressive part; I felt deep vibrations in my chest as wave after sonic wave pulsed over me. This percussive sensation and the actual physical pressure emanating from the massive engines over that distance, were accompanied somewhat surreally by the sound of the Moody Blues' *Days of Future Past* blaring from the back of a van parked on the beach.

Crash Landing in Baltimore

I WAS INVITED TO SPEND CHRISTMAS 1972 in Cedar Rapids, Iowa, at the home of Pat Hutchinson, my counselor girlfriend from Camp Stanley. I headed north on the scenic route through the Okeefenokee Swamp into Georgia, my head still filled with memories of the hi-tech moon launch, only to encounter, once again, the paradoxical nature of American reality. Driving by a row of ramshackle backwoods shacks, I stopped to watch as an old black man in a stubbled field shook a branch at the rear end of a grizzled mule that lazily walked on a circular path, attached to a pole that pivoted on top of a central stone block. What a transition! Within an hour's drive, I'd gone from moon rockets to someone grinding grain as if in ancient Mesopotamia.

Minus-fifty-degree temperatures/wind chill factor failed to endear me to Iowa in the winter. In Washington D.C., along with a few of the other camp counselors who had come from other parts of the world and were still in the country, I stayed with camp leaders Tom and Lee Held in their nice suburban house. After touring the usual Washington sites, I headed to Baltimore and stayed with Dave Beaven, a camp counselor, at his parents' large house.

On New Year's Eve, headed to a party, I found myself perched on a wheel-hub in the back of a solid-top jeep, with Dave and two others sitting on the other hub and floor, and a driver and passenger up front. The driver, who may have already had too much to drink, was driving quite fast and erratically. As we sped down a quiet city street, he failed to notice that the road turned sharply ninety degrees to the left, and wrenched the wheel violently at the last moment to make the acute turn.

David, sensing disaster, shouted, "We're going to crash!" and the unstable jeep started to roll over. The four of us in the back were tossed around violently by multiple 360° arse-over-teakettle rolls before we scraped to a shattering halt, upside down in a driveway, with the roof half caved in. I worked my way to the crushed back window on my stomach, wiggled out, and then helped the three others in the back, to safety. Miraculously, we were all in one piece, apart from some nasty skin punctures, scratches, aches and large bruises, and were all transported swiftly to the general hospital and treated well in the Emergency department. Happy New Year 1973!

I stayed for a week at David's home, healing up, then headed back to New York. It was mid-February, and I felt that it was time to go home, so I sold my car, bought a $50 ticket to Luxembourg on Icelandic Airlines, and returned to London to resume my life there. During my eight-month trip, except for calling my parents a few times, and sending some postcards, I hadn't kept up with the goings-on in England. I was anxious to find out what I'd missed.

Baby, Bootlegs, and Broadcasting

On my return to London after eight months, I discovered I was about to become a father—Sheila had been pregnant when I left but hadn't told me! Quite a homecoming surprise, especially the timing, and on February 21st, 1973, my son Ronin was born at the Whittington Hospital in Highgate. Sheila and I didn't otherwise continue our relationship.

Catching up with my radio buddies, I told them of my experiences in America, and they brought me up to date about the many escapades and broadcasts that had occurred during my absence. The Concord crew had put on an eighteen-hour marathon over the recent Christmas holidays in Islington. It was heard as far away as Scotland, but the New-Year's broadcast celebration had been raided by a large force of GPO and police. The still-original and now-legendary Concord transmitter had miraculously been spirited away in the fracas.

Our joke group, "The Running Sores" (originally put together by Mick, Jeffrey and I, and made up of both good musicians and bad non-musicians [me]), had continued its unlikely proto-punk cacophonic career. Scoring a number of club gigs, the Sores had bizarrely opened for the Tom Robinson Band at The Camden Palace! Their live-audience reception was "spotty" in every sense of the word. Hearing about all this pirate lunacy, I was chagrined at what I had missed, but I'd just had the experience of a lifetime, one that had reinvigorated my spirit after the completion of my training and college sentence.

Coming back, however, I realized I had no idea what I wanted to do with myself. I knew that I didn't want to go back to engineering immediately, so I joined a temporary job agency, which sent me out to work in offices and drive laundry vans. With the financial backing of Mick Lewis's dad, Mick and I started a record stall called Albatross, (Yes, after the *Monty Python* sketch) at a few different London street markets.

Because of ancient Sunday "blue laws," only Jews and Seventh Day-Adventists could work at street markets on the Christian Sabbath—one of the few advantages I ever experienced being a Jew in England! Within a few months we had rented a permanent space seven days a week at the Kensington Indoor Market. We eschewed "Top 40" hits, only stocking the music genres we liked—underground, folk, blues, doo-wop, comedy, and "oldies." This didn't seem like actual work, as we had a fine time scouring record-wholesaler warehouses and estate sales for our market stock, personal collections, and radio shows. While I couldn't think of a better job to do for the rest of my life, I certainly wasn't earning any money in the record biz, so to get back on my feet financially, I reluctantly hired on as a junior engineer at Comyn Ching, a mechanical-services contractor in the West End of London,

One thing that had not changed in my absence was mainstream radio. There was nothing different on the airwaves, just the same old BBC-radio format slogging on, apparently with no awareness of the rapidly expanding music universe. It would be another eight months until, in October of 1973, Britain's two first independent commercial FM stations were launched in London.

After my rich experience of listening to hundreds of small local AM stations across America; the revelatory underground FM stations on both coasts; and the US transcontinental networks; I could now see the bigger picture of what pirate radio could achieve in England. Not necessarily the current American commercial or public model, but one that deliberately connected radio to the community. I also realized that British broadcast restrictions were truly a control and free-speech issue, not a technical, safety or cost concern.

Apollo 17 Launch on 7 December, 1972

Arnold in Grand Canyon

Bison

Camp Tahoe for Kids

Arnold's Court Case Document

After Pirate Radio Case

4

Pirating Resumes, to a Government Broadside!

URGED ON BY MY AMERICAN-RADIO HIGH, my first question to the crew when we all got together was "When's the next broadcast?" In early March we ramped up Concord's broadcasting efforts, which had been mainly moribund since the big 1973 New Year's raid.

Scrambling around among friends, radio connections and relatives, I lined up a few new locations for the re-launch of my pirate career. As I once again donned those tatty headphones, the thrill of being behind the mic again, spiced with the delicious background threat of a raid, brought my muscle-memory back immediately.

Much new British music had emerged whilst I had been away, broadcast extensively by the crew, but, as usual, not by the BBC to any extent. This new content provided a fresh start for my own show with the music I'd soaked up from radio on my cross-country travels, as well as from my American friends' record and tape collections that strongly influenced my new playlist: Dan Hicks, Randy Newman, Jim Croce, Bill Withers, Al Green, Jackson Browne, the Allman Brothers, Harry Chapin, Delaney & Bonnie, Joy of Cooking, Curtis Mayfield, and War. These were just a few of the stars of the maturing US music scene that I began to spin, to a warm reception.

I was glad to see that the British hadn't lagged behind in their creativity in my absence, with the wonderfully stylized "glam rock" scene; performers like Roxy Music and Lynsey DePaul soon earned their place in the album-laden milk crates that I lugged to each broadcast. In addition to my own record collection, there were frequently new releases from sympathetic record labels and agents, and many musical groups submitted cassettes to us for playing on-air. Although most weren't broadcast quality, many got their chance to say they'd been on the radio. From that raw input, I was inspired to start taping live gigs for broadcast, using a cassette recorder— this ploy often got me into a show for free.

Another aspect of my revived show was the creation of short featurettes on various artists or themes. As a rabid Beatle fan, many of my shows were based around the Fab Four. I had a great time, for instance, putting together a live show detailing all the hidden messages said to be scattered through their albums, such as "The Hand of Death" on the *Sgt. Pepper* cover, and the "Paul's Dead" of *Abbey Road*. A highlight was playing "I am the Walrus" on my *Magical Mystery Tour* EP, by spinning it backwards on a turntable with my finger, so that I could prove "I am the eggman, they are the eggmen, I am the walrus" gets inverted to "I'm very high, I'm getting higher, I'm getting there." This procedure scratched and wore out the vinyl quickly and the cheap turntable motors protested fiercely, but that segment was often requested. Perhaps I presaged the rise of the "scratching" genre!

New, Improved, Radio Crew

RADIO CONCORD'S NEXT LEAP FORWARD was caused by an extremely bad technical problem. The transmitter we had initially bought in 1971 had remained, despite much manhandling, trouble-free during my absence, but just a few broadcasts into my return, all of the pirate radio hauling, mauling, and over-modulating caused our severely abused electronic workhorse to break down spectacularly—it went up in an inferno of sparks and flames at the beginning of a broadcast. As none of the present Concord crew had any real technical knowledge, we were in a bind, and desperately needed help if we were to continue.

Due to natural attrition, and to the often-unreliable nature of pirate radio personnel, new volunteers had to be found all the time. A very intelligent chap of eighteen, Simon Newbury (Browning), became our first technical whiz and transmitter-meister. While I was away, Simon and his friend "Dismal Dave" Robbie (Stuart), who had been broadcasting under the name Radio North London, had come to a remote Concord broadcast held at a reservoir in Northwest London.

A tall lad with shoulder-length hair, Simon would work self-lessly and tirelessly over the next years, making and maintaining transmitters for us, for himself, and for other pirates, on top of his own show, a mix of pop-rock and progressive rock. Entirely self-taught in electronics, with occasional reference to books, he usu-ally succeeded by sheer force of experimentation. His hands and fingers, greatly abused in his electric-construction efforts, were very calloused, and his party trick was to stick his fingers into a live light socket—their thick carapace insulated them from shock.

Simon's workroom, located above his parents' off-license in Edmonton, North London, was piled high with discarded com-ponents and transmitters in various stages of construction or destruction. I spent many a night helping him with the work of cutting, drilling and soldering chasses and components as he wove his electronic magic for the next broadcast. His home-built transmitters varied in size from little 8-watt jobs that you could tuck under your arm, to one that was dubbed "The Artifact." This monstrosity, six feet tall and two feet deep and wide, was made up of many Uni-strut modular racks, and meant to operate at 1kW output. As far as we knew, it was the largest transmitter ever used by a land pirate. Fortunately, I had the use of an estate car from my engineering job, and we could slide The Artifact into the back easily, and still transport all kinds of other equipment and crew around London as required.

"Dismal Dave" was a friendly, but self-confessed dark person ("proto-goth" would be his description now), but also a good guy who would help out, and did fine music shows featuring some of the heavier and darker progressive music of the day. Although Simon and Dave were initially attracted to Concord because we had some sort of organization, not a common attribute of pirate stations, perhaps our greatest asset for them was our continuing access to multiple broadcast locations.

The enigmatic Keith Hunter (Keith York or Len Deevish), from Yorkshire, entered the Concord orbit through Simon, and stuck with us through all our later adventures. A thin man/boy with shoulder-length brown straight hair, he played great underground progressive music—Yes, Steely Dan, and the like—accompanied by knowledgeable patter. We frequently roasted him about his dietary habits, as his total caloric intake appeared to consist of sugary soda and salty snacks. A very opinionated fellow, Keith could argue a discussion point for hours; oddly enough, this really helped in keeping us focused and grounded at important times, and in the course of making critical decisions.

Tony Reszka, a friendly chap from West London, called us up during one broadcast and asked to help. He turned out to be one of the few volunteers willing to do the dirty all-night work of being a lookout. Most of the time he didn't even want to do a show. A long-haired blond kid with a perpetual grin, Tony was sixteen and still in comprehensive school, and wore (even in the summer) a sheepskin coat of which he was inordinately proud. His ambition, he confided, was to go to college, study biochemistry (which he did, and has had an acclaimed career), and create a legal hybrid of two related plants—the hop and hemp.

After hearing one of our shows, a fellow named Andre Bell called us and offered his help. Andre was a great boon to us, because he knew and had connections with many of the London underground and progressive music performers like Arthur Brown (best known for his 1968 single "Fire") and the Who, and he was learning the ways of artists, management, and technicians in the rock/pop world. After doing a few Concord shows of his own, he became more interested in helping us behind the scenes.

Our collective ears pricked up when we heard that Andre lived in a flat above his uncle's electronics parts store in Hanwell. He duly invited the Concord broadcasters and techs over to his place, and we went downstairs to the store after hours. Our wizards usually made do with salvaged electronic parts from old pre-transistor equipment, so, as they toured the shelves, they were all but drooling at the electronic bounty on display. Then, unbelievably, Andre urged them to take any components they needed, and without further ado, we pirated transistors and expensive parts that we had once only dreamed about. Concord broadcasted from Andre's flat a few times without problems, our antenna stretched across a parking lot behind his place and attached to the back of a cinema.

Jerry (Dam Blocker) joined our cause through my friend Mick Lewis. He was an odd character, silent most of the time, but put him behind the mic, and he'd play some great prog-rock. Because he was so quiet, I can't tell you much about him, but he worked hard for Concord.

A listener called during a broadcast in North London, said we were coming in powerfully in Wood Green, and added that he had experience as a DJ and wanted to help us. Thus, Don Stevens entered the Radio Concord world. After living in America for a couple of years, he'd married an American woman named Anne and had acquired an interesting "Mid-Atlantic" accent. The American-DJ style Don brought to Concord was refreshingly different and popular with our audience and with the other DJs. Several times a week, much to Anne's chagrin, we would come over to his place and occupy it for long periods for producing shows.

In the late winter of 1975, Don and Keith volunteered to do a stint with Radio Caroline aboard the one intermittingly operating pirate radio ship, *Mi Amigo*. Because of the British laws, in order to reach the ship, they had to go via Holland and catch a ride on the supply boat. They helped out around the vessel, and were allowed to host some shows late at night. That would have been a thrilling experience for me, but it involved a couple of months commitment out on the North Sea, and running Radio Concord on land kept me too busy as it was. (You can read later in Chapter 4 about the episode on the Thames that was, alas, the closest I would get to seaborne radio piracy.)

So, in short order, we had taken on a very strong and dedicated group with technical expertise, radio and showbiz connections, and a greatly expanded musical content. These committed core additions to our crew helped lay the foundation for the next chapter of Radio Concord's development.

Nuns and Space Aliens

WITH THE LUCK OF INNOCENTS, Radio Concord had not had a completely debilitating raid and bust in nearly three years of operating, just the many near misses when we'd had to spirit away the transmitter. Although those occasions were usually accompanied by the loss of all our other equipment, we counted ourselves lucky that we'd had no arrests. Considering all the efforts that the trackers and police had gone through so far, in trying to nab us, as we repeatedly cocked a snoot at them, we had to be prime candidates for a big raid by this time, and it did in the summer of 1974.

Being blessed with law-abiding parents meant I couldn't broadcast from their flat under normal circumstances, but just once, when they went away for a long weekend, I couldn't resist the temptation, and allowed the pirate crew to set up shop in their neat council home. Their flat was on the first and second floors of a four-story building backed with small, enclosed yards and gardens; this required some tricky climbing by our team to get a wire from the second-floor balcony to the desired endpoint.

Our goal was the top of a metal fire escape that was connected to the end of the girls' dormitory of the La Sainte Union Convent School, four floors and about sixty feet up, and five gardens away. To accomplish this precarious feat, Simon, Keith and I, in broad daylight, scrambled our way diagonally across all the back gardens, walls, and sheds without any of the neighbors noticing and calling the police on us.

In addition to the ground-based obstacles, there were also electrical and telephone cables splaying out from poles overhead, so we resorted to stone-age techniques—tying our wire to rocks and sticks, and throwing the clumsy projectiles up and over each obstructing line until we had painstakingly threaded our insulated wire over all the aerial obstacles.

Finally, after heaving the last stone and clambering over the tall convent brick wall, we won through to the base of the building's emergency stairs. Hoping we wouldn't get arrested as Peeping Toms, we scuttled up the wobbly cast-iron stairs past the girls' dormitory windows, and with a flourish, hoisted the wire tautly to the top landing from across the gardens. As we were tying off the end, we heard a "Helloooo!" from below. Busted.

We'd been spotted by two of the teaching nuns; dressed in their medieval black-and-white, they stood at the bottom of the stairs, calling, "Yoo-hoo! What *are* you young men doing up there?" Thinking quickly, I shouted down to them, "We're college students, Sisters, and we're setting up an experiment to pick up intelligent radio signals from outer space." I went on to apologize profusely for not asking their permission, adding that, we had to finish the project by next week, or we would fail our college course. Somehow I sold this outrageous fib to the nuns, who smiled indulgently at us, and one said, in a bright cheery voice: "Oh, all right then, but be careful and don't make a mess; ta-ta!" Waving goodbye to us, they walked off arm in arm. We three pirates, shaking our heads in relief and disbelief, quickly clattered back down, dutifully averting our eyes at the dorm windows, and prepared for the weekend broadcast.

The long, high antenna in this elevated part of London gave us a great broadcast range. We set the audio equipment up on Mum's dining room table, and installed the transmitter in the spare bedroom. A steady stream of DJs dropped by and enjoyed the tea and digestive biscuits we kept on hand during their shows. The signal was unusually far and clear, and with the ongoing party atmo-sphere in the house, combined with great feedback from the lis-teners calling the phone box across the road, it was by far our most successful broadcast session to date.

That is, until the second night, when a barrage of flashing lights appeared out on the street, eerily distorted by the wavy front-door glass, and the cheery two-tone chime at the front door took on a more ominous note. Checking our only getaway option, we found the police had already cut off our rear-garden escape and were gathering at the locked back door, tapping insistently on the glass. Simon, thinking quickly, ran upstairs, turned off the power, yanked out the crystal from the transmitter, flushed it down the toilet, and calmly began to dismantle the other connections with his pliers, rendering the electronics useless.

Meanwhile, the front-door chimes still pealed, so once the crew were settled, I opened it a crack: "Can I help you, Officer?" A uniformed police officer, standing at the head of a phalanx of lesser constables, thrust a piece of A4 paper with a crown at the top and a lot of wheras-es and whereof-ses below it, into my face. "We believe there is an illegal radio broadcast 'ere, and this 'ere's the search warrant!" was the official reply. "What? We're just having a party! Sorry; I'll keep the noise down!" I said innocently.

At the officer's insistence, I slowly and carefully read and examined the warrant that set out in great detail how we had con-travened the pertinent radio laws, all the way down to the judge's signature. At that point, three men in plainclothes moved to the door alongside the chief and identified themselves as GPO radio trackers. With all as ready as it could be in the house, I let the Rozzers and suits file inside, noticing how all the neighbours stood at their doors, curiously watching the kerfuffle going on at the Levines'.

The flood of officials searched and questioned all those in the house, but mainly me, as I was considered the responsible party. The GPO men lugged out all our precious equipment, records, and dismembered transmitter. At least they didn't take my parents' album collection, which was stored in the historic radio cabinet where I'd first heard Radio Odyssey. Once the place had mostly been cleared out, the police officer told me that the rudely awakened Mother Superior of the convent had not been amused by our antics, but would not press charges. I wish my Mum would've been as magnanimous on her return!

Judgement and Repentance?

THE GPO, AFTER PERPETRATING SUCH A BIG BUST at my parents' house, with all the expense of deploying such a large force against us, just *had* to bring charges against me and some of the others involved. With no picture IDs mandatory in Britain, some of the offenders managed to give a fake identity and address, and walk away, but not me. Duly summoned through The Royal Mail three months later, all of the identified miscreants were brought up on charges of transgressing the Wireless & Telegraphy Act of 1967, the very Act that had doomed our beloved ship pirates! To be so accused, and in such heady company, was truly a life highlight for me.

On November 30th, 1974, we showed up as required at the Clerkenwell Magistrates' Court near Kings Cross Station, ready to take our punishment. Despite there being no crystal in the transmitter, the preponderance of evidence won the day. Perhaps if I'd employed a lawyer the result would have been different. After some technical information from the GPO representative was read into the record, we received a stern admonishment from the crusty, be-robed and bewigged judge. When asked, I dutifully told Hizzoner that I'd seen the error of my ways, pointed out that it was my first offence, and that I didn't realize it was an illegal operation, so threw myself upon his hoped-for mercy. The impatient judge fined me £10 plus £10 court costs; the other pirate reprobates got off with lesser penalties. All the defendants took their punishment bravely. For me, it was money well spent, just for the experience alone.

Well. The Forces of Officialdom had given us a stern warning not to do it again, or there would be even bigger trouble next time, so after the trial we naturally redoubled our efforts for the cause. A new Simon-made Radio Concord transmitter had premiered a week after the bust at my parents' house. To confuse the GPO, and our listeners, we changed the time of the station's regular broadcast start from Saturday midnight to 8 AM Sunday.

The Supreme Dialect meets El Supremo

I HAD BY THIS TIME REALIZED THAT I was essentially a Marked Man, and if I were to continue in pirate radio, some kind of metamorphosis was needed to prevent the GPO from discovering that I was on the air again. The solution was obvious: change my radio persona and voice. My original "Tommy Arnold" personality used my own voice, but how was I to change that dramatically enough so the GPO wouldn't recognize me?

Then I had a brainstorm: *Dr. Who* was my favourite sci-fi TV show on the BBC, and the show featured the best hokey alien-creature-villains of all times, the Daleks. Mutants living in a metal shell, they speak with a strident, staccato, metallic voice, are very violent, and want to destroy or enslave all human and other life forms in the universe. The ruler of the Daleks is called the "Supreme Dalek." Inspired by my love for puns, I decided to call myself the "Supreme Dialect." Learning how to speak like a Dalek was challenging, especially without the help of an electronic ring-modulator device, like the one used by the BBC Radiophonics Lab in the *Dr. Who* series.

In a strange way, when my new show debuted, the different character I was forced to play, helped transform my usual music and comedy content into a broader look at the world, culture, and community. On the new show, a typical song introduction would go something like this: "You-will-listen-to- this-Nick-Drake-song-and-you-will-enjoy, you-will-enjoy, you-will-obey!" My fellow-pirates loved the brittle voice effect and usually cracked up in the background of my shows.

I had also realized that I needed a new intro and/or outro song, to go along with my new voice and name re-launch. To set off the harsh Dalek voice, I had to juxtapose something very, very different with it, and found a suitably sappy selection in my parents' dusty record collection. "A White Sports Coat and a Pink Carnation," as sung by the King Brothers, a 1950s British trio (in a more pop-schmaltzy style than the original Tex-Country version by Marty Robbins), was just the ticket.

The Supreme Dialect ruled the airwaves for a year or so. It was a blast being in another character, something I hadn't done in public before, and I found it especially liberating to act like a maniacal metal-coated space alien hosting a radio show. Conducting serious interviews in that dehumanized voice was very challenging, I must admit, and often ended in hysterical laughter by all participants. Despite the silliness, guests understood the situation and were all good sports.

Ultimately, the voice, kept up for an hour or two at a time, was too wearing on my vocal cords, and as my show was evolving to include more community news and musician interviews, I began to feel more and more constrained by the unnatural Dalek honk. To remedy this, I changed my name, persona, and voice again. And so it was that one day the Supreme Dialect time-warped away, and turned into "El Supremo," with my voice and personality taking on the insistent tone and accent of a (hopefully) patently fake American pop-radio DJ.

Brother and Birds Broadcasts

EVEN THOUGH CONCORD HAD BEEN RAIDED at my parents' house, the Levine family seemed more puzzled than annoyed by my antics. My oldest brother Ralph so enjoyed the stories of my escapades in pirate radio that he offered his place to use for a broadcast. Usually we beamed our shows from North or West London, so Bexleyheath, Kent, just off the old Roman Road to Canterbury (the same one that Chaucer had taken a few years earlier) was foreign country.

On a lovely late summer's day in 1973 our crew retraced old Geoffrey's jaunt to Ralph's place. The antenna wire took no time to sling up a tree at the end of his garden, and we broadcast from his living room, with thankfully no raids for the duration—the change in our usual broadcast area may have thrown the GPO detectors off. A workmate who lived in the area called in with a glowing reception report. My young nephews had fun cycling up and down the street being lookouts, but my sister-in-law Valerie nervously paced the house during the whole transmission. As a bonus for their family, I began to use their address to receive new albums from record companies and agents, to be enjoyed until I picked them up for station use.

Most of the broadcast locations we used were family homes or small apartments. However, in the autumn of 1974, Concord literally went up in the world, to a flat on the tenth floor of a twenty-story block of flats in Edmonton, North London. Fortunately, the lift worked, which made light work of bringing up all the live-broadcast equipment. That was the easy part. Exploring the access to the top of the building, we found the door to get onto the high-rise roof was unlocked, and we played out the wire from the edge of the roof and down the side of the building towards the open window of the flat we were using. Even though in this configuration the antenna would be dangling just a few feet from the face of the building, because of its sheer height, we would be beaming out over most of London.

Suddenly, as the wire snaked down, I felt a sharp pull from below. Peeking over the precipitous side of the building, we saw an older lady leaning out of a window a few floors above our flat, grabbing the wire and reeling it inside. Quickly, after calculating which floor her window was on, I cut the wire and we tromped down the stairs and sheepishly knocked on her front door. She actually answered the door draped in our wire. "Wot the 'ell d'y'fink yer doin'?" she shouted.

"Can we have our wire back please?" I timidly asked, dropping into my now usual schtick that we were innocent college students trying to pick up extraterrestrial radio signals for a class project. Amazingly, she believed us and, with a stern face and finger-wag, handed over the unruly, tangled bale of wire, whilst admonishing us: "If there's any more trouble I'll call the bleedin' police!" Appropriately chastised, we went back up to the roof and successfully fed the wire back down into the window for which it was originally destined.

What a strange flat for our broadcast! Pete and Carol, a very welcoming couple, lived there with an aviary of parrots and budgies. Not believing in cages, they allowed the birds to fly around and land on any object or person, even during the broadcast. It was quite a task (and quite hilarious) keeping the birds from hopping onto our record-decks as we were DJ-ing, while also protecting the open transmitter and equipment from flying bird poop! A wonderful and somewhat surreal scene developed when I had a lengthy on-air interview with a quite intelligent talking parrot. Apart from the more serious questions, a lot of gratuitous *aaarrgh!-ing!* went on between man and bird. And yes, of course he was perched on my shoulder.

Aphrodite; or, How We Almost Got No Satisfaction

CONSIDERING THE USUALLY NONDESCRIPT PLACES from which we tended to broadcast, in the autumn of 1974 the next combination was an apex of oddity that swung the pendulum deep into the Funk-and-Flash zone. At a party, I had met Caroline, and her partner Sue. A beautiful couple, they took a liking to me, and subsequently we got together to socialize. The two of them had connections with wealthy debutantes and used to invite me along to parties in the swanky upper-crust flats and houses of Chelsea and Kensington. Considering the social benefits, being their "beard" was no problem for me.

They lived together blissfully in a delightfully cute (but leaky) old flat-bottomed houseboat appropriately named *Aphrodite*. This picturesque vessel was moored, together with a handful of other quirky boats, on a small creaky dock on the River Thames in the shadow of Chelsea's ornate Albert Bridge. Above them, on Cheyne Walk, traffic rumbled busily alongside the river, but below the solid granite parapet the river life was quiet and idyllic. Caroline and Sue lived openly as a gay couple, very rare in those days of extreme persecution. Just a few years before this, when Caroline had been dating straight, she was Cat Stevens' girlfriend—she said she broke up with Cat because of his fragile and troubled psyche.

The houseboat was a fittingly unique place from which to broadcast. The original radio pirates of the Sixties had been out on the ocean, with lots of open sea around them, but we, as if to go one better than them, were planning to broadcast from a river in the centre of London, surrounded by ten million people, and less than a mile from the Houses of Parliament. None of those other political details mattered though, as at last, (*Aaarrgh!*) we would be real high seas pirates me hearties! That is, as soon as the tide came in and lifted us off the mud!

This floating location, however desirable, posed some serious technical problems. A few hours before the broadcast, our attempts to locate a suitable high place to attach the antenna end-point, resulted in a lot of negative headshaking from the techies. The optimum conditions for any MW broadcast are from the top of a tall hill with no obstructions around. Here, our transmitter would be sited below the waterline of a low-profile houseboat on the River Thames, the lowest place in London, surrounded by tall buildings, in a floating hulk with ropey electrical connections, and a dubious earth that in itself was vital for our MW signal.

But, we all agreed, the show must go on, and it went without saying that the location of the long wire would definitely determine the success of this broadcast. At first, the Albert Bridge's vertical suspension rods looked likely, but we soon deemed them impossible to reach because of the many obstacles we'd have to work the wire around between the bridge and the embankment. Looking for creative alternatives, I noticed a four-story Queen Anne-styled terraced house, Number 48, located on the other side of a small service road beyond the main Cheyne Walk road, directly across from the houseboat, with a small grassy park in between. The sturdy Spanish-style wrought-iron balustrades at the upper windows looked like an ideal tie-off location, especially as some metal latticework crept conveniently up the house just left of the desired spot. I was immediately struck with a whimsical vision of myself climbing like Errol Flynn, to the third-floor balcony of my paramour.

When I suggested this location, Caroline's eyes widened, and shaking her head, she exclaimed: "You must be kidding! Do you know who lives there?" With a suitable pause, she continued, "That's Mick Jagger's house!" We were all delighted. The London home of the legendary Jagger! "Why not?" I said hopefully, "Wouldn't he understand what we were doing, free speech, music and all that?" We debated the situation; was this too high-profile a house for us to attach our wire to? Didn't we attract enough attention as it was? Caroline thought about it for a minute and then said encouragingly: "You know, this actually may be a good time. Mick can't be in town right now, because I haven't seen any fans camped outside the house the last few days."

As usual, I was the designated climber of tall buildings, but as we assessed the whole situation, we realized that the climb might actually be the easiest part of this operation. Cheyne Walk is a four-lane major road with a near-continuous flow of double-decker buses, taxis, cars, and lorries moving along it. Not only the heavy traffic, but also the park and the service road beyond would make this escapade our most challenging wire-stringing attempt to date.

On the other hand, no electrical lines ran overhead to interfere with our aerial work, a circumstance that made our task seem faintly possible. We started out on our task, with me carrying a roll of wire casually in my hand, and tools concealed in my pockets. Two of the crew walked alongside me, trying to act as unsuspicious as possible as we strolled to our goal. We crossed over at the Albert Bridge traffic lights, taking note of how long the road in both directions was car-free during the various red-light sequences. As the three of us walked by Jagger's house, I nonchalantly peeled off from the others as they continued to the Mews corner.

Unlatching an ornate metal gate (surprisingly unlocked), I slipped through into a small front garden, and snuck to the left front of the building. Tentatively, I rattled the wrought-iron lattice, which felt strongly attached to the bricks. The plan was for me to clamber up about thirty feet, totally visible from the street. "I'd better get this done right sharpish," I thought.

So, there I was, just like Romeo, but in broad daylight, scaling the outside of Mr. Jagger's house to his bedroom balcony, with wire-cutters instead of a stiletto in my belt, and radio, rather than romance, on my mind. When I reached the third-floor window, I put my left arm through the lattice to anchor myself, quickly reached over with my right, and looped the wire and rope tie-off over the grillwork that covered the lower half of the window. Then, getting off Jagger's cloud, I climbed down one-handed, doling out the vital wire with the other.

Tony and Dave, seeing me complete my mission from the corner of the Mews, hied quickly over to the pavement outside the front of the house, their task being to roll the wire out over the narrow service road, across the small median park, and up to the pavement edge of Cheyne Walk. During the next sequence, the long wire would be at risk, lying vulnerably on the ground with cars, vans, prams, and people passing obliviously over it.

Surveilling the service road in case of any problems, I watched as the wiremen waited for the right moment, then streaked the rest of the way across the main road. We had learned the hard way to be cautious: at a recent broadcast on Rhyl Street in Camden, during this very same maneuver, we had just loosely attached the wire to some unfinished council flats across Malden Road, when a Number 24 double-decker bus bound for Victoria Station, came along and took our entire antenna down the street with it.

The plan was that once the wire was across the street, other helpers would put it through a string loop on a lamppost and hoist it high above the roadway. It was a two-way street, and by our calculations, we had about a 20-second window in which to achieve our complete goal. Luck was with us, and our timing was perfect. On the red light, one person unreeled the wire across Cheyne Walk, while two others, running shotgun on either side of him, waved their arms to stop any stray oncoming vehicles. Slipping the wire through the insulating rope loop, two of the crew hoisted the rope, then pulled frantically on the cable. The antenna twanged up high into the air just before the first double-decker bus roared under it.

The wire was now stretched tautly across from Jagger's house to the ornate Thames-side lamppost, and from there, the end thrown down to the houseboat hidden beneath the embankment ledge. Jubilant at our success, we were just about to board the *Aphrodite* to start the broadcast, when we heard shouting from across the road. At the very upstairs window where I had attached the antenna, an irate woman had appeared, and was shouting, waving, and jerking on the wire.

As we were holding the opposite end of it, there wasn't a lot we could do or say to deny our involvement. Caroline, told of the furor, came up from the houseboat, took a gander, and told us that was Jagger's Italian housekeeper. Three of us crossed back over the road and stood meekly in front of the house as she screamed down at us in unintelligible Italian. As far as we could tell from her expressive but very *un*-Juliet-like language, she wanted to know what the hell we were doing and was informing us that she was going to call the police.

Before we could come up with one of our stock student radio/space-alien experiment excuses, she undid the knot on the tie-off, and the wire snaked downwards to splay all the way across Cheyne Walk. Seeing this, the crew near the houseboat quickly hauled the antenna across the road even as vehicles were running over it.

Despite the housekeeper's florid Neopolitan threats, the police didn't show up, and we decided to continue. With time running out on our 6 PM broadcast start, we went with a quick-and-dirty plan B, co-opting a large London Plane tree near the waterside. Weighting the wire end with a stick, I threw it up as high as possible into the tree, lodging it on a branch, and tossed the other end (also weighted) across the swirling river water and into the prow of the houseboat. Concord came on the air just a few minutes late that day, but our desperation tactic had worked, and we were broadcasting!

At last! Just like our watery radio heroes of the 1960s, we were now actual pirates on the high seas, or at least on a low river. As we went giddily about our work (or was it seasickness?), we couldn't stop saying "*Aaarrgh!*" to each other, in that inimitable Robert Newton/Long John Silver manner. A few hours later, our water-borne fantasy came back down to silt when the tide went out, and the flat-bottomed converted coal barge *Aphrodite* re-settled herself squishily onto the muddy river bottom.

Incredibly, considering that the broadcast wasn't reaching as far as usual because of the antenna difficulties, the number of phone calls we received at a nearby callbox reassured us that people were listening across central London. This was an especially vulnerable location, with only one narrow wooden gangplank as an entry and exit, so if raided we couldn't just jump over a garden wall or scramble up a roof to escape, as we usually did on land. Although I had become quite the adventurer, leaping into the filthy, cold River Thames at night to escape the police was not an experience I would have savoured. Fortunately, we had a steady stream of willing lookouts and regular changes of shift, so everyone stayed alert to their duties.

This inspired location gave us an extra boost of excitement for our shows, and we joyfully tossed out as many watery puns as we could think of. The one recurring technical problem we had was blackouts, when the old electrical cartridge fuse would blow if someone turned on an appliance or bulb too many, or when the bilge-pump came on to suck out the continuous hull leaks. Broadcasting at this location was most enjoyable, with Caroline and Sue keeping us going day and night with tea and bikkies. The successful show went on throughout the whole weekend without (happily) the sniff of a raid, or (sadly) the sighting of a Mick.

Radio Dynamite

WITH SIMON NEWBURY, DAVE ROBBIE, Keith Hunter, Don Stevens, and some of the crew from Radio North London added to the Concord mix, as well as other casual helpers on board, we now had a solid personnel base with which to operate powerfully and regularly. The autumn of 1974 was also the time (as recounted in other chapters) where we'd begun to suffer from a series of debilitating raids, so we decided to confuse the authorities by changing the station name to Radio Dynamite, with a new crystal that gave us an operating frequency on 235 metres.

To further fake out the trackers, we also moved our broadcast time to Sunday 10 AM to-4 PM. The younger and newer members of the crew took all this change as a signal for a fresh music-programming start, and brought in more of the growing punk and progressive music scene. A workmate of mine, Karl Downes, designed an exploding-stick-of-dynamite logo for our bumper stickers and letterhead. For a few months, this rebranding gave us a new energy that helped transcend the depressive effect of the Concord raids.

However, rather than the "a change is as good as a rest" effect we'd hoped for, the ultimate scenario was more like "from the frying pan into the fire." Although naively, we only wanted to project an innocent whimsical radio usage of the word "dynamite," in the sense of "exciting" and "unpredictable," we should really have foreseen that the provocative name was an insane idea. It was an especially ill-fated choice because of the contemporaneous rise of the pro-active Angry Brigade and the IRA in Britain, the Bader-Meinhof Gang in Germany, and the PLO in the Middle East.

This was way more than an image problem. From the first, we got feedback from our audience about the dangerous connections and connotations of our new name. A couple of other pirate stations had also heard, from their conversations with GPO trackers, ominous comments about our "radical turn." We began to feel the heat was being turned up on us, and after a few months we decided to switch back to "Radio Concord" and damn the torpedoes.

Other Pirates

FROM 1967, PIRATE RADIO GROUPS had coalesced into stations such as Radio Jackie in 1969. Following Jackie's emergence, Kaleidoscope, Odyssey, Sun, and Belinda also began providing pop music and some community programming over large areas of South London and Essex, along with Atlantis in Brighton, achieving dedicated followings. North London, on the other hand, didn't have a strong, organized station until Radio Concord.

Beginning with our initial contacts with those young Radio Odyssey pirates in 1971, members of Concord met or chatted with pirates from other stations fairly regularly. As described in other chapters, pirates would often track us down at our broadcast sites. As time went by, some of those rebels were integrated into our crew, and many of our crew had worked at other pirate stations, so the small secretive community kept well in touch.

From what I heard from most of the other pirates and from the grapevine, Radio Concord was looked on somewhat askance by our contemporaries. The majority of pirate stations had started from a young, nerdy, tech-centered base, and they were, we discovered, somewhat wary of Jeffrey and me—we were older, and had no technical training, nor particularly wanted to acquire any. Our eventual move into being the Squatters' Radio, and our plunging into controversial political issues, only confirmed their suspicions. For us, radio was a means to an end, not the process, which was where their love and interest more lay. The organized pirates liked to create a sound as that of a "real" pop radio station, and that more structured mainstream-programming format suited them. That was never Concord's forte, and the free-form music, news, and features of our fluid programming style quite shocked some of those purist outlaws. Despite that, I believe we had earned the other pirates' respect by our tenacity, different pirating methods, and success. Any stylistic clashes between us never deterred them from helping out when asked, and vice-versa.

Radio Concord at a Crossroads

By the late winter of 1974, Radio Concord had become a working group of about ten dedicated people, aged from 16 to 25, who produced shows and helped at broadcasts, with a few other occasional helpers. Despite our apparent (and comparative) success, the station's existence had reached a crucial point. Public awareness of us was certainly growing, along with the number of raids, even with the ill-fated Radio Dynamite name-change interlude. We of the core group began to realize that, in order to improve our quality and variety of presentations, we needed a recording studio, a secure base where we could produce shows, and maintain a central meeting/equipment-storage place.

We had learned the hard way that we couldn't leave all of our live broadcast equipment exposed to capture with every raid, but if we had studio-production capacity, we figured, a raid on one of our temporary sites would "only" net our transmitter and a cheap cassette-player. A studio would also provide us with the ability to put our shows on cassettes efficiently, with consistently good production quality, which would be a vast improvement over our jumpy and individually bedroom-produced tapes. Our other great need was for a steady supply of safe broadcast locations. We assumed this would always be a problem, as you can only ask your friends and relatives to host your pirate radio station so many times.

This studio-search plan for a secure base marked the formalization of our pirate endeavours, and our intention for Concord to have a more significant role in the social upheaval that was happening all around us. The problem was that none of us had any money, and, even if we'd been lucky enough to find and afford a place in London, most of us were not leading lifestyles conducive to standard renting, not to mention that finding that perfect place was going to be tough in rent-controlled London, where no one moved unless they absolutely had to.

The big problem, as I saw it, was that if we didn't succeed in our quest and gain some stability soon, we were in real danger of falling apart. At this low point, some friction had developed among the crew members, and a few of them had hinted at moving on to help other pirate stations. Spurred on by this Concordian discord, we began the studio-search in earnest, asking all our friends, relatives and contacts for any spare garage, room, storage shed, rabbit-hutch or cardboard box we could use, but we came up empty. Winter was ending as damply as our spirits.

BANNED BY THE BBC!

**Aphrodite in the Mud
Caroline and Sue's
Houseboat in Chelsea**

**Mick Jagger's House
He Didn't Invite Us In**

**Dynamite GPO
Information Sheet**

Alternative London Survival Guide by Nicholas Saunders

Nicholas Saunders

5

Air and Land Pirates Join Forces!

O N A DREARY LATE WINTER DAY IN 1974 as spring threatened to arrive, Mick Lewis, Jeffrey, and I met in the jumble of Mick's dad's seedy Finsbury Park storefront mail-order company. Located near Arsenal Football Club's old Avenal Road stadium, the store sold odd items like mechanical pocket calculators and miracle-warm socks, the kind of things often advertised in small back-of-newspaper classified ads. As we sat amongst the tatty jumble, dismally discussing our quest of getting a central studio and sites to broadcast from, so as to prevent the break-up of Radio Concord, Mick suggested calling up an underground alternative information center called BIT and asking them for some advice.

BIT was an information service, publisher, travel guide and social centre founded in 1968, by John "Hoppy" Hopkins. It pre-dated the Internet as a free service that would try to find any information asked for, and derived its name from the smallest unit of computer information. With nothing to lose, I called their public number, and explained our unusual plight, briefly describing what Radio Concord stood for. Surprisingly, the blokes in the office didn't think I was some crackpot, but actually seemed quite interested. At the end of the call they asked that we come down to the BIT office, a squat in an old three-story building at the corner of Westbourne

Park Road, and the Great Western Road, near Portobello Road Market, and meet their core members.

Squatting: Banned By The GLC (Greater London Council)

FOR THOSE UNFAMILIAR WITH THE TERM "SQUAT," in Britain it basically means taking over an empty property and living in it without permission of the owner. The squatting movement burgeoned in the 1970s, with a huge rise in the exercise of that ancient common right. At that time, the practice of squatting properties was still technically legal, according to rulings dating back to 1215, in a little document called the *Magna Carta*. This legal perquisite had been eventually combined with common law that declared the squatter of a property could claim its title after seven years of continuous occupation. With this hybrid custom/law in place, squatting had become, down through the centuries, a small but viable political, legal, and social option.

The recently well-organized squatting movement in Britain and Europe at that time was a direct reaction to the huge housing need that had coincided with a lack of homes and flats available for rent at reasonable prices. This situation had come about, partly because of the demographic bulge of the baby boomers, and partly from a lack of planning for future housing after WWII bombing had destroyed so much of London and other major cities.

Also in play, was the continuing financial malaise that had afflicted the British economy during most of the 70s—a result of oil embargos, legacy industry job losses, and union busting. The deteriorating housing situation added to the extended economic downturn that put numerous young people on the dole for an entire generation. The British punk movement emerged directly from the despair and rage that were a natural reaction to a bleak future with no homes and no jobs. With nowhere to live, squatting became more or less inevitable.

London became a center for squatting, with strong local groups and leaders emerging in areas such as Brixton, Camden, Islington, and Westbourne Park/Notting Hill. Most of the squats were in varying degrees of deterioration and dilapidation, made up of thousands of units of mostly older inner-city housing stock—blocks of council flats, entire housing estates, and individual homes. These were homes that had been boarded up by local authorities because of a sub-standard condition, such as no hot water or inside toilet. For private owners, because of a tax loophole, an empty building meant they didn't have to pay property taxes or rates on their assets.

Despite the often-poor physical condition of many of them, the squats were at least a dry, mostly safe place to live for tens of thousands of people who literally had no other option. If necessary, squatters bridged wires across the back of electrical meters and connected to the power mains for free. Plastic hoses hooked up to gas and water pipes provided heat, cooking, and water, with no need to feed the infernal gas and electric coin-meters, ubiquitous in nearly every rental in Britain. (Sadly, new concrete bunker blocks of flats that were eventually built to replace much of the older housing stock, didn't stand the test of time aesthetically or socially, and many have since themselves been demolished because of the ensuing rise in urban blight and crime resulting from their dour design.)

Squatting a property itself was usually quite simple, and not much legal risk unless you were very unlucky. The squatting directions were: 1) find a long-empty house or flat, either through a squatting organization or by just roaming a likely neighborhood; 2) break into it through the front door or open a window with a jimmy; 3) immediately change the locks; 4) move in with a mattress; and 5) illegally hook up the gas, water, and electricity if (as they often were) still turned on. This "how-to" information was readily available from squatting organizations and from BIT.

According to the law, if the police didn't actually *see* you break in, and if you stayed, then it wasn't technically a breaking-and-entry crime. An example of this quirky law: one night I and a couple of friends had just breached the front door of an historic Georgian row-house on Perrin's Lane, right in the center of exclusive

Hampstead Village. As we sat on the floor talking in the empty living room, lit only by some candles, there was a loud pounding at the front door. A few seconds later, two uniformed policemen came thudding into our room. We calmly sat and waited, until one said "'ello! What's going on 'ere? Someone called us that people were breaking into the place." As nonchalantly as possible I said, "We're squatting here." They looked at each other, shrugged, and one said "…Oh! All right," turned on their heavy heels, and walked out the house, politely closing the doors after them.

Disregarding law and custom, private, institutional, or commercial building owners often performed illegal evictions; this is what happened to us at that Hampstead squat. On a lovely Sunday morning, a few weeks after we took possession, suddenly we heard a loud hammering downstairs. Taking a gander from the upstairs window, I could see some burly men, accompanied by big dogs, breaking down the front door and window with axes. Eventually, despite us putting our shoulders to the door, they broke in and frog-marched us outside; our belongings were thrown unceremoniously out of a top-floor window.

Back then, under normal circumstances, it usually took official legal proceedings to get a squatter out, but this could take months or years and cost the owner a lot of money. As a result, some owners just ignored the occupation of their buildings for years because of the cost and trouble of evictions. Those squatting in publicly owned structures, including entire apartment-building complexes, were often legally challenged by the councils *en masse*, and when the landlords won, a luridly emotional eviction might be seen on the news. Although squatting still occurs today, the laws have been changed, in reaction to the 70s movement, to make it easier for owners to evict.

References: *Squatters Handbook* on-line

Squatting the Airwaves BIT by BIT

A COUPLE OF DAYS AFTER MY PHONE CONVERSATION with the workers from BIT, Jeffrey, Mick and I went to the redevelopment-headed building to meet with Dave Kelly, who helped run the place. Dave led us into their back office and introduced us to BIT co-founder Nick Saunders, and as we were getting acquainted, the notorious Heathcote (pronounced "HETH-kut") Williams burst into the room.

Heathcote was the archetypal curly-haired, wild-child, public-school-educated hippie-poet-satyr, roughing it as a squatter. Life for Heathcote was always bursting forth, and always for *Art*, as he was literally a one-man anarchistic army with connections at all levels of London society. He lived near BIT at 217 Westbourne Park Road, in a third-floor squat with his partner Diane Senior (of the Senior Service cigarette family), and their young daughter China. I later discovered there was a running feud between him and the artist David Hockney, who lived directly across the back gardens from his squat. When I was visiting Heathcote, I often observed him playing silly pranks on Hockney, mooning him, or sending catapult-loads of stones and/or other odious materials through his windows.

Declaring the immediate area of his squat the "Independent Country of Frestonia," Heathcote issued stamps and money to back up his claim, just like in the old film *Passport to Pimlico*. The blue stamp featured a dark Buddha-like head and the words GOD WILL PROVIDE. I quite often pasted these on outgoing envelopes, which the General Post Office always obligingly delivered for me. After becoming a Concord regular, Heathcote injected poetry, politics, satire, stream-of consciousness prose, and even more anarchy than usual into our broadcast schedule.

While we were giving the BIT management our sales pitch, asking them to help us look for a studio and places to broadcast from, we could almost see Heathcote's mind lighting up, as he immediately recognized the potential of a pirate radio station linked into the burgeoning squatting and underground arts movements in London. His eyes took on an impish glint, one that we would get to know well over the next few years.

The mass communication methods currently in use among the homeless and squatting population took the form of crude, hand-written, small-batch mimeographed newsletters; distribution was erratic. Radio, thought Heathcote, could be the long-sought means to bring the far-flung squatting community together. Following our presentation, Dave, Nick, and Heathcote, asked many probing questions, thoroughly vetting us politically and socially. When they were satisfied we were not moles sent by the authorities, all went well, and it was left that they would get back in touch.

A day after our meeting, Dave called and said that all the BIT workers loved the pirate radio/squatting link-up idea, and wanted to begin the relationship by donating their offices at BIT as the first broadcast site! Great elation among our pirate crew! We set up a date for a continuous transmission over the 1974 four-day Easter Bank Holiday coming up in just two weeks, from Friday through Monday April 12-15th. What a break! The stars had aligned for the station.

For this significant opening opportunity, we planned a live broadcast, using all of our current studio equipment—two ropey record decks, a crackly Radio Shack four-channel mixer and mic, and a small portable battery-operated cassette tape recorder. On April 12th, we set the sound equipment and transmitter up in a corner of BIT's public hang-out room facing the Great West Road. Their chaotic front office was stuffed into another corner of the space. In this situation, we'd have to be ready for whomever, or whatever came through the door, or called on the phone, at any time of the day or night. This broadcast was certainly upping the ante in our efforts, embarking on a level of political pirating that we'd never before attempted.

As a council-flat lad, I was not fazed by this seedier world, but this move prompted some internal discussion, as not all our crew were happy with this new association with London's *demi-monde*. A few of them, before turning pirate, had come from nice middle-and upper-middle class homes, and this type of politics and subculture was quite new, and a bit intimidating to them. In the interests of the greater good, they bravely put aside those personal misgivings, and soon were abuzz as the rest of us with radio passion and anticipation of the upcoming broadcast.

The equipment set-up was no problem, but we were faced with our usual antenna location conundrum. BIT was located in a very built-up area, with large London Plane trees stretching closely and leafily together along the road on both sides of the BIT corner squat. In the inner block behind the building, while there were no gardens to trample through, there was also no obvious space to string up the wire. After reconnoitering the whole block, we came to realize that our only chance for a good signal was to attach the long wire to the top of a 20-story 1960s-era block of council flats (now gone) almost directly across the Great Western Road from BIT headquarters. Luckily, there were no overhead electrical wires on either side of the road, and we found a fortuitous small gap between two trees where the wire could be hoisted up without much leafy obstruction. Nonetheless, we faced the major double challenge of navigating through the heavy two-way traffic, with multiple double-decker buses rumbling along the street, and then gaining access to the flat roof of the tall building.

To raise the antenna, we obviously needed to start at the top, so, as the designated climber, I was loaded up with two spools of wire, some string, and the tools needed to secure the wire onto the roof. Dave from BIT offered to come along with me, and he, (let us say) "helped" me get through the locked high-rise doors with surprising ease: The rest was almost *too easy*; a lift to the top floor; a door to the fire escape stairs; some handy rungs ascending to an unlocked roof hatch. Bingo!

Once on the roof, we assessed the possibilities. The two-foot-tall outer parapet was set back a couple of feet from the lattice-work overhang of the roof, and we realized that in order to secure the wire on a likely-looking pipe upstand, visible beyond the building's edge, I had to lean *way* out over the abyss to accomplish my task. "Hold on real tight, Dave!" I implored. Dave held firmly onto my waistband, and I prayed that the seams of my Singapore-sewn jeans would also hold firm as I dangled precariously over the edge of the building with a 250-foot drop below.

I managed to secure the antenna-insulating rope to the metal strut, and Dave deftly pulled me back to dry land. Next, I then carefully uncoiled the wire down to the plaza in front of the building, where helpers on the ground grabbed hold of the end, and, as I doled it out, they walked it to the edge of the road, with me estimating the length of the hypotenuse difference between the two rooftops. After a few excruciating minutes' wait for a break in the traffic, two helpers, surrounded by a phalanx of scruffs frantically signaling to the oncoming cars, lorries and red double-decker buses to slow down, rushed the end of the wire safely across the street.

At the BIT house, a crew member at a third-floor window hoisted up the wire, slid it through another short insulating-twine loop, then began to pull it taut, as we watched with bated breath as it rose to its intended height and tightness. The dangling slack end was pulled into the broadcast room, snipped to size, and connected to the transmitter. Total success!

With enough time remaining before the official broadcast start at 6 PM, we tested the signal. Because of the stunning height and optimal length of the aerial, we knew it would be beaming powerfully, even with our small 12-watt transmitter, but how far? Reception-check calls (CQs) from friends all over London reported its strength as close to, or even louder than, the BBC reception levels on all their radios! We were warily ecstatic, and not a little apprehensive: what would be the consequences of plunging into the shadowy alternative underground in such a public way?

BIT Broadcast to the Underground

As THE BROADCAST STARTED, WE BRAZENLY GAVE out BIT's main phone number, and from the outset, calls came in continuously with requests and comments. Our transmitter wasn't very well shielded or filtered, so I imagine most of the occupants of nearby houses on the block and in the tower flats were stuck with Radio Concord all up and down their MW radio dials and teeth fillings.

Meanwhile, the BIT staff went about their everyday work of helping the many travelers and squat-seekers coming through the door. The staffers didn't seem to mind the risk of a raid, as they felt that they had developed a kind of hands-off attitude from the local Harrow Road Police Station. The front room was open all day and night for assistance in everything from locating crash-pads, to counseling, advice on squatting, referrals for drug problems, STD information, and particulars about underground London events or organizations. At the very least, the BIT headquarters provided couch space for visitors to have a cup of tea, chat, or just sleep for a while.

The homeless persons, squatters, runaways and foreign visitors who arrived during our stay all took part in our continuous on-air party. During the four days of the broadcast, members of the crew stayed awake for as long as possible, not wanting to miss anything, before crashing on the floor for an occasional short nap. A rock band was rehearsing in the basement below us for two days straight, and we would sometimes patch them through live on the air. Ladies of the night would often stroll in and have a cup of tea to warm up, chat with us, and be very open over the air about their tough street lives and work.

DJs from other pirate stations dropped by, having tracked us down by triangulation and field strength meters (just as the GPO could do at any moment, we noted). Live music, interviews, news, poetry and prose were interspersed throughout the broadcast, along with recorded music to tie it all together. The phone calls kept coming in from many parts of Britain, and even as far as Aberdeen in Scotland. The Scot won an album in a spontaneous "how far" competition, although a few weeks later we received a couple of letters from Sweden about this broadcast. Surprisingly, despite such a strong signal, there was no raid over those four days. With the front door wide open, we were, in effect, sitting ducks for any officialdom listening in, but the GPO trackers must have been chasing another pirate station, or off on their much-deserved Bank Holiday break, giving us a free pass to start our new squatting pirate radio chapter.

This superb broadcast secured our credentials as pirates, which in turn opened the door for us to go deep into the underground scene. Heathcote Williams knew all the English progressives, and I was delighted to meet many of them, like Steve Abrams, a leading British Yippie, and one of my heroes, John Michell, influential new-age writer of *View over Atlantis* and subsequent books. Tony Allen, the first alternative British comedian, was in the scene, along with Sid Rawle, founder of *Maya* newspaper, and known as the "King of the Hippies."

Sid was later the founder and leader of the infamous, and still extant "Travellers." (From Wikipedia: New Age "travellers" [sic] or "crusties," are people in the *UK* who often espouse new-age beliefs and the hippie culture *of* the 1960s, and travel between music festivals and fairs in order to live in a community with others who hold similar beliefs.)

Then there was the mad savant hippie civil servant, Bill (Ubi) Dwyer; the mythical philosopher and free festival organizer Wally Hope, and finally, *Alternative London Survival Guide* publisher, and BIT co-founder, Nicholas Saunders (who greatly influenced me)—all these leaders, and more, gladly helped us with our cause.

Nick Saunders, to me, seemed to genuinely want to live the archetypal hippie lifestyle while living and creating in the real world. One time I walked through the unlocked front door of Nick's squat, just as Nick (a fine specimen of manhood) strolled out of his room naked. The rooms at the top of his house were virtually devoid of furniture, curtainless and almost carpet-free. In the center of the "living room" was a small rug, and sitting on it was Nick's beautiful naked girlfriend. Nick sat down unselfconsciously next to her, so I took my clothes off, and sat down with them. As Nick and I chatted casually about our business together, his girlfriend got up and made us all some tea on the old gas stove by the sink.

The Squatters' Radio

WE BEGAN TO REALIZE THAT THE SQUATTING movement could provide an endless supply of locations from which to broadcast, free of any ownership responsibility for all concerned. In return, we could help the movement by acting as the "Squatters' Radio." Following a few more broadcast successes from different squats in the Westbourne Park area, we made a group decision to connect formally with the local squatting group, which was headquartered a half mile up the road from BIT on Elgin Avenue. The group was headed by the charismatic Trotskyist Piers Corbyn, who was always working (and still is) at the center of the homeless and street politics world.

Piers knew everything and everyone in this milieu, and topics at the weekly Elgin Avenue management meetings were wide-ranging: helping people to get a squat; fighting evictions; planning major rallies; summarizing court battles; and organizing council-meeting protests. When going about his good works and helping those in need, Piers never pushed his philosophy on us, or anyone else as far as I saw. His brother, Jeremy Corbyn, whom I met many times at homeless meetings and street protests, was as passionate as Piers, but was the least wild-eyed activist of the family, and had decided to work more within the system to effect change for the future.

The important paralegal aid group Release was located nearby at Elgin Avenue on the corner of the Harrow Road. Release provided an incredibly supportive network of volunteer lawyers and paralegals, that helped all those in the squatting community who had no money and no way to fight back against the authorities. They worked closely on all the squatting legal issues, such as evictions, drug busts, and immigration status. Later, after more GPO raids, they would help Radio Concord avoid charges and recover our illegally seized equipment.

This local community came together at The Café, which operated out of a squatted corner shop on the Great West Road opposite the Bingo Hall, next to the ancient Grand Union Canal, and near the mysterious bean-sprout factory. A collectively run place, charmingly decorated in rustic skip-found country-style furniture, The Café was managed by a couple named Dave and Gail, who provided the primary energy and impetus that kept it going. The food was tasty, wholesome, and inexpensive. These four grassroots organizations—BIT, Elgin Avenue Squatters, Release, and The Café—were actively helping thousands of people every day.

These new connections deeply affected our programming. Meeting those involved in the various street movements gave us a whole new perspective on the power of radio, and access to a seemingly bottomless reservoir of people, stories, and news. At this time, the other pirate radio stations in London were playing the usual "Top 40" pop music, with no real news or deeper community involvement. As Concord evolved from its tentative beginnings, our crew had come to realize we did not want to just follow that formula, and all along we'd been organically expanding our programming to bring more voices, community stories, and new music to the air. Now, inspired by the selfless squatting movement, we embraced social justice as our platform.

I remember someone saying, during an early crew discussion on our political content: "What are we doing this for anyway? It can't only be for EMI's or CBS's (record companies') benefit!" That sentiment, shared by all, enabled us to proceed with what we felt was a higher purpose. The authorities' severe reaction to us, our desire for community involvement, and the accessible simple reality of radio broadcasting, showed us that there was something worth fighting for, and we were (sort of) ready. As for me, I felt that what we were doing had come full circle from the days of the original British radio pirate ships of the 1960s. In a way, we were replicating those brave wake-blazers; our ongoing series of broadcasts from dilapidated squats was perhaps the equivalent of those myriad rusty pirate ships and sea forts in those inspirational days, except we were bobbing in the concrete sea of London.

Windsor Free Festival & King Kong

THE SQUATTING MOVEMENT, BEGUN AS THE RESULT of a housing shortage, had eventually combined with other underground movements to create ingenious ways to confound the law while making social connections with each other and with the greater youth movement happening in the country. Certainly, the most flamboyant and authority-irritating form of social connection was the establishment of the "free festivals."

The Windsor Free Festival was originally just a small crowd of anarchistic and politically active members of the British hippie underground who defiantly squatted and partied on public lands near the Queen's Windsor Castle home in 1971. This was obviously an idea whose time had come; in 1972, there were one thousand festivalgoers, and twenty thousand in 1973. In the year of which I write (1974), the organizers had totally outdone themselves: the Festival was squatting on the Queen's very own well-kept Horse Guards' marching grounds, with participants camping on the manicured lawns under the very shadow of Windsor Castle and among the ancient towering royal oak trees.

So from August 23-27th 1974, The encampment commanded an excellent view of the castle on its hill above the incongruous proceedings, and vice versa. But squatting was squatting, and even the Royals and police had to tread lightly around those ancient laws. A two-lane public road bisected the park and made access to the site very easy, so tens of thousands of hippies straggled in from all over Britain and many other countries.

I drove Keith, Simon, and our transmission equipment to the festival in my car, and we made camp behind the main stage under a huge oak tree. The stage crew allowed us to plug our transmitter into their (quite small) generator, which was already straining to supply the stage sound, lighting, and tea-making equipment needs. They also agreed for us to plug into the main mixing board at the rear of the stage and get a live-audio feed cable to the transmitter sitting on the grass in the shade of the magnificent tree.

As always with our broadcasts; antenna location, height, and length were the major issues. Since we'd arrived early, we could easily scope out the still somewhat-empty grounds. From the tree at our camp, we could see another regal specimen about 250 feet away, to which we could fasten the furthest end of the wire. I found myself risking life and limb by climbing 80 feet up the trunks of two 600-year-old trees, but in the end, the installation running from our camp to the far tree was a triumph and a thing of beauty.

The height and 250-foot horizontal length of the aerial, coupled with the open area surrounding us, except for Windsor Castle, and the hill it was built on, meant we were going to be heard well in London, and all the surrounding Home Counties during the day. Thus, by climbing a tree or two, we'd secured a potential audience of twenty million, and at night, many more in Europe.

At least six scaffolded stages were scattered through the grounds, each with canvas tarps pulled over the top for weather protection, and a small petrol-generator snorting on the ground behind it. Sometimes during the festival, multiple bands would be performing simultaneously on all the stages across the sward, bringing happy cacophony to the proceedings, as the audience strolled through this real hippie dream.

The event, which featured dozens of underground bands and musicians, went on all day and most of the night. I can't remember much of the music I heard as I staggered around the site on my breaks from radio-related activity, but the atmosphere was one of unity and joy. Heathcote, of course, decided to streak the festival, and I kept getting glimpses of his bare bum twinkling through the crowds as they parted, cheering him on.

Did the Queen peer out from behind her fine lace curtains in the castle to see us threatening the decorum of her empire? If Her Majesty had by chance turned on her radio to listen to the latest episode of the BBC's *The Archers,* during the course of the festival, she may not have been amused by the unfiltered Radio Concord broadcast she would have heard, as the BBC's signal was most probably blocked out by proximity to our antenna!

The Windsor Festival also became a great opportunity for local entrepreneurs to show up and offer dubious British fast food and drinks to the thronging crowds. It was an unusually warm holiday weekend, and residents from nearby towns arrived to set up food wagons and impromptu knick-knack booths along the public road, to cash in on this hungry and very thirsty gathering. (The lack of sufficient toilet facilities, I prefer to forget.) A soft ice-cream wagon driven by a chap named Bob pulled up next to our camp on the first official day of the festival, and set up shop. The rusty vehicle became a veritable gold mine, what with the thousands of stoned hippies in dire need of sweet munchies. Bob was an easygoing chap and we struck up a friendship, with much free ice-cream thrown in for the radio lads.

On Sunday, running out of ice-cream supplies and fuel for his generator, Bob needed to go into town, so he asked me if I could look after his ice-cream wagon until he returned. Little did he know that to run a soft ice-cream machine in an ice-cream truck had always been one of my boyhood fantasies. Ah! The pleasure of watching the practitioners magically swirl the creamy mix into a cornet. I spent some time getting the machinery to make the right dairy-rich slurry consistency for pleasurable eating—this process surprisingly required some skill, but it was *so* much fun sampling the mistakes.

When the magical substance was ready, I turned on the wagon's irritating Tonibell-like advertising chimes. Festivalgoers, inexorably drawn by the awful tintinnabulations, gathered expectantly in front of the sliding window of the van. Since I was giving out the ice-cream for free, I ran out of everything within half an hour, but when Bob came back, he didn't mind a bit that I'd used up the rest of his supplies, as he was making a lot of money anyway.

We broadcast successfully from the main stage over the long weekend, and interviewed not only many of the performers, but also many of the unwashed squatters. When nothing live was on the stage, recorded music played from our small cassette player set on the grass next to the transmitter. In this situation, located nowhere near a public phone, we couldn't immediately tell how far we were reaching and who was listening.

On the second day, Keith went into Windsor Town to get some supplies and batteries for the cassette player, and phoned a few scattered friends, receiving rave reports. From freshly arriving crew members, the uplifting news was that we were booming out over the London area as loudly as the BBC. Later, we received dozens of letters that showed our audience had extended over a large part of Southern England, bringing the biggest and most notable squatting event ever to the British public.

Despite being in plain sight of the main road, we'd gambled that broadcasting from such a large event would dissuade the Post Office trackers from conducting a raid. This proved to be the case, but since we'd started the festival broadcast on the previous Wednesday, by late Sunday evening we were reaching the limits of our money, supplies and will to continue, so we packed up our gear and left, not waiting for the official "end" of the festival on Tuesday morning.

As it turned out, this was a fortunate move. The concert organizers had begun negotiating with the police and Palace officials since they'd first set up their camp, and by Sunday had come to an agreement that all the ruckus would be gone by Tuesday afternoon. Sadly, on Monday morning, as dawn was breaking, the authorities betrayed their agreement in brutal fashion.

Hundreds of police, brought from all over the southeast area, started to walk abreast in a single line through the sleeping concert-goers, beating people with batons, ripping open tents and rousting everyone, children, possessions and all. This vicious harassment kept up until everyone had fled the park, and by the time the sun had fully come up, there was nothing left behind but a chaotic mess. Some of the organizers regrouped and sent the word out that they were starting another festival near Virginia Water, to which a few hundred hardy souls made their way.

As for Radio Concord, the most significant event of the festival happened as I was doing my duty watching over the transmitter, trying to keep acid-tripping hippies from impaling themselves on the glowing radio-valves. A longhaired, bushy-bearded young man walked up to me with a gleam in his eye and asked in a public-school voice: "Are you part of Radio Concord?"

"Yes" I said cautiously.

"Great! I've been looking for you!"

"You're not the GPO are you?" I asked a little too late.

"Good god no!" was his amused reply.

His name was Graham Barnes, and on the way to the festival he had picked our signal up strongly on his car radio, and just had to find out where we were located. It turned out that he too was a radio pirate, using King Kong as his DJ handle. He'd been operating his one-person station under the name Radio Aphrodite, just one of those radio enthusiasts broadcasting alone from a bedroom. Graham subsequently proved he wasn't just any electronics nerd, by revealing his impeccable music credentials to me (he played underground music like Frank Zappa and Cream). This was a man after my own ear, giving an outlet to the important music of our time that couldn't be casually heard anywhere else on the official British radio dial.

Graham and his sister Geraldine, who later fell in with us as well, were from a comfortably middle-class family in Hertfordshire, north of London. He had gone to Tonbridge Public School, where they had shot the film *If*, directed by Lindsay Anderson and starring Malcolm McDowell. He said the horrid antics of the boys shown in the flick (apart from the machine-guns, thank goodness), were pretty much normal at that upper-class British public boarding school. As we spoke, I could see he was obviously very bright, an impression that was confirmed when he said he was in his first year at the prestigious Imperial College in London, doing a B.Sc. in electrical engineering.

At the festival, crouching over our glowing transmitter under the oak tree, Graham had at first marveled at it, but within a few minutes had begun to point out various technical things that were wrong with the design and how it could be improved. When he asked if he could come to our next broadcast to help and do a show, I eagerly agreed, and we exchanged phone numbers. Little did Graham know into how many crazy adventures this innocuous meeting would lead him over the next two years. Having the input of a *bone fide* engineering student was also a first for Concord, as all the tinkering transmitter-builders we knew and used (like Richard Courtney, or Simon, who had built our present transmitter) were self-taught. I'd watched Simon turn a useless pile of metal and valves into an illegal glowing working device in literally minutes. Graham could not only do that, but at the same time also tell you the equations and formulas behind the equipment's operation.

Graham's friend, John Hallam (John the Baptist), soon also joined the fray. Slim, with short brown hair and a goatee, John was born in Kenya of British parents who were living the old Empire dream. He remembered the British leaving Kenya before independence, taking everything that was of any use, and training none of the indigenous population to take over. (No wonder it's been a struggle for ex-Empire countries to climb out of their post-colonial depression.)

John, with his plummy British accent, added a great amount of dry wit and variety to Concord broadcasts; his tastes ranged from folk and early music to the recently popular folk-rock genre. John was also proud of his taste for real, non-sterilized ale, and was one of the first supporters of the Campaign for Real Ale (CAMRA), that has transformed beer-drinking habits and swept around the world. With our overwhelming broadcast success at the festival, and the subsequent addition of three valuable members to our crew, Radio Concord was beginning to create its own future.

Taking the Mantle

MY FRIEND AND CO-FOUNDER OF RADIO CONCORD, Jeffrey (Matt Black), hadn't particularly liked the more activist turn we had taken, and since he was also busy working in the film industry, he only occasionally helped with the broadcasts at this time. Thus, by default I was left with the job of Station Manager. Coming from the British engineering tradition, I sketched out what I thought was needed to make it all work. Leadership was not a role I had taken on before, really preferring to be a back-room boy, but even though everyone worked together collectively, the crew had begun looking to me for direction in the operation of the station.

My regular duties included: finding and scoping out broadcast locations; negotiating with the residents of the buildings we set up in; setting up and taking down the wire; being a lookout; taking phone calls; helping to build transmitters; speaking to the media; recording and producing interviews; being interviewed; meeting with record-company executives and agents; replying to fan mail; and attending our regular meetings. These multiple roles, though thrust upon me, turned out to be excellent training for all my future community activism.

Apart from all the location getting, antenna raising, and security outlooking, there were the actual radio shows I produced. Certainly, with so many hats to wear, my time in front of the mic was perhaps the most tranquil part of the whole Concord experience for me. I was able to focus on the music mix, interviews, associated trivia and the general announcements, rather than operating in the constant flight-or-fight mode induced by my many other station-related activities.

Playing my favourite music and comedy and getting positive responses on the call-in/request line kept me awake on many a cold late-night shift. For an expected interview, I'd scribble down a few notes and hope for the best. With more impromptu chats, I learned how to quickly adapt to the interviewee(s) on the phone or in person, and, as an added perk, I always enjoyed having someone else with whom to test my repartee!

Operating the ever-changing configuration, position, type and number of audio equipment components was always challenging with every change of site, as muscle memory alone could not be trusted to keep the show's live production smooth. On any given day I could be spinning discs from atop a bathtub or a kitchen sink; broadcasting from the paneled library of a stately home; or doing my show while confined in a small cupboard in a derelict building while attempting to keep my intense shivering from the cold from affecting my vocal delivery.

Sheepdip, Hole in the Wall Gang, P.C. Samantha and Jake

UNLESS WE USED THE TOWER OF LONDON, and enlisted the Beefeaters to defend the doors, we knew that for every attempted broadcast, wherever we were, there was a good possibility of being tracked down and raided. In mid-winter of 1975, one location stood out because it was virtually raid and bust-proof, yet enabled us to maintain an extended broadcast time, powerful signal and long range.

Brian Sheepdip (Yes, that really was his name; can you imagine the teasing at school?) was a slim young man with Beatle-cut dark brown hair and a ready smile. He ran a semi-official crash-pad/doss house on Dartmouth Park Hill in Highgate, near The Archway, London's version of the Golden Gate Bridge for suicides. His operation was set up in a large empty shop-front, and with the whole block destined for demolition, Camden Council had given him the building for the overnight housing of the homeless. Brian was engaged in significant groundbreaking work, including directing transients to medical care or other available social programs, as well as providing a safe floor to sleep on, and some filling grub and tea. He enthusiastically supported what we were trying to do on the radio, and happily allowed us use of the dusty premises.

At night, inside the shop, dozens of homeless men slept on the floor, packed closely together on single mattresses. We rejoiced when we first saw this setup, because in the event of a raid the police would have to tiptoe their way through some very disgruntled and sleepy street people, before they could make their way upstairs to the top floor at the back of the shop, where we were to set up our broadcast equipment.

There was an office on the second of the upper two floors, but they were otherwise used only for light storage. As we gathered on the top landing during our initial visit, we were a little confused;

some of the empty rooms on the floor looked more than adequate for our use, but Brian didn't lead us into one of those. With a mischievous twinkle in his eye, he beckoned us over to a large clothes cupboard at the end of the corridor, and pulled one side of the heavy armoire away from the wall; we all whistled and sighed with admiration.

A jagged crawl hole had been carved through the plaster and the Victorian-era orange-clay Fletton bricks—we were obviously going through the clothes cupboard to Narnia for *this* broadcast! For reasons only known to him, Brian had broken through the common wall between the empty buildings. What could be better for us than entering one house, then broadcasting from the building next door? Any search warrant would be useless, as it would be for the wrong address, and they'd still have to find us behind the cupboard!

Brian had hooked up the electricity in the other building and brought up his office phone with a long cord for our use during the broadcast. We stretched an antenna over to an empty house across the back of the block, and got ready for a great weekend. Since we were near the top of Highgate Hill, the highest elevation in London, this was one of our strongest broadcasts ever. Phone calls came in continuously during the entire transmission, day and night, and for a week or two afterward letters came from all over Britain and Scandinavia. All the DJs were in good spirits throughout, as we felt we had complete security.

During one of my turns answering the phone, I got a call from a woman named Samantha who wanted us to play some soul music. She sounded friendly and had a sexy laugh. We chatted some more, and discovered we'd both gone to the same school, she a year ahead of me. She gave me her phone number, and we arranged to meet for a date a few days later. She turned out to be an attractive and shapely woman with short red shagged-cut hair, a salty sense of humour, and an interesting story. Leaving school early, she'd gone against her parents' wishes and got herself a steady job by joining the Metropolitan Police Force. She'd been a policewoman for just a few years when an "indiscretion" caused her to leave the Force. Since then, she had been living with her mother in a council flat in Stamford Hill and working in private security at big stores in the West End.

Being with a beautiful cop, even an ex-cop was weird, considering all the pursuits in which I was then involved, but I discovered that she had an abiding irreverence for the law and loved to smoke pot and hash (possibly why she'd had to leave the police force—I didn't want to ask). We got on well and saw each other regularly for a few months. One of the good things about knowing a cop well is that they know where you can get good drugs. One evening, Mick Lewis and I wanted to get some grass or hash and asked Samantha's advice. She gave us an address and a name in a seedier part of already seedy Dalston in East London.

As we walked with trepidation up to an old terraced bay-windowed house, we could hear the throb of a deep bass guitar sympathetically rattling the dusty front windows, which appeared to be draped in thick blackout curtains left over from WWII. After we rang the bell a few times, one of the curtains in a bay window shifted, and a thin fortyish black man peered out through the steamed-up windows. I yelled that we'd come to see Jake, and that Samantha had sent us. "Who?" he mouthed.

Fearing a Cheech and Chong "Dave's not here!" situation, complicated by the pounding music, I repeated her name much louder. He nodded, and after a minute or so, opened the front door. Jake, for it was he, led us down the darkened hall and into the front room. As he opened the door, I felt that deep throbbing, electric-bass-guitar sound slam palpably into my chest.

For me, a working-class Jewish kid, it was quite shocking to drop into a whole different culture without preparation. We found ourselves in a dimly lit room with about a dozen older black men and women sitting around amid battered furnishings. I could see, behind a screen, beds where young children were sleeping and playing. Large professional-type speakers were scattered around the room, all on and blasting away, playing music that Jake said was direct from Kingston. He turned out to be a DJ in the black dance clubs of London, very much into spacey bass, dub-heavy, early reggae á la Lee Perry. Jake wanted to know how Samantha was; I chatted casually with him and a couple of the other people, who were quite friendly, but Mick looked petrified through the whole thing and didn't say much.

Jake passed joints around, and the air, already redolent with grass smoke, became even more so. After an appropriate amount of time, I asked him what he had to sell, and he went behind the screen and came back with some flat paper sachets of strong-smelling Jamaican grass priced at £1 each. Considering how difficult and dangerous it usually was to obtain herb in those times, a reliable source like Jake was, for us at least, a positive byproduct of our radio efforts.

Squatting With Radio Concord

THE ORIGINAL POINT OF JOINING UP WITH THE squatting movement had been to acquire a studio and multiple locations from which to broadcast. Although we had gone on the air from a number of squats so far, an ideal situation for our permanent studio hadn't turned up as yet. Then, at a regular Elgin Avenue squatting meeting in midsummer 1975, we were told of a small empty Victorian-era two-story red-brick terraced house, owned by the local Westminster Council and located just a few blocks west from Elgin Avenue, off the Harrow Road. Some of the homes in the area were squatted, while others still had actual council renters in them.

That night, with the invaluable assistance of Sharon Wright from the squatting organization, we broke into the house at No.12 Alperton Street. An import from California, Sharon was dedicated to helping people out, freely sharing her confident squatting knowledge and her formidable jimmying skills, apparently *not* picked up in the sleepy suburbs of Woodland Hills in the San Fernando Valley. I picked a sunny room overlooking the street for myself, while Graham, John, and Keith claimed their own digs. We threw down some grungy mattresses in the bedrooms, and scrounged locally for basic furniture.

To make the house completely livable, I hooked up a plastic garden hosepipe to an ancient gas stove I'd found on the street, and duct-taped it to the main pipe. Bridging across the electrical meter with thick wire for free electricity turned out to be quite easy. The water on the street was already turned on, and just needed the valve opened. So, at long last, we set up our own rudimentary studio in a room at the back of the second floor, and enhanced it with 24-count paper-egg-crate-lined walls for sound deadening. The resulting sound quality was quite good for making our show tapes, and our audio output was improved additionally by the generous loan of a professional mixer and a special-effects box.

For the first time, just as we had hoped months earlier, Radio Concord now had a real studio production space, combined with a secure common place to live and hang out. Being able to produce a show with better equipment and provide a safe interview or performance space was an enormous improvement, one that enabled us to begin what was to become our most productive stretch of pirate broadcasting.

Now that we were *bona fide* squatters, most of the crew went to the regular Elgin Avenue meetings held by Piers Corbyn, and got into the everyday squatting life-flow. Since Concord had become the accredited squatters' radio, we now had access to more information, news, and music than we could ever broadcast. Travelers from all over the country and from many other nations were squatting in London at this time, and were either managing or relying on these vital support organizations and services. In this netherworld, the population was a mash-up of traditional tramps or dossers living rough and in filthy dumps, runaways, refugees, and economic victims, all rubbing shoulders with young middle-class hippies, living out their proletariat dreams in their "liberated homes."

Certainly, the main thing I learned from being part of this world, was that, for the basic human rights for all of the many and varied homeless people in this world, for whatever reason, there's no excuse for governmental agencies not to provide access to a safe place to live for all, for their health and dignity—whether it be a tent, a dry floor in a derelict house, a mobile home, a warehouse, a tiny home, a flat in an apartment building, or a family house.

Feminism Comes to Concord

AMIDST ALL THESE ADVENTURES, and in this improbable way, I met Sharon Wright (she of the very useful talents in regard to locked doors) when she helped us squat our studio. She would be my future partner and wife for the next fifteen years, and the mother of my daughter Rose. Looking vaguely Native American with her long dark hair and strong features, she'd traveled the now sadly defunct Asian hippie route for nearly five years, and had gone to India and back overland in the days when you could hitchhike fairly safely through Turkey, Iraq, Iran and Pakistan. In the midst of a journey that was intended to take her back to America, she stopped in London, and stayed on, not sure what to do next. She had begun squatting, and, after making friends in the movement, began to help people like us find homes, and to navigate the mysteries of squatting.

I liked Sharon's lively, playful personality, and the worldly determination that lay underneath it. As a bonus, she laughed at my many bad jokes and puns. I was captivated by her wonderful tales of traveling the Mysterious East, and her accounts of the hippie happenings in 1960s Los Angeles and San Francisco. She had absolutely no shyness, and that helped me overcome my natural reticence and boost my sociability quotient in public situations or when meeting new people.

After we grew to like each other during our meetings at the squatting headquarters, one thing led to another, and we officially became a couple. Sharon moved into my Alperton squat bedroom and began to discover the adventures-plus-activism good times we were invoking with our pirating. She began to help with the radio station, and when launched on-air as "California Sunshine," produced a delightfully whimsical, woman-themed show that brought a new American-feminist air—a view not present at the time on any other station, pirate or not—to Concord's operations, showcasing, between riffs of contemporary American music, important women's issues and activist interviewees.

Like other world travelers, Sharon used to get her mail from *poste restante* in any city she might have been headed for, but was not obsessive about picking it up regularly. One day she brought an accumulated pile home and opened an older letter from her parents first. Sharon didn't have a good relationship with her parents, so when she shrieked, I could only assume someone had died. When I asked her if that was the case, she replied: "it's worse than that! My parents are coming to visit me in London—tomorrow!"

Her suburban parents had no idea of Sharon's living conditions or lifestyle, so she was frantic: "What shall I do?" She wailed. I offered to show them around town in my little car, and even had a shave and trimmed my curly mane a bit before meeting them. The dreaded parents turned out to be very friendly, and loved being perched in the cramped back seat of my open-topped car, as we took in all the sights of Central London for a couple of days. We avoided taking them to our squat!

Squatting with Sharon

SQUATTING ON ALPERTON STREET GAVE the radio station (and Sharon and me), some stability in our lives. One short block away was the busy Harrow Road, a still very old-fashioned blue-collar High Street. The small grocery shop around the corner from us had no refrigeration—the milk, butter, and eggs were kept cool under terracotta earthenware covers. The Victorian-era Harrow Road public baths, with their individual bathing rooms, were still open, which was wonderful, as many of us were squatting or renting without access to a bathtub, shower or hot water. The old Grand Union Canal ran parallel to us, one block south of Harrow Road, and was still used for floating-freight commerce. I spent many a pleasant afternoon perched on one of the bridges, dreamily watching the barge traffic drift by the mysterious bean-sprout factory.

During our downtime at The Café, we talked with fellow squatters and planned future radio adventures. With Portobello Road Market a short distance away, we had great fun looking for forgotten treasures that we could use or resell elsewhere. Ceres, the first organic food store in the country, founded by Gregory Sams, was our grocery-shopping choice when we had enough cash. If not, we were usually successful in finding end-of-day bargains from the old market stalls on the street outside.

Heathcote Williams

Piers Corbyn
Squatting Leader

Graham Barnes
aka King Kong

God Will Provide
Postage Stamps

Windsor Free Festival
Leaflet 1974

Windsor Free Festival
Police Violence

**Twisden Road TV Antenna Still
Pointed to East Germany**

Date 23.02.75

I have rcd yur tx to 15.01.75_____. lease report cfm QSL!

Rx   : SH1o
Ant : W3DZZ
QTH : Oberdorla near Mühlhausen/GDR   QRA: ACHIM FRESINO
Freq : 1305khz   5707 OBERDORLA GDR
mez : 0010
RSTPO: 44354
wx   : no rain
StWraender: XXXXX
Uni tnx for your ans!

                              7y 73,55 de   Achim Fresino

                         achim fresino

Reception Letter from East Germany

6

Pirating Infamy: Fighting for Recognition

IN THE FIRST HALF OF THE 1970S, most other pirate-radio stations had not been overtly political, and any leanings in that direction were focused primarily on changing the broadcasting laws. These stations felt that their prime purpose was providing good pop music to their many loyal listeners, while at the same time relishing the cat-and-mouse shell game with the GPO trackers.

Concord also wanted the rules changed, of course, but by now, our social message had become much more important than either the music or the thrill of being chased by civil servants. Don't get me wrong, music still held together the relationship between our DJs and the listeners, and we loved playing it, but the station had become much more than a source of tunes.

As we moved deeper into the many street movements, broadcasts of squatting news and reports became a major feature of the station. We also dispensed messages, phone numbers, and addresses for help with health issues, politics, drugs, arrests, immigration, housing, and food. Activists from all over London were brought into the live broadcasts, or to our recording studio, to tell their stories and share their art and opinions. In the real spirit of community radio, musicians, poets, storytellers, artists and charlatans all got their chance to go on the air. Our somewhat loose research methodology at this time consisted mostly of searching out those political or cultural stories not being told by the mainstream press. With cross-squatting media co-operation, our programming, raids, and exploits were reported by the various squatting newspapers in London, often leading to stories picked up by the legitimate press. We were aware, from a few daring mentions of us by DJs on The BBC and from the new commercial Capital FM radio shows, that the music and radio business kept up with our exploits.

All through this chaotic period, new helpers came onboard, drawn by our activity and growing notoriety. Our vetting for any "moles" was mostly done quite casually, just relying on our instincts when evaluating their motives for joining us. As for any such individuals breaching our inner circle, as far as I know, that never happened.

Being part of a vibrant underground movement during those radical years brought with it access to many eccentric characters. An outstanding example of the complications of our open-door policy was one Lord Amory. (He was neither a Lord, nor an Amory, but had just decided to take that *nom de plume*.) His Lordship joined up to help at broadcasts, and then went on to produce a talk show that was very eclectic even by Concord standards, with long ravings about the state of the world. He was ahead of his time; his inflammatory ranting style would have been perfect for the US talk-radio shows of the 2000s. He was also at the centre of one of the most hilarious scenes I ever witnessed at one of our radio piracy court cases. Of the five of us in the dock, three gave silly fake names. Already well known by the authorities, I had to use my real name. Then Lord Amory stood up in the dock to face the charges, and when asked his name, he replied: "Lord Amory" in his stentorian voice.

Amidst giggles from various parts of the court, the prosecuting barrister, already irritated by the previous irreverent and blatantly fake names and answers by others, leapt to his feet. An impressive figure in his traditional be-wigged, and black-robed splendour, he loudly bayed: "Your Honour, I object! It is patently obvious that this is not his real name, and he should be forced to reveal his true identity for the court."

The old judge, looking amusingly shrunken in his ponderous red judicial robes and dusty peruke, was already appearing quite fed up with this whole ridiculous trial that was making a mockery of his court. He assessed the strange collection of freaks and hippies that had been dragged in front of him, and gave out an audible sigh. Leveling his gaze again at the barrister, he said slowly, with a hint of exasperation, "I honestly don't care what his real name is! He was brought up here on *this* charge, and under *this* name, and by George, in *my* court, *that's* what he's going to stand on! Objection denied!" Down came the gavel. The barrister sank meekly back on his chair to the accompaniment of much guffawing from the accused and the spectators.

As Concord activities changed to reflect our more radical posture, we didn't think much about what the establishment could, or would do to us. Apart from the usual broadcasting raids and busts that had become almost humdrum for our crew, we had to contend with new and somewhat disquieting surveillance measures aimed at us.

Even in regular homes, phones could take a year to get installed, so having one put in a temporary squat was not usually possible. The Concord crew mostly used their parents' or friends' homes as phone bases for messages, or reluctantly resorting to those famous red street-telephone kiosks if they didn't smell too bad.

It was only by chance that I discovered that my parents' phone line was tapped. I was talking with my brother Ralph, now a phone technician with a private communications company, about the station and our security system. He told me of a number that phone workers call at the end of a service visit to check if the line is working correctly. If, after replacing the phone in its cradle following a call to this number, there was an almost immediate callback from the automated system, it was working correctly. If the test number *didn't* call back, Ralph said, it either meant something was wrong with the line, or that the phone being serviced was being tapped and diverted.

Happening to be at my parents' home the next day, I just *had* to test Ralph's information. With rapidly pumping heart, I dialed the test number, heard it ring a couple of times, then make an electronic sound. As instructed, I then put the phone down. Ten seconds went by with no return call. "Shit!" I tried it again, at different times of the evening, with the same distressing result. Armed with that unsettling information, I called four of the crew from a phone box and left messages to call me immediately at that number from a public phone and not from a personal or private line. On their returning the calls, I gave them the instructions for checking their primary-contact phone number. Depressingly, two others had the same result as mine. Wow, this was serious. If the Government were tapping our phones, what else would they do? Now forewarned, we told all the Concord regulars to be *very* careful about what they said on phone calls.

Our activities, after all, were increasingly heading in a political direction, and by giving voice to many small causes, lost or not, we were providing opportunities for the public to tap into real human stories from the streets. Michael X (Michael Abdul Malik), for instance, was a self-styled British Malcolm X, but with a very lurid and dubious gangster past. He was well connected with the hippie underground and, during a brief period of reformed intentions, started the Notting Hill Festival (with Hoppy Hopkins) in 1967. By the mid-70s, Michael was on death row in a prison in the Caribbean, and we gave his sister, who was carrying out a forlorn quest for a stay in his sentence from her small flat near Gospel Oak, a radio platform to plead his cause and for her many other concurrent civil protests. Sadly, this didn't prevent Michael's execution in 1975.

One interesting cause we brought to the air was the "Free George Davis" campaign. George Davis was an East End (of London) dweller with a shady history, a member of one of those all-white, blue-collar gangs who had come up from the same type of hard streets, council flats and tenements as the infamous Kray Brothers. I was introduced to the Davis family by Heathcote Williams, and as a result of this connection, I got to meet some of the members of another London *demi-monde*, in which blue-collar unionism, Marxism, Irish Republicanism, and street gangs came together in an odd mashup.

Strangely enough, the current charges against George that had led to his arrest were dubious at best, considering all the other illegal pies the gang had their fingers into, but the police were determined to get him on *something*, no matter how spurious. To fight this injustice, his family and friends had begun to mount a vigorous campaign to free him from charges they firmly believed the police had fitted him up (framed him) on. They daubed "Free George Davis" slogans on bridges, overpasses, and walls all over London.

Their biggest exposure came in August 1975, when they desecrated the grass pitch at Headingley Cricket Grounds in Leeds the night before an international test match, etching their slogan in acid on the pristine turf of one of the world's most hallowed cricket stadiums. George was released in 1976 but went back to prison a number of times over the years.

As can be seen, some of those quixotic causes and people we aired in our quest for fairness were quite challenging subjects, and often uncomfortable to deal with, but it was an ongoing learning experience for me and for the other pirates. We were just following our ethos of providing everyone with a voice, wherever it was coming from, as "community" for us meant "all the community."

So, to sum up our philosophy and programming arc in 1974-75, Radio Concord had, in a fairly short time, gone from playing tasty music in our bedrooms to involving ourselves in greater community issues, and then helping to create and support grassroots issues and social movements. No wonder the government and the BBC wanted to keep a lid on this simple, inexpensive, and effective freedom to speak and organize. Surprisingly, even with the phone-tapping, surveillance and raids, the majority of our core group stayed committed to the cause, realizing, if only from the sheer level of opposition, the pressing need for non-governmental sources of our kind of radio information and news.

Banned By The KGB: TV Antenna to East Germany

THERE WERE MANY NIGHTS, especially when we were working in the cold, wet, rain, sleet, or snow, where we questioned our commitment to the cause. People were listening, but was it changing anything? Were we closer to influencing actual changes by our presence on the radio dial? Some events and broadcasts did help reinforce our faith in what we were doing. One of these was the Twisden Road, Tufnell Park broadcast. This transmission took place out of a three-story terraced house squatted by a pleasant couple who had claimed the cozy place as their home, and had lived there untroubled for three years. After showing us the layout, they took to their bedroom for the night, leaving us the whole downstairs in which to set up.

This broadcast was Graham Barnes's first self-built transmitter test for Concord since I'd met him at the Windsor Festival, and this rig was perhaps not up to his later electro-concoctions. We had also switched our show time, broadcasting from 6 PM Friday to 10 AM Saturday. The big problem at this squat was that we couldn't get any kind of decent antenna up to any height without causing too much attention. Our 6 PM start-time was fast approaching, and it was too late to go anywhere else and set up.

Our spirits sank, in fact, to the floor, as there were not enough chairs to go around. Then Graham, having racked his brain to the obvious point of desperation on this, his floundering maiden voyage, jumped to his feet, yelling hysterically: "I've got it! Let's attach it to the TV aerial!" The current squatters must have got into the house before the cowboy wire-and-pipe strippers had raided the inviting empty building: This important fact, Graham informed us, had left an innocuous-looking coaxial cable going up from the living room to a TV antenna on the top of the roof above the upper floor. "It'll do *something*," Graham reassured us through gritted teeth. For my part, if I didn't have to climb a tree or tall building to put up the wire, it was a good day, (or in this case, a cold winter's night). The coaxial cable was adapted to fit the connection on our transmitter.

A TV antenna is designed to be a directionally fixed receptor of signals emanating from a particular location, rather than an emitter of signals. From the street, we could see that the antenna was facing east, so that was, arbitrarily, to be the direction of our outgoing audience tonight. We walked the neighborhood to check on the signal with a transistor radio, and found that it sounded scratchy even just 100 yards away. Spirits sinking yet further, we called a couple of people around town and learned that our signal was barely being heard, even on a good radio set in East London. At least with this pitiful range, we didn't worry that the GPO trackers would bother to pick us up that night.

Despite the grim reception, we all did our assigned live shows. I fell asleep on the floor at some point, waking about 3 AM to see that everyone else in the temporary studio was fast asleep, including Keith the DJ, comically nodding off in the creaky chair in front of the record decks. We later heard from puzzled listeners that the same Yes LP side had been playing over and over again for some time. I woke Keith up gently, so as not to cause him to lose his balance in the chair, and he continued with his show. I then stumbled out for some fresh air and discovered the front door had been left wide open all night!

Although we bemoaned our poor broadcast, a gratifying surprise bonus came about a week later, in the form of two letters from young radio hams, who had heard our pathetic transmission deep within still-Communist East Germany. How could this be? Graham postulated that because it was a directional TV antenna, it had beamed our MW signal all the way to East Germany without bothering to touch down anywhere else of interest in between. Our pirate efforts had been heard behind the Iron Curtain! That revelation was very significant for me and for the others of the crew, in some way reconfirming why we were doing this crazy thing. If brave East German kids, facing prison if caught listening to us, could tolerate one side of a forbidden Yes album played perhaps five times in a row at 3 AM, then that was the very least we could do for them!

Panned By The Press?

APART FROM THE RADIO MONOPOLY OF THE BBC and its implicit censorship, the British press, though known to be quite freewheeling in its celebrity and political-scandal coverage, was and still is, severely constrained by government censorship when "National Security" is involved. (In which case, a D-Notice—now a "DSMA-Notice"—is issued to newspaper editors, ordering them not to publish a particular story). Though complying with a DSMA-Notice is supposedly voluntary, the press almost always follows its directions.

I'm sure there are also other good-old-boy non-D-Notice ways to coerce silence or minimalization of stories, but my only previous glimpse into the practical effects of that shadowy domestic power came when I was in Europe on holiday. Even without knowing French or Italian, I could see that lurid stories about the British Royal Family were particularly popular with the local European newspapers, featuring front-page articles about the Royals' antics and proclivities, the likes of which were certainly not published at home.

It was perhaps inevitable that Radio Concord, with our powerful broadcasts, all the police raids, and our presentation of underground music, alternative news, and squatting information, would begin attracting serious press attention, first in the London rags, and then the national newspapers. In those pre-Rupert Murdoch union-breaking days, the offices of all of the major newspapers were located on or near Fleet Street in the City of London. (Although this is no longer the case, "Fleet Street" is still used as a generic term for the national press.)

As mentioned, I was a busy chap at that time. Being the station's designated spokesperson, I gave interviews in newspaper offices, from secret broadcast locations, outside of court buildings, and over the phone. Along with my pirate radio efforts, mind you, I was still working at my job as a mechanical engineer at a company in Feltham. One workday, a call from *The Times'* chief crime reporter, whose name I recognized from reading the paper, was put through to my desk. He had a deep, spooky James Mason-ish voice, and the fact that he'd found my phone number at work freaked me out, again confirming the level of surveillance being conducted on me and on the station. He was persistent in his request for a feature article, and, I must admit, was intimidated by him, but finally declined the interview, telling him that what we were doing was not a criminal act, so it really was not in his "crime" bailiwick.

Escape From Northern Ireland: Going AWOL

ONE EXCLUSIVE NEWS STORY THAT I BROKE—and I'm sure the powers-that-be hated us for—was the dirty secret of British Army soldiers going AWOL in significant numbers from the very violent and sectarian armed conflict then taking place in Northern Ireland. No word about these defections had come out in the Fleet Street Press, as they were most probably pressured to repress the information in order to avoid government embarrassment, public censure, and the debilitating effect on troop morale.

The provocative piece of news about the rebelling troops in Northern Ireland came to me from one of those army deserters. John Murphy (not his real name), was hopscotching between various squats around Elgin Avenue, hiding out from the military police, who were scouring the area for him. John, a thin man with short-cropped dark hair and a few days' beard growth, was introduced to me by Piers Corbyn at a squatting meeting, and, speaking in his soft Northern England brogue, cautiously opened up to me. He described his growing discontent with the often-brutal acts he was forced into by the Army, and with the conditions under which he was made to serve. He also provided details of his dramatic escape, along with fifteen others, from his barracks. Upon hearing the startling full story, I checked back with Piers and others for his trustworthiness, and they emphatically assured me of the truth-fulness of his story.

The May 23-26th Spring Bank Holiday broadcast from the Piano Factory in Chalk Farm (detailed later in this chapter), was approaching, so we arranged for John to come to my show there for a live interview. We spent about an hour of airtime talking about his experiences in the British Army in Northern Ireland, and about what was truly happening on those dangerous streets, and in the Army barracks. Fearing a raid by either the military police or the GPO trackers, I kept the interview short, then drove him back to his safe room near Elgin Avenue.

That broadcast was one of our more powerful, not only because of John's contribution, but also because our signal during that long weekend went out strong and clear, reaching a large audience. The very next day, I was contacted by David Pallister, a newspa-per reporter for the *Guardian*, who had heard the interview, and wanted John's story. After I called him back at his office at the *Guardian* to make sure this wasn't a sting, we arranged to bring them together.

To avoid Army surveillance, John and I took random circu-itous routes from our squats, meeting finally on the eastbound platform of Westbourne Park tube station. From there we took a train to a secret after-hours meeting at the darkened newspa-per offices, near Fleet Street. The lone security guard called up to David, who appeared quickly and ushered us hurriedly through the almost empty main newsroom, and into his private office.

After the introductions, David wanted to know some facts from John that would confirm his AWOL story—this was too big a scoop to get wrong. He asked the deserter to give him detailed information about his Army outfit and the method of his escape, and John obligingly showed Pallister, on a wall map of Northern Ireland, the location of the army bases at which he'd been sta-tioned; information on other deserters he knew; and when and from where they had fled.

John also recounted the anguished personal story of his desertion, and how his hatred of what the Army was doing in Ulster had kept gnawing at him until, late one night, he had clambered over the walls of his barracks and made a fraught journey back to England, to lose himself amid the throngs of London. Pallister called me a couple of days later and said he had verified all the information given by John, and that they were going to publish the hot story in the *Guardian* the next day. Pallister was extremely grateful, and asked me to let him know of any other stories that might be of interest (which I did).

We expected the blockbuster news to kick up some dust, and, sure enough, I noticed an even bigger increase in the number of suspicious-looking characters with polished shoes haunting the squatting area and coming to the general meetings. John had been concealed in another safe house, stayed inside for a couple of weeks until the initial heat was over, and finally left for a secret place in the country.

The Balls Pond Road & the *Melody Maker*

ONE CALL I WAS VERY HAPPY TO TAKE was from the *Melody Maker*, a weekly national music paper, as they wanted to write a feature article about Concord. Our reaction was ecstatic. In those days, the now defunct *MM* was the *Times* of the music press. Offering erudite and authoritative music journalism, it maintained a smaller but much more respectable circulation than the tabloid-like *New Musical Express (NME)* and *Disc*.

Rather than holding a conventional interview, we arranged with *MM* editor Chris Welch, for reporter Brian Harrigan and his photographer to embed with us during a broadcast from a cramped third-floor flat just off the Balls Pond Road in Islington on March 7th. Brian was new to the *MM*, and this was his first big feature article, and he and the photographer, fascinated, no doubt, by the truly glamorous world of pirate radio, stayed for the entire night. There was a slight hitch when we realized that the presence of a photographer meant (duh!) photographs, which was a problem, as we didn't dare expose our real identities.

Rising to the occasion, most of us resorted to obscuring our features with hair. In my case, because I had so little hair on top to hide under, the reporter's disembodied hand covered my face in the photo. Another shot was taken, upon my earnest request, to fulfill an absurdist dream of mine of having a black horizontal bar—as frequently utilized in the garish Sunday tabloid *The News of the World*, when exposing, say, the likes of a drunken vicar stumbling out of a brothel at three in the morning—placed across my recognizable visage.

On the morning of March 15th, a few days after the broadcast and visit, I rushed round to the newspaper store and snatched the latest *MM* from the rack. And O my! I was stunned to see a good-sized block-teaser on the front page that shouted:

"PIRATE RADIO —MM Spends a Night in the Secret Hideaway of the Airwave Buccaneers – page 22."

And there we were, next to the big Robert Plant and Led Zep lead article, and the same size, and right above the Peter Gabriel and Genesis interview block teaser (though we had the more impressive black shading!). Ripping the paper open, I shrieked when I saw that the article covered over a full page, including a photo with me in it! I eagerly scanned the piece, my shaking hands fumbling to find the "Continued on page 38," where yes, just as Brian had promised, there was that photo of me doing my show at the kitchen sink, with that wonderfully damning black rectangular bar over my eyes (see cover). I bought six copies.

Brian had written a droll article that managed to capture the flavour of the characters involved and of our cause. On closer reading, it turned out that some haphazard editing had caused particular quotes, events, people, and places to get mixed up, so I must make one disclaimer: it was Joe Lung, and not I, who ran the "Big Tits," and "Disease of the Week" contests!

Here's the exact text of the article:

Page 22-MELODY MAKER, March 15th, 1975

Pirates of the Air

You won't find Radio Concord's programmes listed in your newspaper. That's because they're one of Britain's pirate stations, broadcasting for 12 hours each weekend from a different secret location. MM's Brian Harrigan entered the illegal world of El Supremo, King Kong and Joe Lung to see how – and why – they do it.

Picture a radio station where the transmitter comes biscuit-tin size and often has to be rebuilt before broadcasts.

- Where the deejays go under false names and avoid identification like the plague.
- Where record requests are taken at a public telephone box manned by the deejays in strict rotation.
- Where the aerial, all 180 feet of it, has to be put up before each and every broadcast by one of the deejays.
- Where broadcasts are made from a different location every week, from squats and tiny one-roomed flats, and where every knock at the door brings a sudden dryness to the throat and a cold knot of panic in the stomach.

Picture this whole tapestry and you've got Wonderful Radio Concord, the station of the people, and for the people – well, at least those people who can actually pick up the signal on 225 metres on the Medium Wave between 10 p.m. Friday and 10 a.m. Saturday.

I joined Concord and its merry band of faceless dedicated men for last week's broadcast and discovered what life is like on a land-based pirate station.

But first, let me introduce you to these radio renegades. There's El Supremo who, apart from delivering shows in a deliberately phony American accent, also takes responsibilities much of the time for erecting Concord's aerial – all 60 yards worth of wire.

El Supremo said, "That's the most difficult part really. Once we got to the top of a block of flats and started paying out the aerial down the side. We'd lowered about 150 feet when we realized that it was disappearing about halfway down.

"We went to see what was going on and found that a little old woman had seen it come snaking past her window, so she opened it and pulled the wire in." Then she cut it.

She gave it back when we told her we were scientists conducting an experiment to pick up radio waves from intelligent aliens. She was very impressed.

Supremo's got a fund of stories about aerial-building, including the time he was chased up the fire escape of a convent by a very irate nun. She was told a story about Supremo being a student who was testing the atmosphere for humidity.

"She seemed quite pleased about that. For the next two hours I kept on getting little waves from smiling nuns on their way to prayers and what have you."

Next up is King Kong, who is the station's technical whizz-ape and seems to be the only one who knows how the Heath Robinson collection of diodes, triodes, fourodes and fiveodes that make up the transmitter actually work. King Kong said, "You don't need size. The transmitter we've got here once broadcast to Sweden. We've got a postcard to prove it from someone who lives there."

Then there's Joe Lung, a Rasputin-like figure who looks as sinister as his name, but in fact is a very pleasant person and the most professional of the deejays on Concord.

Matt Black comes next, an idiosyncratic figure who makes films for a living and puts out a 100 per cent oldies show.

Making up the rest of the pirate crew come such colourful names as John the Baptist, Dan Blocker, Len Deevish, the Saskatoon Kid, Wolfman Fred, Captain Banana, Vilfin, Snoopy and anyone else who cares to go along for the broadcast.

Their broadcast last week started in typical style with Joe, Matt, Supremo and Kong building a new transmitter. Said Kong,

"We had problems last week and it turned out that for most of the time we were broadcasting at about ten watts, which is about good enough for the bottom of the street."

That done, we took to Supremo's car laden with transmitters – the new one plus a spare – a mixer, microphone, record decks, a transformer, records and the aerial – worth its weight in gold. The whole lot would have fitted neatly into the boot of a Ford Escort.

That week's chosen site turned out to be a tiny one-roomed flat. It was short on room, but it was warm and private, which are two big plusses for Concord. "Last week," said Joe, "we were in a squat in Islington. We set up all the equipment but when it started to get a bit cold we switched on the electric fire and all the power practically disappeared."

King Kong solved the ensuing problem of a blown fuse by replacing it with a lump of copper. It seemed that everything electrical was glowing rather orange by the end of the broadcast.

We were ushered in by the owners, a taciturn bearded guy who was to provide some live music that night and a fair-haired girl who seemed to be tickled to death by the whole circus. The location was "somewhere in North London."

The studio was their kitchenette, with the record decks resting on the kitchen sink, the transmitter on a cupboard and the deejays plus spectators perched anywhere where there was more than three square inches of buttock space.

"It's aerial time," said Supremo and deftly changed into his plimsolls. He set off in the direction of a nearby block of flats. After about an hour he came back, frozen and blue-nosed, but happy. He'd strung the aerial from the top of the flats to a tree in the garden.

"If anyone complains I'll say that I've asked some friends to put up a washing line for me," suggested the bearded flat tenant.

All he needed was 50-foot-long arms, two-foot clothes pegs, and underpants the size of a Zeppellin and it would have been the perfect excuse. Since he's relatively normal in shape and size he's just ignored as the Concord men set about their work.

One by one they look at the aerial out of the window and say dutifully, "Nice aerial." Supremo looks delighted.

It's 10.15 p.m. when the show finally gets on the road – slight problems with the earth, which King Kong deftly handles. "Hi everybody, this is Radio Concord coming to you on 225, and we're sorry we're a little late but we had some technical problems and pretty soon we'll have a phone number for you to phone in your instant requests, and in the meantime here's a little record for you called, um . . ."

Supremo's nervous as a kitten and makes endless mistakes, but there's something tremendously appealing about it. Someone once said that all the fun went out of TV when they started pre-recording programmes and eliminating all possible mistakes. They were right. Concord, with its comedy of errors, proves it.

The night continues in the same vein with each deejay taking his turn. A telephone box is located, and the requests start pouring in when Joe Lung reads out the number. The response is astonishing. Before long the number is jammed, and they have to pick a new one.

Despite the gimcrack appearance of the equipment Concord really get heard – it's not just the next-door neighbour, Mr. and Mrs. Scroggins from number 38, who can tune in. They get telephone calls from south Yorkshire, Lancashire and all over London, including Leyton, where a caller says they're coming through ten times louder than Capital.

And speaking of Capital, Mighty Joe Lung, so-called because of his long-standing $1 a day nicotine habit, has a valve to pick with them.

"They keep on nicking all our ideas," he complains. "Or at least it seems that way. It's happened so many times it can't be a coincidence.

"We were the first station to feature instant requests. Capital said it was impossible, but we just went right ahead and did it. A few weeks later so did they.

"Then there's Kenny Everett's competition where he plays just the first note of a record and asks people to guess what it is. We started that weeks before they did.

"They're loads of other little things. Maybe they are just coincidence, but I don't think they can be."

It's now 1.00 am on Saturday morning and anyone with a modicum of sense is safely tucked up in bed. Not radio Concord and me.

Supremo decides to take a drive around to see what reception was like. King Kong and Dan Blocker join us. In fact, the signal is surprisingly strong almost everywhere we go – and that's on a car radio.

When we return Supremo leaves the car near the telephone kiosk, we pass two of the look-outs and get back to the studio.

As yet they've been raided only once in four years of broadcasting. "And that was during the day when we weren't actually putting anything out," comments Supremo.

He was taken to court and given a conditional discharge. He also had to pay costs of $1, much to the disgust of the Post Office who send out detector vans to try and track down pirate stations.

Comments Joe: "I really don't know why they don't try more often. I think it's because detector van duties are classed as overtime, so if they put us off the air there'd be a lot of blokes who would be short of a bit of extra cash.

"I mean, we broadcast a telephone number so I should think it would be quite easy to track that down.

"Tracking the signal is a different matter. We've got lookouts and we know the cars and vans the Post Office use so they're easily spotted. When we see one we just pull the plug and the signal's gone so they can't trace it."

They tend to have more problems with accidental discoveries like when King Kong was on the roof of a block of flats – no, not tearing it down with his bare hands – checking out the aerial.

"A policeman tapped me on the shoulder and said 'Hello, hello, hello, what's going on 'ere then.' I told him I was just getting a breath of fresh air and then ran. I managed to get downstairs, grab the transmitter and get away."

On another occasion in the murky depths of the morning the Concords were slightly surprised to see their transmitter suddenly leap three feet in the air.

King Kong looked out of the window and saw a puzzled policeman at the other end of the aerial giving it a hefty tug. "We just cut the wire and made a run for it."

Fortunately, nothing happened last week, apart from the man in the flat next door demanding to know what was going on. At 3 a.m. he made his third visit and pleaded, "I just want to know what's happening. I won't tell anyone, honest. I just want to know."

John the Baptist and Wolfman Fred turn him away yet again.

By now it's live broadcast time, and the bearded flat owner and his huge black friend treat us to 15 minutes of their own numbers. Mr. Beard perches in the living area, while the black guy sings in the kitchenette. It may not be Top Of The Pops, but it's live.

All the way through the 12 hours of broadcasting there's a continuous coming and going of deejays and look-outs, alias telephone answerers. The ones coming in are blue with cold and they make a bee-line for the small gas fire.

The ones going out look depressed – it's not surprising, since the calls have dwindled to a mere telephonic trickle and there's not a lot you can do in a North London phone box at four in the morning.

Supremo, happy now that he's near the fire, says: "It might seem mad but we are doing this for a good reason.

"We don't see ourselves as pirates as much as alternative radio. We play absolutely anything on the station and we think it is a real alternative to Radio One and Capital.

"They just play their top thirty playlists or whatever, but we play anything. And anyone can come and have a go. They've all got as much right as anyone to broadcast.

"The Post Office say we interfere with other stations and emergency broadcasts but that's just not true. We're very careful about that."

King Kong adds that with unidirectional aerials there could be thousands of stations throughout Britain. Supremo nods and then lies down on the floor and falls asleep.

Dawn breaks slowly and now there are no phone calls at all. I've got the horrible feeling that there's just no-one listening. It doesn't seem to bother Concord though. They just keep on.

The transmitter is still glowing away in the corner and King Kong looks at it appreciatively. "That's a bloody good transmitter," he keeps saying to no-one in particular, and then reaches for a chocolate biscuit, one of about 100 that John the Baptist brought to help us through the night.

By seven I've just about had it but for Supremo and John the Baptist it's time for the Completely Mad Breakfast Show.

Says Supremo, in between mistakes, "We run a Big Tits competition and a Disease of the Week Contest."

"Another quiet night and no raids," he says later, obviously a bit disappointed that there hadn't been any action. "It's very funny really, because if they do raid us they can't legally arrest us. They confiscate equipment but that's it."

Looking at their gear it hardly seems worth it. Besides, they could knock up another transmitter for less than £30.

"There's no money in this," says Matt Black. "It's just an important thing to do." He means it but doesn't look all that convinced since he's just spent three hours curled up in the car by the phone box.

"And its good fun, if you don't get caught," adds Supremo.

The calls start coming in again but soon its 10.00 a.m. and time for closedown. King Kong wanders over to the block of flats and climbs to the roof – by the stairs, I hasten to add.

As he's uncoiling the wire a woman wanders out onto her balcony and sees it snaking down past her window. She summons her husband and he comes to have a look.

Pretty soon every balcony is full of people gazing at the wire like it's a giant anaconda, but no-one does anything. Kong, nonchalance itself, emerges and the lads pack up and go.

"Every day's a holiday on Concord," comments Supremo as he drives off. Everyone else seems to be asleep.

Reproduced with permission from Time Inc UK

The article was very well received in the music industry, spinning off more interviews for us in the Fleet Street papers; it also turned out to be a big break for Brian, who would later become an editor at *Melody Maker* and write many books. There had never been such massive media exposure for land-based radio pirates before; the whole country was reading about us. That exposure also meant we had defiantly placed ourselves in the bright spotlight of the governmental authorities, and we knew that they'd not allow such open mocking to go unpunished.

The week after publication, we were raided at 7 Matilda Street N1. Three weeks later we were raided and busted at 115 Westbourne Park Road W11. Following that broadcast was the 1a South Villas NW1 raid. All these raids resulted in complete losses of our equipment, except for the transmitter I ran across the Islington rooftops with, but that went in the next raid anyway. The next broadcast was cancelled when the police were called to 12 Lancaster Road W11 during the antenna installation. The government obviously wanted to squash our presence on the airwaves and were going to concentrate on Concord until we went away one way or the other. Despite these setbacks, our spirits were not dimmed, and we continued broadcasting weekly for the rest of the year, only sustaining one heavy raid and loss of equipment in late August.

Free Radio Association

In the early hours of the morning, during the quieter times surrounding a broadcast, those hanging out in the location would usually huddle around the transmitter to talk shop and gossip. At one particular broadcast in the summer of 1976, we were idly waiting for the first shortwave BBC Overseas Service broadcast of the morning, hoping to get some news items to pass on to our listeners. With the radio still hissing nothing but static in the background, our talk was about the incessant raids on us, and what we could do about them.

The crew agreed that, since our audacity, political stands, and content were obviously not going to change, we had to consider changing our operating methods to avoid the ongoing harassment. One good idea thrown out was to use a microwave link that would allow us to send an audio signal to the transmitter from another remote location, but cost and technical line-of-sight issues between sites made that problematic. Then we brainstormed another method that could almost guarantee us not getting raided. This brilliant (and difficult) ploy consisted of not just moving the transmitter for every regular or weekend broadcast, but instead, moving or switching the transmitter multiple times during the broadcast itself.

We assumed this novel tactic would hopefully flummox the GPO's tracking methods and send them running around in a tizzy to different areas in ever-changing directions as we switched locations. Finding our stationary broadcasts usually took the trackers only a few hours, but with this scenario, by the time they got close to the location or managed to get a search warrant, we would be switching the transmitter site. By sending the trackers off on wild-goose chases across London, we hoped they'd just give it up for the day.

This multi-location effort could not be achieved by Concord alone, but there were many land-pirates broadcasting around London. Most were individuals in an attic, operating whenever they wanted, without much regard to competing frequencies, signal strength, content, time, or locations. Stations like us, who broadcasted at the same time and on the same channel every week, had very different needs. To make our scheme work, we needed to contact all the disparate pirate broadcasters we could, and combine our technical and human resources.

Since there were already resource groups, such as The London Region Free Radio Campaign (LRFRC), and the Southern Independent Radio Association (SIRA) that helped pirates, we decided to try this new broadcasting ploy, and making this decision got us motivated to phone, cajole, write, and knock on all the pirates' doors to arrange the first meeting of the Free Radio Association.

For the meeting we came up with a practical plan: If we could persuade the other pirates to agree to our method, they would still be able to operate individually as usual, but under the loose FRA umbrella organization, they would pool some of their resources and time to create a pirate network with much better security for us all. The meeting was arranged for a room above a pub in Hampstead Village, and about twenty-five pirates attended. We went around the room for introductions, everyone sharing different reasons to be a *clandestina*. Some did it for their ego, others for the sheer anti-establishment thrill, others for the music. By the end of the meeting, with a few more beers under our belts, we had enlisted more than enough pirates willing to try our new approach for thwarting the authorities.

Our first effort was launched two weeks later. This weekend test would see Concord broadcasting for three hours from a squat in Belsize Park, then switching off to a different transmitter in an entirely different location in West London, and jumping to South London for the next, on a different frequency. The preparations were quite complex, to say the least, and we spent a crazy anarchic weekend with the FRA members, including Radio Kaleidoscope, careening around London to put up three antennas at widely distant locations.

For this broadcast we decided on a mix of live and recorded shows at our secret locations. We coordinated the critically timed switchovers from phone boxes *en route*, or, if there was no phone available, by directly announcing them over the radio. Somehow, although the quality of the programs and the strength of the stations varied wildly, it worked; at the end of the long day *no one* had been raided. This coordinated approach had never been attempted before, and Concord had successfully spearheaded and managed the debut broadcast. The FRA broadcast a few more times as a unit, but it was hard to keep a bunch of mainly young rebellious kids to a plan so complicated, with so many moving parts, and with such limited resources. The experiment, though short-lived, at the very least, provided a chance for pirates all over the London area to get together, to get to know and work with each other, and network for the future.

Be Careful What You Wish For!

SEVEN YEARS LATER, IN 1983, A LAW, impelled in part by the continuous pressure of the land-based radio pirates, would be passed by Margaret Thatcher's Conservative party, creating Britain's community radio system. At the time of its enactment, many of the stable pirate stations that had continued from my days, actually became legitimatized.

Sadly, some laws are flawed and don't necessarily realize their original purpose. Because of an extremely high yearly license fee, to this day, most volunteer radio organizations simply can't afford to operate within the legitimate system. Minority groups in particular have been excluded by this artificial constraint, and pirate radio has once again become a hugely popular medium for them. After all these years, the use of exclusionary tactics, such as fees now, shows that there have only been minor changes in Britain as far as the true breadth and possibility of a community radio system are concerned. Lacking policies to the contrary, the British government still exerts more control of freedom of speech on the airwaves than is merited in this era of multi-platform communications.

Raids, Roofs, and Hoofs

Some of our broadcasts were just plain surreal. One *Dickensian* location—a combination of all those dangerous nightmare factors you'd expect to find in a dilapidated squat—was, for me, the equivalent of Alfred Hitchcock's *Spellbound*.

Number 7, Matilda Street was a 200-year-old two-story ramshackle Georgian terraced building located a street away from the old Caledonian Market in Islington. The five squatters who lived in the house were delighted to have us there, and gave us a tour of their home while describing for us the housing situation in the surrounding buildings and streets. Not all the buildings on this street were squatted they said—there were still a few rentals scattered in between abandoned and boarded-up frontages.

As we set up our equipment on March 14th, 1975, we were faced with the fact that there was just *one* working electrical outlet in the entire house, a ceiling fixture with crumbling braided-wire insulation dangling from a badly chipped plaster rosette. Two double-outlet sockets, inserted into another double socket, enabled us to plug all our gear—transmitter, lights, electric bar heater, and audio equipment—into that single overtaxed source. It was a bitterly cold night, so we needed the electrical heater on in order to keep our hands warm enough to change the records on the turntable and operate the equipment—hard to do in thick gloves!

When said heater came on, if the light bulb was on as well, the fuse would blow, and all would go black. We took turns stumbling down to the fuse-box in the basement to wrap another piece of aluminium foil across the many-times-previously blown cartridge-fuse and push it back in again. Fortunately, the friendly squatters had hooked up the gas line into the house, and a stove in the back kitchen provided us with hot tea and the opportunity to warm ourselves at the open oven door.

Our wire for this broadcast stretched from our roof to another roof on a squat located diagonally across the road. Although perhaps half the desired length and not very far off the ground, our aerial's location in this hilly area of Islington enabled us to broadcast quite powerfully (apart from the frequent in-house power outages). A week later we received a letter from a listener in Scotland who said the signal had been coming in strongly all broadcast long. Moreover, according to the frozen volunteers answering our on-air number in a smelly phone box on the Caledonian Road, the calls from listeners requesting songs and words of encouragement were pouring in fast. To keep all the strolling lookouts and phone-box scribes from getting frostbite, we kept rotating them back into the house every half-hour to warm up and have a cuppa.

This chilly rotation paid off at about 2 AM on the second night, when a lookout stumbled breathlessly into the transmitter room and panted: "There's-gasp-a-gasp-shit-load-gasp-of police-gasp-on the Cali-gasp-Road-gasp!" Since the pubs had closed three hours before, the news sounded suspiciously as if the rozzers knew where we were and poised for a raid on us.

Having that much time to prepare for their knock was an unexpected luxury, so we put into action our sophisticated escape-act, which consisted of shutting the broadcast equipment down without a closing message, and disconnecting all power wires, except for the much-needed heater, from the ceiling outlet. The squatters readied themselves for a brave face-off with the police and GPO trackers at the front door, and the rest of the Concord crew dispersed through the house to pretend to occupy empty rooms.

During the initial set-up, while scoping out the best antenna location, I'd noticed that there was an empty boarded-up house two doors over and decided to check it out. On investigating the top landing of our broadcast squat, I'd found a small, hinged access hatch in the ceiling. Intrigued, I stood on a chair, unbolted the hatch, pushed it open, and pulled myself onto the slate roof. Tiptoeing across the slippery slope of the occupied rental next to us, I found a similar (and—yes!—unlocked) roof-hatch in the empty house. I opened it with great care and shone my torch down into the room below. From a quick sweep of the beam, I could see that this hulk had been mostly stripped down to its bare wall studs, with parts of the rail-less stairs to the top floor missing. I dropped down inside to explore the building, and realized swiftly that — Bob's your uncle!—I'd discovered a great bolt-hole.

So when the expected Bobby-knocking started on the front door, I was already up the stairs with the still-warm transmitter under my arm. Climbing out of the hatch, I lifted the transmitter up through it with some rope as a crew member moved the chair away from below. Then, setting the metal box to one side, I waited at the opening, wondering what kind of scene would unfold below my feet.

When all the movement to the rooms had stopped, I whispered down to the squatters at the front door that we were ready for them to let in the unwelcome visitors, and soon began to hear the heavy footfalls and echoing voices of many police officers entering the house and spreading throughout the ground floor. When they began to come up the stairs to the second floor, I thought it was past time for me to move.

Gently closing my escape-hatch, I sidled, transmitter under arm, carefully over the frost-slick slate roof of the house next door. As I slithered past blackened clay chimney pots and brick stacks, with the sweat fast cooling on my brow and my heart beating like a sparrow's, I felt like some desperate miscreant out of *Oliver Twist*.

I finally made it onto the roof of the abandoned house. In my previous reconnoiter, I'd found a ceiling crawlspace just below and to the side of the roof-hatch, and figured this niche would act as a cave where I could hide safely, even in the event of a very careful search from below. Closing the hatch and slipping into the cobwebbed rafters, I crawled over the joists and shoved the transmitter into a far nook. When I dropped down to the upper floor from the interstitial space, I had to lean against the wall for a few minutes to catch my breath, and settle down from the adrenaline rush of the raid and my mad rooftop flight.

Outside, I could hear a babble of voices from the direction of our broadcast location, and see the flashing lights of the police vehicles leaking through the boarded-up windows of my hideout.

Suddenly, my heart jumped at the sound of a muffled knocking, accompanied by the unexpected flash of a torch into the abandoned house. Then I heard a thudding at the boarded-up front door, accompanied by the painful squeal of nails being pulled from plywood.

The police were going to search this building! Padding back to the overhead hatch, I climbed very carefully back to my dark lair in the rafters, trying desperately to quiet my breathing. As I crouched there, I could track, by the creaking of ancient floorboards, the footsteps of someone walking through the house and occasionally stopping, presumably to listen for any untoward sounds. The footfalls made their way up the last flight of stairs, even negotiating a way past the broken parts. Then, shockingly, the beam of a powerful torch blazed through the cracks in the ceiling directly below me—the searcher had come into the very room above which I was hiding and was sweeping the bright light around in search of hidden culprits. Damn!

PC Footsteps was very professional; he stood there for an excruciatingly long time, listening for giveaway noises. Barely breathing, I kept stock-still amidst the coarse and dusty rafters, praying not to sneeze. At the end of what seemed an eternity, the Police Constable finally walked out of the room and, it appeared, out of the house. I stayed alert up there for over an hour, my extremities getting colder and colder, just in case the Bill was faking his exit. When I felt absolutely sure that the police had gone, I descended into the dark again, leaving the transmitter safely in the rafters.

Here was my next dilemma: going back to the squat across the roofs was probably not wise, in case the police were still lurking. There was also a good chance that the neighbours in the house between the squat and my hiding place were probably now alerted, and would hear me crunching across the roof-slates. Leaving by the boarded-up front door was also out of the question, as the cops were surely out there watching for unusual movement.

Fortuitously, as I explored the ground-floor rear kitchen area, I found an inner-bolted back door that wasn't otherwise locked, and stepped cautiously out into a small garden area. Surrounding it on three sides was a six-foot tall brick wall, on which I could just make out the glint of glass shards mortared into the top as a deterrent to casual illicit entry. Because of the brouhaha of the raid, I felt I shouldn't climb over the intervening walls to either side, because the neighbors might still be up watching the police activity and catch sight of me.

Lacking other ideas, I scrambled up the back wall of the courtyard, and lurched to the top. Covering the sharp security glass with the sleeve-ends of my thick winter jacket, I somehow managed to settle my legs and torso gently on the broken shards without causing any lasting damage. As there was no moonlight, I could see nothing in the area into which I was about to jump.

Geronimo! I dropped over the wall into the darkness, falling much further than I'd expected, and landing off-balance on rough cobblestones. As I sprawled on my hands and knees, I felt what seemed to be straw between my fingers, and then received one of the biggest frights of my life—a sudden loud metallic clanking, accompanied by the shuffling, neighing, and snorting of large animals clattering in the dark.

As my eyes adjusted to the ambient light, I realized that I'd landed smack in the middle of an open horse-stable, and was now surrounded by six wide-awake and spooked Shire workhorses thrashing their enormous dinner-plate-sized hooves about. As they bucked and swirled around the corral, I managed to duck and dodge their flailing feet, but found myself thrown roughly against the wall several times by their heavy bodies. The chances of getting caught up in such an equine dance must have been very slim; the stable was probably one of the last horse-and-cart businesses still left in 1970s London.

Lunging and weaving, I managed to sidle my way along the wall to a simple wooden gate, over which I hastily scrambled, only to fall into a small courtyard, where a ten-foot tall metal-gated archway led to the street. "What's bloody next!?" I muttered under my breath, panting and shuddering from a combination of cold and fright. The gate was locked, but I managed to shimmy up the ice-cold slippery bars, squeeze (with only a few jacket rips) over the rusty-barbed wire laced on top, and scoot down the outside of it to freedom.

The sky was lightening to reveal another cold wintry morning as I peeked around the street corner; no police cars in the vicinity. Plucking up courage, I casually walked past the broadcast house to the next street corner. No one accosted me, so I doubled back, tiptoed up the well-worn front steps of the broadcast squat, and discreetly knocked on the door. The dirty front-room curtains soundlessly rustled apart, then the door opened, and I was yanked inside to safety. A crowd of Concord crew and squatters surrounded me, all asking at the same time what had happened to me, and, more importantly, where was the transmitter?

As I huddled next to the oven to thaw out and sip a hot cup of tea, I recounted my adventures, detailing my escape from the police in the abandoned house, to the last horse-hair-raising surprise. Although the police and GPO trackers had done their usual search and questioning, they didn't find the transmitter and couldn't bust anyone, or even take away our equipment and records for evidence. Once warmed up, I retraced my slippery steps across the roof slates and climbed back into the rafters of the abandoned house to retrieve the transmitter for next week's show. All in a night's work for a dedicated pirate!

Police, Walnuts, Dogs and Axes

FREE SPEECH IS A WONDERFUL INVENTION, but it does come at a cost on many levels, a fact that we learned at one particular broadcast on April 11th, 1975. While at a meeting at Release, the squatters' pro bono legal organization, Jim from BIT told me we could transmit during the upcoming summer bank holiday from a four-story Georgian terraced house/squat almost directly across from the BIT office at 115 Westbourne Park Road.

As with our first broadcast from the BIT building, I had to do some real antenna installation acrobatics, dangling precariously from yet another twenty-story tower block (still there) across the road. How the crew pulled the wire safely over the main road without electrocution from the overhead wires and continuous traffic mayhem, I have no idea, as I was too busy teetering over the edge of the roof, untangling the line from obstructing pipes!

This squat was primarily a place where transient people lived with the barest of amenities—I counted about a dozen sleeping bags and personal-effects bundles in the otherwise empty rooms. The place was in poor condition, but the electrical system worked well enough for our needs. Following an early broadcast test from the temporary studio we'd set up on the third floor, a crew member who'd been stationed in the phone box down the road came running in excitedly. It seemed that because of that beautiful high and long antenna, Radio Concord could be heard clearly across a huge swath of Southern England.

Starting at 6 PM, and buoyed by the heady knowledge that we were a major blip on the dial that night, our shows and interviews became very jovial and went relatively smoothly, with fewer technical problems than with the average Concord broadcast. A stream of DJs, lookouts, techs, interviewees, squatters, and just the passing curious, flowed freely in and out of the *al fresco* studio during the evening.

Around about 10 PM, Heathcote Williams came romping up the stairs, with a newly written prose piece clutched in his hand, and a wicked grin on his face. He began his show by reading his essay, which was all about the revolution that was coming, and how the fascist governments would fall. The Metropolitan Police were *not* shown in a flattering light. One piece of this epic I remember, had the Queen fleeing from a burning Buckingham Palace, aided by a Chinese rickshaw driver who stopped in the middle of the Vauxhall Bridge Road over the Thames, ravished her, then planted in her vagina a walnut that sprouted and started a whole new world disorder. Not, in retrospect, the most judicious application of the tenets of free speech.

Sometime after 2 AM, the crew were wanting eats and drinks to get them through the rest of the night. In those years, the only all-night food store in the whole of central London was a few miles away from us, in Bayswater, so Tony Reszka and I jumped in my car with the orders for everyone's either very sweet or salty junk food and/or drink. As we sped back through the quiet London streets, rejoicing at the strength of Concord's loud signal on the car radio, a sudden chilling shout erupted from the speaker, as on-air DJ Keith York began screaming into the microphone "We're being raided! We're being raided!" Then, nothing but static.

Driving west down Westbourne Park Road, we couldn't believe our eyes. The whole street outside the squat was cordoned off, with dozens of police cars, police, police dogs, plainclothes detectives and/or GPO trackers milling around, and an amusing *Keystone Kops*-like queue of Bobbies spilling down the steps and into the street, all waiting to barge through the narrow doorway into the building.

This time it looked like they'd thrown the kitchen sink at us. Wordlessly, Tony and I looked at each other and came to a silent agreement: curiosity was not good right now; flight was good right now. Just before we reached the cordoned-off street, I screeched into a left-hand turn onto a side street, accompanied by loud shouts of "Stop! Stop!" from uniformed police running towards us. In response, I accelerated out of the sharp turn with a loud squeal of tyres. As I wove down the many back streets of the area (fortunately ones that I knew well), my heart was pounding hard and fast. Tony, keeping a careful watch behind us, finally announced that no one had managed to follow our circuitous route. About an hour later, we came back to the broadcast area, parked the car far enough down the road so we could see what was happening and not be seen, and promptly both fell asleep.

At sunrise, we woke, stiff and cold from sleeping rough in the car, and, seeing no obvious police presence, walked down the street and darted up the stone-flagged front steps, to what remained of the now battered and splintered 200-year old Georgian door. I shouted my name through its jagged vertical gaps, but nothing stirred inside except the ghostly echoes of my voice. After a long wait, a disheveled Keith stumbled down the stairs and, heaving together, we got the door open, crumbling it into even more pieces in the process. Keith was extremely glad to see us; yes, to know that we were okay, and to let us know what had happened, but mainly because we'd brought the fast-food snacks. Leaving him rabidly rummaging through the feedbag, we went up to the erstwhile transmitter room. Not a lot left in there. On hearing our voices, other Concordians began to straggle in to compare war stories.

The incident was told piecemeal, with each member adding his or her *Rashomon*-like account. With the roaring success of the broadcast and the late hour, no one had been methodically watching the street. Hearing loud bangs on the front door presaged the first signs of trouble, but these were not the usual knuckle-rappings we'd heard on other raids. The crew ran to the front of the house just in time to see a cluster of burly pissed-off policemen slamming a battering ram into the front door. Presumably, the search warrant was stapled onto the front of the sturdy knocking-stick, a device usually reserved for the many forceful home evictions in this area. Waiting on the lower steps were some very agitated drug-sniffing police dogs, the rest of the police, and the GPO men.

When Keith had given the last warning shouts on-air and turned off the equipment, the Concord staff, guests, and inhabitants of the squat had hightailed it to remote corners of the house. Members of the crew found empty rooms, lay down on the wooden floors, threw a blanket or jacket over themselves, and feigned waking from a deep sleep, yelling "Who the hell's making all the noise?" and the like, at the police bursting into the room. "What radio broadcast?" was the common puzzled reply to questioning, "We just live here!"

The police and their dogs swarmed through the house looking for something official and gruff to do. (As always, per our no-contraband-at-the-location policy, there were no illegal substances in the building; at least not externally.) Much to their chagrin, there were also no revolutionaries to chase over the rooftops, no drug or gun haul of which to boast. Not even a parking ticket! From the looks of it, the police were furious at the GPO men for bringing them out for no good reason, especially at this unearthly time of the morning on a Bank Holiday.

Keith, chatting with some of the police during and after the raid, managed to get much of the story from their side, which explained why there was such an overwhelming response. Contrary to our wishful thinking, the GPO meanies had been specifically tracking us that evening, and knew our exact broadcast location early on. They went to the nearby Harrow Road Police Station for a search warrant and some Bobby backup for their bust. To sweeten the pot, so to speak, the GPO posited that there might be dangerous radicals and drugs on the premises. To prove we were broadcasting, a GPO man then put Concord on his portable radio at the Police Station, just as Heathcote's lewd and seditious story about the Queen happened to be airing.

Timing is everything. The police, very patriotic lads, were immediately incensed by this blasphemous tirade against their Monarch, and rushed the search warrant through with a rudely awakened judge. All available units and major raid equipment were called out to launch an attack against this impudent and probably violent radical gang, perhaps giving them a *Siege of Sidney Street* moment.

Well, at least the GPO had something to be happy about from the raid: in the initial confusion, no one had pulled the incriminating wavelength-setting crystal from the transmitter, so the Man had all our gear fair and square, and with the necessary proof. There was some small payback for the Concord crew when the GPO men then had to strain their backs carrying the transmitter, albums, and heavy DJ decks down to a waiting Black Maria.

It was only by sheer luck (and fast driving) that I wasn't at the squat for that big raid. Being well known to the trackers, and with my past capture and record, I surely would have been summoned for the broadcast violations. In the end, no charges came down for any of our crew or squat inhabitants, as most gave false names and addresses, but as usual, the unkindest cut was the loss of our equipment and records. Arrogant and lax in our security, we had not kept enough lookout during the broadcast, and that was our downfall. The next workday, Westbourne Park Road was shut down once again as work crews removed my beautiful antenna handiwork from the airspace across the street.

The 101ers; A Most Unexpected Clash

IN THE LONDON OF 1975 AND 1976, music was still the key binding factor in all the new street movements, and the squatting movement was no exception. Just as Concord was known as the "Squatters' Radio," there was an unofficial "Squatters' Band" called the "101ers;" inevitably, we were destined to meet. Following an introduction by Piers Corbyn, three of us went to their eponymous 101 Walterton Road squat, where the band lived communally on all four levels of the old house. As we talked, the musicians began to see the advantage of radio exposure on Concord, since there was no chance of any play for them on the BBC. We all got on very well, and planned some live and taped broadcasts of their performances. As a great bonus, they all agreed that we could do a live transmission from their squat!

The lead singer and guitarist of this motley crew was a charismatic, hard-working, Orbison-coiffed musical dynamo, with the squatting name of "Woody Wooderson." The 101ers were unashamedly, a very basic pub-rock/R&B/rock & roll band, with nary a nod to the punk movement emerging at the same time. The number of members varied from gig to gig and from day to day, which naturally made the quality of the music just as wildly variable, but the danceable beat was always there in any iteration. Along with all the old rock & roll chestnuts, they mainly featured Woody's original songs, delivered in a powerful throaty emotional voice, and accompanied by slashing guitar riffs.

When I saw him for the first time, at a gig in a squatted bank by the old Tolmer Square Cinema, I felt immediately that he was special, and definitely on his way somewhere in showbiz. The 101ers would often play in such abandoned squatted halls, banks, and buildings, as well as in regular-world clubs like Ronnie Scott's in Soho, where I witnessed a truly wondrous gig in which Woody and the band had the crowd in the palm of their collective hand. His (their), "Gloria" was the most powerful live version I have ever heard. Personally, Woody's own "Keys To My Heart" was always my favourite of his original 101ers songs, and I always requested it at shows. I recorded the Ronnie Scott's gig on a cassette, and played it on my next show.

On Friday night, May 14th, 1975, we set up the transmitter and equipment in an empty third-floor back room of 101 Walterton Road. The antenna was strung quite easily from the roof of the house and across some back gardens to another squat, and we proceeded to broadcast non-stop for three non-raided days. Woody, who was hanging out in his fourth-floor pad watching the proceedings, came down to the transmitter room a couple of times to play solo sets on his guitar, and I interviewed him between songs.

The London Evening News newspaper had contacted me after seeing the recent *Melody Maker* article and wanted an interview, so I had arranged for reporter Barry Wigmore and a photographer to come to the 101 broadcast. As we were setting up, the photographer began taking shots of us and our studio setup, and Barry spent quite a bit of time talking to the participants and band members. To our great surprise, they put Radio Concord on a full inside-page spread the next week, with a small teaser on the front page next to a photo of Linda McCartney fighting yet another pot bust.

At this broadcast, Jean-Claude Nadry, a young waiter from northern France, had begun helping us after picking up our broadcasts at his work in London. His legs can be seen up a ladder in *The Evening News* shot of the broadcast, with me in the foreground holding the transmitter, my face purposefully whited out to prevent recognition.

A few weeks after that broadcast, I was hanging out with a couple of 101ers in Woody's room, when he drove up on his motorbike and came bounding in. He proudly announced to us that he had just married an American woman for £200 so she could get a work permit, and flashed the wad of notes at us. Did she later realize whom she had married? I never found out.

Eventually, wisely realizing that the squatting-band scene was way too limited for his talents, Woody began to cast around for another musical outlet, and started to play with a couple of younger guys. One afternoon during this time, as I was hanging out in his room waiting for him to return, he came in, flipped a tape cassette over to me and said casually, "Hey Supremo," (El Supremo was my then-current DJ name) "Check out my new band!"

He had finally broken with the 101ers, changed his name to "Joe Strummer," and formed a new band called the Clash. Yes, at that moment I had in my hand Joe's very own cassette of the master of their debut album. I played the tape on my next show, a first for the Clash, Radio Concord, and the world! (Oh, how I wish I had that cassette, but it was taken in a raid a week or two later.) With Woody/Joe's ensuing fame, we found out his real name was John Mellor, and that he was from an upper-middle-class family, not from the blue-collar roots he professed. With all the good work he did while squatting, his origins were ultimately irrelevant. So, that was perhaps my most exciting pirate radio musical achievement: witnessing the transition of Woody Wooderson of the 101ers to Joe Strummer of the Clash, and debuting the band's first album on Radio Concord.

On February 8th, 1979, during the Clash's last American tour, I went to their gig at Temple Beautiful, an old disused Jewish temple right next to the Fillmore West in San Francisco. Working my way to the side of the stage, I got a message back to Joe that El Supremo was here, and was ushered back to the "green room," where I joined Joe, the band, and other members of the entourage as they prepared themselves, mostly quietly, to go onstage and rock the house. Temple Beautiful collapsed all on its own shortly after that gig. Coincidence? You decide.

Sid Rawle, Maya, and the Travellers

ONE OF THE MOST CHARISMATIC LEADERS of the British hippie underground and the squatting movement was Sid Rawle, dubbed "The King of the Hippies" by the media. Along with the loony civil servant Bill (Ubi) Dwyer, and of course, the infamous Wally Hope, originators' of the Windsor and Stonehenge Free Festivals, Sid was a ubiquitous presence at all major events.

As to Wally; at events with nothing going on, every so often, in a ritualistic manner, some stoned hippie would struggle up to his feet and shout out loudly and hoarsely "Wally!!!!" This hog-call would be followed by the crowd shouting out: "Wally!" in reply.

Piers Corbyn had recommended that we contact Sid, as he had his fingers on the pulse of the Borough of Camden's squatting movement. In the early spring of 1975, Graham Barnes went along with me to meet him at his squatted home/office/publishing house (for his underground newspaper called *Maya*), at 26 Grafton Road, Kentish Town, next to the old ornate red-brick indoor swimming pool I swam in as a kid.

Tall, bearded, with thinning straggly red hair and a generous touch of Irish blarney, though he was actually English, from the West Country. Sid manifested just about all the street cred possible for those days. He was deeply involved in the 1960s hippie scene in London, and helped start the Hyde Park Diggers movement. He also led the New-Age contingent to John Lennon's Dorninish Island off the coast of Ireland; (known as Beatle Island or Hippie Island, Dorninish was the dream island of John Lennon, who owned it until his death; it became a colony for idealistic New Agers whose tepees were eventually defeated by the County Mayo winter); and formed the Peace Convoy that became called the Travellers, as noted earlier.

On top of those achievements was Sid's pioneering work in the squatting movement. His partner Minke, was younger, gamine-like, with short black hair, and they had a young child together.

From our conversation over tea, Sid could see that Radio Concord was a natural ally for his alternative newspaper, and for squatting in general. From that meeting, and with Sid's generous help, we located many squats to broadcast from in the greater Camden area. I struck up a personal friendship with him, and we had many long far-ranging talks on all manner of subjects.

Not long after the 1975 Stonehenge Free Festival, (see Chapter 7), I went around to his place to catch up and make plans for future collaborations, only to find the house partially empty and Sid's two *Maya* helpers looking very upset. It seemed Sid and family had run off to somewhere in Wales with a substantial amount of *Maya's* cash. The passionate *Maya* newspaper workers, left scrambling to keep on publishing their serious social-issues newsletter, were rightfully steamed at this plain old-fashioned rip-off by their influential leader.

Piano Factory, Chalk Farm

SOME BROADCAST LOCATIONS SHOULD NOT HAVE WORKED because of their sheer audacity, or the technical and antenna-related gymnastics required, but somehow did; the Piano Factory was a wonderful example of this. Despite its many complications, this became one of our most powerful and meaningful broadcast outings.

The 1975 Spring Bank Holiday weekend was coming up, but we had no prospective location until I got a call from Heathcote Williams a few days before the holiday: "I've got a *great* broadcast location for us!" he gushed. That afternoon, Graham Barnes, Keith Hunter, and I rode the tube to Chalk Farm Station with him to check out the proposed site. Across from the old Roundhouse entertainment venue there is Belmont Street, a quiet cul-de-sac. In the center of the street was a small grassy sward with a fifteen-story 1960s-era, square block of council flats erupting from it. Surrounding the outer ring were some small timeworn Victorian-era homes, and light industrial buildings.

Heathcote led us through a set of big black wooden double doors set into high brick walls topped with broken glass. Beyond them was the small cobbled courtyard of a blocky, coal-smoke-darkened five-story brick building that straddled the whole south corner of the street. In the front of the building, with its industrial sash windows, was a large loading dock with a rusty roll-down door. Heathcote opened a man-door in the roll-down and we followed him in. Our smiles just got bigger and bigger as we checked out this ideal walled-off location; it was a veritable castle, certain to thwart any but the biggest police raid. It seemed that Heathcote's friend Michael had audaciously squatted the entire historic Chappell Piano Factory!

As we ascended to the top floor in the creaky piano-lift, I made a mental note to take the stairs in future, as the first three floors we passed yawned open, dusty, and unused. The occupied fourth floor was very different. A few privacy partitions had been installed around the edges of the large high-ceilinged space, and within them, in an attempt to create some intimate living areas out of this utilitarian environment, furniture clusters had been set up on carpets to form three different "rooms." Michael, an artist, greeted us excitedly at the lift, showed us around his creation, and, once we'd filled him in on what we would have to do to stage the broadcast in his home, he immediately offered the place and his help.

The next day, along with Tony Reszka and John Hallam, we came back, bringing some 200-foot reels of silver-coated copper antenna-wire and our arsenal of tools. As we secured an insulating rope loop to a metal strut outside one of the windows of Michael's "living room," we saw our host, along with Heathcote and another man arriving, laden with boxes of electronic equipment, TVs, and stereos. They were laughing and high on the fact (they said) that they had ripped off the gear from a department store using fake credit cards.

Brief Fanboy Interlude—The third man turned out to be author John Michell, and meeting him was a very momentous occasion for me. I was very much into sci-fi books and ancient legends, and had read and agreed with Gerald Hawkins' popular 1965 book, *Stonehenge Decoded*, which maintained that the ancient monument had been constructed as an astrological clock. This logical treatise rang true to me, and, with my subsequent engineering training, I became increasingly convinced.

Reading Michell's 1969 book *View over Atlantis*, as well as many of his later publications, helped piece together for me the web of ancient knowledge that I felt was still present if only we could recognize it. My discovery of Alfred Watkins' Ley Lines concept as a teen, combined my love for geography and history, seemed to have a valid connection to older, now lost truths, and searching out those invisible lines that carry that old wisdom between them, became a passion of mine. I pored over detailed ordinance-survey maps for countless hours, looking for ancient ruins, churches, tumuli, earthworks, and Roman roads.

My interest in those arcane subjects had started about age ten, when I learned the tumuli, or burial mounds, on Hampstead Heath near my home, were reputed to be that of Bodaceia, the warrior queen who led the Britons' unsuccessful rebellion against the Roman invasion in 60 A.C.E. (Although her forces massacred some 70,000 Romans and their supporters, they were ultimately defeated.)

John suffered my star-struck adoration, and fielded my questions like the gentleman he appeared to be, fake credit-card theft notwithstanding. Interviewing him during our four-day broadcast was one of my life's radio highlights.—**End of Interlude**

Before the Piano Factory broadcast could happen, we had to negotiate an antenna route that was potentially brilliant, but our most challenging since we'd bamboozled the nuns at the convent school into thinking we were looking for signs of extraterrestrial communication. Our target was the top of the fifteen-story block of flats across the road. Graham and I slipped through its unlocked main doors, took the lift to the floor below the roof, and by methods not necessarily seen as legal in most jurisdictions, opened the door to the top of the building. Leaning out over the vertiginous 150-foot drop, I could see a mass of overhead telephone wires splayed out from a single utility pole on the side of the road to the surrounding flats, houses, and the factory—in short, the worst tangle to overcome that we had encountered to date.

From my perch on the roof, I unrolled the wire down to the waiting helpers at the foot of the building, and secured the insulated end to a strong plumbing vent-pipe. To succeed, we had to get our wire over *all* the overhead lines, then lift it clear to the top of the block of flats at one end, and the fourth floor of the piano factory on the other. With no crossbow handy to send the wire over all the obstructing cables at once, we reverted to type, tied a rope to a stone, and began throwing the stone over each cable as we came to it, tying the wire to the dangling rope, and pulling the rope and wire up and over. We started this process early in the day, and thought that we had time to accomplish this tricky installation before the late-summer sunset.

By the time we reached the middle of the road and had managed to throw our line successfully over about half the overhead wires, our presence was definitely being felt on the street. What a ridiculously suspicious sight we must have been now with: six scruffy reprobates draped with wires, toting rocks and weird electronic equipment, playing our bizarre toss-and-haul game in broad daylight. Even to a casual onlooker, the scene could have implied terrorists, or the very least, wire-thieves.

As we gazed skyward, looking for the next cable over which to hurl our rock, a police car squealed around the corner from Chalk Farm Road. With some heavy-footed braking, the Panda pulled up right next to us, blocking our path to freedom (which would have been difficult to achieve anyway, festooned as we were with equipment, and fastened by wires to immovably fixed objects). How could The Bill have tracked us down so soon? Who had tipped them off? A neighbor looking out of a window and making a 999 call? This had happened to us before, but we'd never been caught *so* red-handed. Conning a gullible nun or neighbour with a silly excuse was one thing; police inquiries were something else entirely. We all thought the jig was up for real this time.

Two policemen got out the idling car, and one of them said, surprisingly: "Why, hello, Mr. Levine," in a friendly, cheerful voice. In one of those divine and incredible coincidences, I suddenly remembered a night about two weeks before, when I'd been unloading the radio-station equipment from my car at about 2 AM on a Sunday morning at my parents' flat, where I often stashed the gear after a successful broadcast. At the suspicious sight of a bloke illegally parked in a bus zone, and pulling bulky items from the boot of the vehicle, a police car pulled up behind me. Two policemen got out, and one, a short blond-haired chap, started asking me questions. They wanted to know what I was doing with the equipment (subtext: was I was stealing it?). I explained to them that I was a DJ returning home to my parents' flat after a gig, and with some noisy radio-checking to HQ, they appeared to believe me. As there wasn't much crime happening in the area that night, they visibly relaxed, chatting with me in a quite friendly manner about my DJ work.

So now, of all the policemen, in all the Holmes Road Police District, and on that shift, the short blond-haired cop was literally the only copper in London with whom I had a chance of explaining away this guilty-looking tableau. I decided to bluff it out and greeted him cheerily, covered in wires, innocently asking him how he was doing. He said that they'd received a call from a concerned neighbor who was worried about our activities in the street. Thinking quickly, I began spinning the (technically impossible) story that we were having a holiday party at the Piano Factory, and were stringing wires for speakers in different places. And goodness, he actually fell for it.

I'm sure this only worked because he'd met me before in DJ mode, and knew I was involved with such things—any other Panda crew would have been much more skeptical and checked us out further. Continuing to chat calmly with the officers, I brazened it out further, as the other pirates stood there in abject shock, not quite understanding or believing what was happening. Promising the lads in blue that, for the neighbours' sake, we'd not make too much noise, we sweetly waved them goodbye as they backed out of the narrow street.

Exuberant at our close-call escape, we finally hoisted the wire joyfully up to Michael's fourth-floor window, hauling in the line like real pirates raising a mainsail. Once tightened down, the wire ascended at about a sixty-degree angle to the top of the block of flats and looked magnificent.

The broadcast started at 5 PM Friday, and because of the length and height of the wire, our elevated and obstacle-free location at Chalk Farm, and a newer 24-watt transmitter, the Piano Factory weekend turned out to be one of our best broadcasts, putting out some excellent music, arts, and political content including my interview with the British Army deserter. Early excited reports from far-flung friends and other pirates, told us the broadcast was being picked up all over London, as loud and clear as the BBC itself.

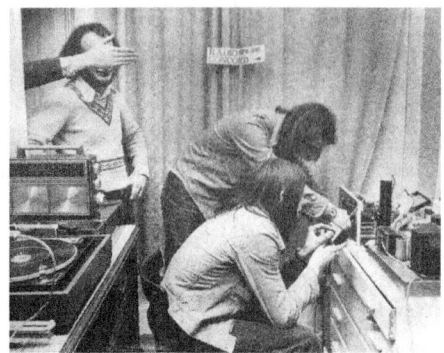

MM Broadcast: Arnold, Keith (front), Graham and Reporters Hand (back).

Free Radio Assn. Meeting Keith Hunter, Ed Hatvany, Mark Aston (King), Nick Catford (back), Anne Stevens, Steve (?), Mick Lewis (back), Arnold

Joe Strummer

Essential equipment for pirate radios—a ladder for a lookout who watches for the Post Office through a hole in the roof.

Evening Standard Article 101ers Squat at 101 Walterton Road

Piano Factory

Westbourne Pk. Rd. Antenna from 20-Story Apt. Block

Sid Rawle at Stonehenge

Concord Squat and Studio at 12 Alperton Road

Arnold, Sharon, Sue, and Jeffrey

7

Fun & Games in
Life & Broadcasting

OUR MOTLEY CONCORD GROUP AT THIS TIME mostly consisted of students, lads on the dole, or blokes like me, working at low-paying jobs. Without the luxury of advertising, sponsors, or any other visible means of external support, our normal everyday operating costs were barely within our fiscal capabilities. In addition, because of raids and equipment breakdowns, we were always in need of funds for new transmitters, antenna wire, records and tapes. The fact that our broadcasting locations were free, along with the low cost of our home-brewed radio transmitting and audio equipment, meant it was all just about possible—with, that is, a few additional fundraising efforts.

Luckily, we were often asked by listeners to provide music for their parties and events, and seeing this as an opportunity to earn cash while creating additional community exposure, we began to provide DJ services. To put on a good visual show behind the sounds provided, we scrounged up some flashing lightboxes that varied their colours and sequencing with the music. The turntables, amps, speakers and light show were heavy, cumbersome and bulky, so it was always a struggle to lug all this, plus our crates of albums, to gigs. To make it easier on everyone, the crew would descend on the event by car, bicycle, or on foot, each carrying the equipment piecemeal.

This was an entirely different aspect of our work; instead of just sitting behind a mic in an empty room, tensed for a raid, we were visibly out in our community, watching people dance and have a good time. It was a joyful experience for us all, and the shows brought in new supporters and put us in direct contact with the many different music, social, and political groups of the time.

Another way that we made some money was by putting on our own benefit concerts in accommodating church halls and squatted spaces. One memorable event was a benefit at the old Hampstead Town Hall on Haverstock Hill Rd, near Belsize Park Tube Station. We rented it for £60 and ordered some barrels of real ale from Fuller's Brewery in Chiswick to lubricate the evening. (As it was real ale, and contained real sediment, we had to treat the barrels very gingerly in their pick-up and delivery under the scrutiny of John the Baptist, our resident expert.)

For this event, I called up Viv Stanshall of my favourite group, The Bonzo Dog Doo Dah Band, and he agreed to do the gig to help us out. A few days before the benefit, however, Viv called to say he had broken his leg by putting it through a bass drum during a gig, " But, not to worry, I've called Roger Ruskin Spear, (his fellow Bonzo), and he's agreed to stand in for me."

We charged £2 for entry to the benefit, but we were hoping to make most of our money on the beer and ale sales. To get around the alcohol-license issue, we sold drinks tickets at the door, which people could then redeem for beverages inside the hall. It was quite an evening, and, as a result of some mentions on the legit radio by sympathetic DJs, a big crowd turned up. Many attendees were a little disappointed that Viv was not there, but only a few turned away, as most were glad another Bonzo was to perform. Three excellent friends-of-the-station bands played some good blues and R&B to warm up.

Roger Ruskin Spear, the replacement Bonzo, was his usual outrageous self. To my delight, he came clad in the horizontally blue-and-white striped sweater worn on the cover of his *Electric Shocks* album. Roger had also brought, along with his many saxophones, his full complement of weird robots, and odd electronic equipment and devices. The show relied on a precisely timed stage routine, with primitive robots speaking, gesticulating or exploding at certain times, as he interacted with them, augmented by a crazy flashing lighting system. His pay for all this? £50, and all the Fuller's Ale he could drink. Luckily, his robots were teetotal!

To the Manor Squatted

THE SQUATTING MOVEMENT IS USUALLY DEPICTED as inhabiting decrepit old flats and houses, but there were actually no bounds to their perceived abodial rights. Here are some of our posher broadcast squats in the summer of 1975.

1) Through the squatters' network, we heard there was going to be a great party and music gig happening at an impressive manor house north of London, complete with acres of splendidly landscaped grounds. The unanimous decision? "Let's broadcast from there!" The old Tudor-style house was majestically appointed, with about twelve bedrooms and wood-paneled walls and staircases. Despite occupation by the squatters, the carefully sculpted lush grounds were still looking like something straight out of a *Town & Country* magazine spread.

For the party itself, live groups played continuously in the Great Hall, while ecstatic hippies frolicked on top of a huge flat bouncy balloon out on the elegant terrace. We set up our gear in the library next to the Great Hall, plugged into the main soundboard next door, and began a weekend-long live music broadcast. During breaks we played recorded music and talked to the performers. Added to that, were interviews with some of the bizarre characters who, intrigued by the glowing valves, and wires running from the next room, wandered into the library.

2) "What?" I couldn't believe my ears with this phone call. "A squat on The Bishops Avenue in Highgate?" ("The" with a capital "T" is actually part of its name—that's how posh it thinks it is.) My incredulity rose. Someone had squatted a big house, at the very intersection with Highgate Lane, on the most expensive street in

England. We of course saw this as the ultimate achievement over capitalism. How could we not broadcast a party from the very visible heart of ostentatious wealth? And what a delightful party it was, of, and by free people, with music and revolution in the air! The broadcast went well all night, with no raids. Although the police stopped outside a few times in their Panda cars, they didn't seem to want to mess with a bunch of music-crazed squatting hippies. Transmitting from the highest part of London was extremely effective, judging by the many letters we subsequently received from as far away as Scotland, France and Sweden.

3) For a bit of international flavour, Sid Rawle introduced us to the squatters who had taken over the majestic old New Zealand Embassy on the south side of Regents Park near Madame Tussaud's and the Planetarium. It was a massive beige building with dozens of rooms, and a full communal setup that included free food, a crèche, and lots of music and art. The five-story building provided good height on one end of the antenna; the other end was hitched without too much difficulty to an obligingly tall London Plane tree across the road, and beyond the wrought-iron fence inside Royal Regents Park (even our aerial site was posh!). Our broadcast from an empty room in this impressive structure went smoothly, with many visits from its colourful inhabitants, both young and old, keeping us and the listeners entertained.

4) By now, our fame had spread widely through London's underground. Scouting for future locations, I remember going to a squat in an impressive old mansion house on the corner of Parkhill Road and Haverstock Hill. When we told the squatters who we were, and why we were there, their faces lit up, and they declared with smiles that they were totally chuffed, and honoured to be chosen. The crew became friends with the multi-cultural inhabitants right off and some excellent non-troubled broadcasts emanated from that safe haven.

Our Very Own Eviction

WELL, IT WAS BOUND TO HAPPEN. In the summer of 1975, the Royal Borough of Westminster, the owners of our little house-cum-radio studio on Alperton Road, finally served us with an eviction notice. We woke one morning to a loud knocking on the front door, and I looked out of my second-floor window to see three men standing on the doorstep. They shouted up that they were delivering said notice, which they then thrust through the letterbox. We could have ignored the papers and moved elsewhere, but out of curiosity, we decided to go to the eviction hearing a few weeks later. From what we'd heard by others who had been through this process, we could get at the very least a month's grace, just for bothering to turn up.

The proceedings were held at a beautiful courtroom on the west end of the Nash Terraces near Regents Park. When the clerk read out the official notice, I was most upset that the bailiffs, during their description of the serving of the notice, described me as "bald" when I still had a bit of hair on the top of my head at that time! When it was my turn to speak, I let them know my displeasure.

Sharon, Keith, and I, the three household members in the dock, each gave our pre-rehearsed, earnest, and legitimate reasons for squatting. For a change of pace, I decided to go on the attack, and threw back a question to the judge. "Your Honour," I said politely, "How do we know they are the rightful owners of that building? Where's their deed to prove it in the records?" The judge started upright in his ornate seat, and appeared to be quite taken aback by that question. After about ten seconds of thought, he shuffled the file in front of him, rubbed his chin with his hand, and said: "Hmmm. An interesting legal point, one that no one has ever asked me before..." My hopes soared for an unexpected legal glitch, until he added: "...but I'm going to ignore it!" The judge finally permitted the eviction proceedings and gave us thirty days to leave.

Squatting Stonehenge—Naked

As had been demonstrated the year before when we took over the Queen's Royal Park in Windsor, the squatting movement was no shrinking violet in its disregard of limitations. Its inevitable extension from housing-only to "public" lands was envisioned by its organizers as a publicity masterstroke, one intended to force the government to deal with the very real housing crisis. Even though the movement's sole resources were bravado and *chutzpah*, these they had in spades, and this extension of rights proved a powerful device to bring the scattered fledgling underground communities and tribes together. The flippant leaders of the movement had no fear of the media or the authorities, and skillfully used the government's own ancient squatting laws against itself.

In mid-June of 1975, Sharon and I heard that a free festival was going to squat Stonehenge, so we immediately took a break from broadcasting for the week. Driving down to the monument's site on the rolling Salisbury Plain, ninety miles southwest of London, my 1956 light-blue Standard Vanguard estate car was packed to the gills with our camping equipment. This wasn't going to be all fun, as I brought our cassette recorder for the music, and interviews, that we hoped to record during the event for future radio shows.

Turning off the main London Road, we bumped over a shallow (and most probably fragile) prehistoric ditch, maneuvered through the gap that the Stonehenge Free Concert organizers had opened in a simple wire fence, and drove onto a fallow grassy field, chosen because it was directly adjacent to the ancient stones. A low flimsy two-wire sheep fence separated us from the monument. The squatting organizers had breached this ineffectual barrier, boldly defied the private landowner, and argued with the convening authorities about the need for permits. Concern about this unprecedented activity, involving as it did the most famous prehistoric icon in the world, quickly went up the chain of local legal command; the Constabulary were alerted, and judges roused from their beds.

As you may imagine, the local homeowners and farmers were also up in arms at the thought of scavenging hippies rampaging through their fields and backyards, but with the hordes of people arriving, the authorities didn't bother to protect the stones themselves from intruders during the festival, as back then, there were no entry gates or continuous barrier around the dolmens.

Our friends Dave and Gail, from The Café, were already busy with their mobile cooking equipment when we arrived, and had set up their establishment with three long tables to prepare and serve food and drinks for the attendees. There was always a long, but agreeable line at The Café's tables, and Sharon and I helped by chopping vegetables, cooking rice, and doling out food. My most satisfying task was to make and serve tea, using a giant gas-heated urn. From the many compliments received, I apparently saved quite a few lives during those days and nights.

Latrines were the nearest woods, about 400-yards away. Firewood was very scarce. With no on-site water, whatever liquid you'd thought to bring was the only liquid you had, but people generously shared their food and drink in this entirely peaceful event. By mutual consent, the event became clothing-optional, and several hundred of us took to this circumstance seriously. Working at my kitchen tasks stark naked, despite the sharp knives being wielded, was delightful, with, fortunately, no nasty slips-ups, burns, or unintentional re-circumcisions.

The weather was unusually sunny and warm, which made being unclothed in England a lot more comfortable than usual. Naked and wandering the grassy field, I rejoiced in this new gathering of the tribes, with its connection to the mystical past and the hope for an enlightened future. It seemed as if a whole new way of unconventional, but communal life was forming around me. Interviewing performers and participants in the buff made for a radio first, and even seemed to make the process smoother and friendlier, substituting the old reality-show situation of: "What do you say to a naked lady?" with "What do you reply to a naked interviewer?"

At the first opportunity, Sharon and I hopped over the low wire barrier to the standing stones, and cavorted starkers amongst them as spacey rock music played. There was nothing to stop us from touching, lying down on, or just reveling amongst these ancient survivors. Of course, the Japanese tourists just loved taking pictures of the naked hippies frolicking on the stones. The music (the main reason we were there) was played from three scaffolded stages. Most of the thousands of freaks who had made their way to the festival stayed up listening and dancing until the early hours of the morning.

Hawkwind, already a big name in the progressive music world, was very sympathetic to the squatting movement, and played one evening with their full stage-lighting effects. During the performance, I turned away from the dynamic band to enjoy the psychedelic stroboscopic light from this modern pagan space ritual playing out on the somewhat startled-looking sacred stones.

Stonehenge: The Druids

FOR A NUMBER OF YEARS BEFORE THIS EVENT, I had gone to Stonehenge by myself to celebrate the summer equinox quietly, and to watch the New Druids circle the obelisks in their flowing robes, as incense smoke belched from large brass censers swung on long chains. The yearly expedition connected me with the books and articles I was reading on the meaning of Stonehenge, Ley Lines and other evidence of earlier civilizations on the ancient Salisbury Plain.

The affinity I had for this old ritual and tradition tied in with my childhood, growing up as I did at Parliament Hill Fields. From my bedroom window, I could see, embedded in the gradual grassy rise of the second field in the park, a six-foot tall, two-foot-square white stone obelisk with a pointed pyramid-shaped top. The stone had been placed there many years ago to commemorate the foiling of the Guy Fawkes Gunpowder Plot of 1606, some part of which had occurred nearby.

By increasing custom, that simple white commemorative totem, had for many years been the informal gathering place for Druids who couldn't make it to Stonehenge for the equinoxes and solstices. They would descend from London buses, taxis, and cars, carrying staffs and already dressed in their elaborate priestly robes and headdresses, then stream up the park paths to collect around the stone for their rituals. I became quite fascinated by this regular unusual showy display in post-war drab and dowdy Britain.

A New Way of Life?

ON THE LAST AFTERNOON OF THE STONEHENGE FESTIVAL, Sharon and I packed up our car, and followed some new friends who said they were going swimming in a river near Amesbury. Coming upon a magically archetypal Thomas Gainsborough-like English countryside scene—except for all the naked hippies—we joined in. The friendly grassy banks of the softly flowing river were defined by willow and oak spaced along a shoreline perfect for basking and slipping easily into the silky water. As if to complete the perfect scene, an old stone road bridge crossed the river, just downstream from a parallel wooden weir that created a safe swimming and diving spot. The water was warm, and we all played as unselfconsciously as children. Mounds of wild watercress grew along the banks, and we stuffed bags full of the tangy leaves to take home.

On leaving the local village after buying petrol, I remember seeing a leaflet advertising an appearance by Rolf Harris at a local town. After our experience at such a wild, yet peaceful, festival, the vision of this mainstream and supposedly "safe," form of entertainment seemed so alien. (In 2013, Harris was charged with nine counts of indecent assault and four counts of making indecent images of children).

The euphoria brought about by this spontaneous free festival "happening" provoked us to ponder on the way back to London, whether this new/old lifestyle, in which we were immersed with our hearts, and were espousing on the radio, could actually take hold in the increasingly consumer-orientated world we lived. My rational engineering mind and prior experience probably understood the ultimate futility of that hope, but I had to believe in *something*, and this community was at least trying.

Crashing Concerts: Pink Floyd at Knebworth

ONE OF THE PERKS OF BEING IN THE "ENTERTAINMENT" business was getting free records, comp concert tickets, and interviews with stars and celebrities of the music scene. We soon discovered that the official-looking Radio Concord business cards that we'd gotten printed up, also helped us crash many concerts and events. Back then, compared to the tight systems in place today, security was lax, and bluffing our way into events usually worked, as the promoters and guards didn't want to annoy members of the "Media."

Certainly, the best major concert-crashing coup had to be the occasion on which most of our crew went up to the July 5th, 1975, Knebworth Outdoor Festival without tickets or money. Pink Floyd was the evening headliner, with many other great acts scheduled through the day. As we drove up to the backstage area in a rented van with no side-windows; Graham Barnes and I were up front, and six others were crouched in the back, holding up a blanket behind our seats to block the view. When stopped by the guard at the gate, I showed him my Radio Concord card and cassette recorder, and said we were going to be interviewing celebrities for the radio.

I must have been convincing, as he waved us inside without hesitation. The whole gang cheered softly as we drove to a quieter parking area, where I discreetly let everyone out. A marquee set up on the backstage lawn was furnished with tables laden with delicious drinks and food, and we had fun all afternoon mingling with the stars, their backing musicians, and assorted roadies and hangers-on. In those days, our scruffy selves fit right in with the other rock back-stagers, as old Levi's and ragged clothes were now *de rigeur* for progressive underground stars and fans alike.

I drifted casually around with my cassette recorder and interviewed some of the assembled celebrities. The various band members gathered at the sumptuous food tables were quite talkative. Linda Lewis was very friendly, Steve Miller extremely surly, and folk-rocker Roy Harper as enigmatic as ever. I was too intimidated by Captain Beefheart to even try to speak with him. As the sun set, we found places in the audience to watch the Floyd spectacle, savouring our crashing success.

How Many Pirates it Takes to Hijack the Albert Hall

OVER ABOUT A FIVE-YEAR PERIOD, my friends and I perfected the art of crashing the Royal Albert Hall. At that time, in addition to the more elevated entertainments, The Hall was producing large rock concerts with the biggest stars (that lasted until a raucous Who concert in the early 70s that led to a "pop and rock ban"). One evening, a group of us, having failed to score tickets for a concert, were dejectedly rambling around the circular perimeter of the building, where the many entry doors led up to the different audience levels. Usually all of them were guarded on concert nights by sour old-time uniformed attendants, obviously used to a more genteel clientele, who took the tickets and conscientiously locked the doors once the event had begun.

During our stroll, I spotted a half-glassed side door that was slightly ajar. I crept over, and saw nothing but an empty stool protecting the door against intruders. I called the lads, and we nervously tiptoed up some long stairs, which brought us to a tier of private boxes. We started trying the handles; a few were locked, and some were occupied, but then, as the music was already beginning to crash around the hall, we found an empty box, and enjoyed the concert in velvet luxury.

We had inadvertently discovered that it was the habit of the door guardians, once the event had begun, to adjourn *en masse* to their cafeteria for a cuppa and a natter, but for some unknown (to us) reason, they always left a single (never the same) door slightly ajar. Armed with this knowledge, we attended literally dozens of free concerts at the old Albert, featuring performers that we could never have afforded to see on our meager wages, such as the Pink

Floyd, Led Zeppelin, the Moody Blues, Simon and Garfunkel, Santana and Ten Years After. It wasn't always easy; a couple of times we were challenged by attendants before we'd found a box, or managed to mix in with the crowds up in the Gods, resulting in some hilarious Hitchcock-like *39 Steps* chases into the boiler room, and other dark bowels of the Hall.

Only once were some of us actually caught squatting in a private box. It was the premiere concert for Ginger Baker's Airforce, and because there were about twelve of us who bunked in, we broke into two groups and managed to find boxes across the Hall from each other. As I was waving to Mick Lewis and the others in their pirated box, a number of attendants burst into the narrow space, and, after a struggle, manhandled the squatters out. It turned out they'd had the bad luck to crash the private box for the Royal Society for the Blind, and their obvious non-blindness had led to their expulsion.

Big Bust at The Vale - Floods, Commies in the Loo, The Missing Crystal and a Pummeled Piano

RETURNING TO THE AIRWAVES after some much-needed summer cavorting, we experienced our most bizarre broadcast and raid, the second police action at Jeffrey's house at 86, The Vale, in Golders Green.

During the summer Bank Holiday weekend on August 22nd-25th, 1975, we had planned the usual broadcast extravaganza from Friday mid-day to Monday evening. If you'll recall, Concord's very first transmissions and first (unsuccessful) police raid, had taken place at this ordinary two-story semi-detached residence. Jeffrey *really* hadn't wanted to do another broadcast from his place, but it had been nearly three years since that failed raid, and our planned location had fallen through at the last moment. (Almost literally fallen through, as the squatted building we were to use was found to be in too dangerous condition, even for us!)

Yes, we should have known better. To begin with, on the Wednesday before the broadcast, all the houses along Jeffrey's side of the street were flooded by a freak local cloudburst. A small and usually placid spring-fed stream had flowed down from Golders Hill Park, spilled into the Vale, and flooded the homes there to a two-foot depth. The next day, I helped Jeffrey and his mum take all the moveable furniture pieces and carpets out onto the lawn, so that the wood floors and plaster walls could dry out before mold developed. The somewhat surreal sight of formal furniture and carpets scattered randomly on the lawn was an appropriate start to this Dali-esque weekend.

By the time of Friday's broadcast, the house was still quite damp inside, and our booted footsteps clattered on the bare wood floors, as we set up our temporary studio downstairs. Jeffrey's Mum was in an even more agitated state than usual because of a) the flood; b) all the unknown, hairy people wandering around her devastated house; and c) the actual illegal nature of the radio broadcast. Fussing about, she finally went up to her bedroom at the front of the house with Reggie, her eternally pink-butted Jack Russell terrier.

Using the same antenna I had installed that very first time, we started the live broadcast, but now with a three-times-larger transmitter. As a result, our signal could be heard *hundreds* of miles away. Friends called in glowing reports on the quality of reception. Listeners phoned into the familiar, but now even more worn and smelly, phone box at the corner of The Vale and Hendon Way. Many DJs from other pirate stations came in for guest spots, and participants arrived for interviews or to relate news items.

Apart from a few forays to an all-night store for snacks, the crew stayed in the house the entire time DJ-ing, sleeping, and taking turns sitting in a car to watch for the GPO trackers. Jeffrey's Mum occasionally made slow trips downstairs to the kitchen, or to the garden with the dog. As her shambling hunched-over form, clad in a worn purple bathrobe, passed us by, her head would shake from side to side, as she muttered "Oh Jeffrey!" in her slightly creepy German accent.

The shows were going very well until about 9 PM Sunday, when reality came a-knockin'—literally, with an insistent pounding and ringing at the front door, and flashing lights strobing through the living-room curtains. Still hoping it was *only* an army of zombie Belisha beacons, I parted the curtains to see dozens of rozzers and GPO trackers arriving outside in police cars, vans, and wagons. Our street lookouts had either fallen asleep or gone home, and we were well and truly screwed. Jeffrey's Mum was told not to answer the door yet, so she played dumb from her upstairs bedroom window, stalling for time with a hilarious/absurdist "Who's on First?" routine (conducted in several languages and incomprehensible non sequiturs) with the head detective standing below her in the driveway.

Those few minutes gave us some time to 1) panic, and 2) think of how to evade capture. The house, as we discovered, was already blocked in front; reconnoitering the back, we could see the forms of police lurking in the garden amongst the displaced furniture. Although three years ago I had successfully fled over the fence with the transmitter, this strategy was obviously a no-go this time.

Gathering in the front room, frantically trying to figure out how to escape prosecution, we realized—aha!—that the only item that made the transmitter illegal was its little quartz crystal. This tiny item, if discovered, would constitute irrefutable proof that we had been broadcasting illegally on that banned frequency, and the GPO could use it to win a court case against us. Without the crystal, however, the transmitter itself wasn't necessarily proof of any wrongdoing.

Thinking quickly, Jeffrey pulled the tiny object out of its setting, looked frantically around for a hiding place, and spied the small wooden pyramid-shaped metronome sitting on the upright piano (left in the damp house because of its cumbersome weight). Opening the wee door of the metronome, he dropped the crystal into its hollow base and closed the miniature brass door-latch.

We shoved the actual transmitter into the equally bulky drinks cabinet, then, passing the word to Jeffrey's Mum to open the door, sat down, assumed our most innocent faces, and prepared for the onslaught.

A torrent of uniformed and plain-clothed policemen, police-women, and police dogs swept in, with the GPO trackers skulking timidly behind the coppers, in case there was any trouble with this "dangerous bunch of revolutionaries." As we were also the nominal "radical hippie" station, they'd brought dogs along to search for illegal drugs, but, as per our usual policy, we had no contraband in the broadcast location.

The plainclothes detectives sent the boys in uniform off to search the house, and the investigators started in on their usual intimidation techniques, the first being the old "divide-and-conquer" routine. This consisted of taking us separately into the hallway and trying to convince us that the others had blabbed, and you'd better talk, or they'd go harder on us. Knowing that they had nothing on us as yet, we easily resisted their ineffectual attempts.

Then, with a shout of glee, the GPO agents found the transmitter in the drinks cabinet. Their joy soon turned to anger after a closer inspection—the telltale crystal was not inside. We could see that the police were getting very frustrated with us, but even more narked with the GPO. Where were all the subversive, gun-toting, drug-chewing revolutionaries they'd been promised? They'd staged this big expensive raid with all their fancy equipment on a public holiday, with overtime for all, and found nothing they could charge anyone with except possibly lack of carpets!

Jeffrey, always the provocateur, upon seeing their growing frustration, jumped up from his chair and lumbered over to the piano. Standing in front of the keyboard, (the piano stool was outside) and staring directly at the metronome, he began to bash the keys in a discordant Jerry Lee Lewis fashion. The jagged honky-tonk sounds echoed through the damp room, which was now filled with a miasma-tainted scrum of scruffy hippies, GPO trackers,

Metropolitan policemen, policewomen, and police dogs of undefined gender.

Two uniformed officers ran over to Jeffrey and tried to pull him away from the piano; he comically responded with the archetypal stretching motion of someone trying to keep playing the piano while being dragged away. The absurd scene made the Concord crew double up with mirth that was simultaneously uproarious and quite uneasy, since the very object they were looking for was now so exposed. The cops were enraged at Jeffrey's antics and our mocking of them, and, since all this time we had been trying *so* desperately *not* to look at the metronome, one detective suddenly and triumphantly misinterpreted our anxious guilty glances.

"It's hidden in the piano!!" he proclaimed.

With a couple of uniformed men holding Jeffrey, while protesting loudly about being able to play his own piano in his own house, two other officers began to take all the wood panels off of the instrument. To our somewhat agonizing amazement, just before they started to do so, one very large officer leaned over, cupped the metronome in his ham-like hands, and, with great care, moved it to a wall shelf out of harm's way. How we refrained from pissing ourselves with laughter, I'll never know.

Jeffrey's mother conveniently added to the distraction by standing in the doorway wringing her hands, loudly bemoaning the destruction of her piano, as the coppers, with surprising skill, took apart and probed its stringed innards. After searching the instrument down to its lowest dust-ridden bilges in vain, they deliberately left the dismembered pieces for Jeffrey to put back together, perhaps seeing this as some kind of Pyrrhic victory.

All this time, I was sitting on a chair with my feet stretched in front of me. The meanest-looking plainclothes cop, a heavy-set fellow, walked past and deliberately tripped over my feet. "You did that on purpose!" he screamed furiously. Knowing they only needed the slightest provocation to have a go at us, I didn't rise to his ploy. He stopped shouting at me after a while and walked away in a huff. A few minutes later he purposely strode back my way, and, as he walked by, silently trod down hard on my feet and twisted his foot back and forth, glowering at me all the time. Refusing to react to the severe pain it caused (I limped for several days), I just laughed at him, and at his childish "revenge."

While all this foot-stomping, and piano-dismembering was going on, the uniformed police had been searching the rest of the house for other offenders or incriminating evidence, and had found the upstairs toilet door locked. They called down for a detective, who banged on the door shouting, "Come out of there!" Finally, Piers Corbyn, the most radical Commie activist in Britain, strolled out calmly with his Buddy Holly glasses askew, his dark curly hair in its usual messy nest, and his ubiquitous sheaves of leftist papers tucked under one arm.

When the raid began, Piers had been about to start a squatting news session with me, and had slipped away and hidden out in the upstairs toilet. Two uniforms escorted him downstairs to the front room, where the detectives demanded his name. After checking up on Piers' identity on their squad-car radio, the 'tecs came back, presumably having been informed that he was one of Britain's foremost leaders of the hippie, political, squatting underground, and an avowed Trotskyist to boot! The head detective's demeanor noticeably changed from one of annoyance to one of nervousness. Into what Commie plot had the boys in blue stumbled?

Piers, who had been shaken down by the best of the police on so many occasions, proceeded to tie the outmatched detectives up with his glib tongue and knowledge of the law. After much radio-ing back and forth from their HQ, and a little more half-hearted searching of the house, the raid formally concluded. The police helped the GPO men take away our transmitter, record equipment, albums, and tapes, to be held as evidence in case charges were filed (which they weren't).

So, as the door shut behind the last of the invaders, there we all were, left somewhat gob-smacked in the bare living room of the ransacked house, staring at the jigsaw puzzle-like state of the piano. Jeffrey was the first to move. He retrieved the metronome, shook the crystal out, and we all cheered in ironic celebration of our small victory. After cleaning up the house and restoring the piano (with not too many bits left over) to placate Jeffrey's mum, a few of us drove over to Graham Barnes's college dormitory room, to build a new transmitter for the following week's broadcast.

No Home, No Job: Grape Picking and Camden Lock

WITH THE EVICTION FROM OUR HOME and radio studio, our temporary squatting bliss came to an end, but Sharon and I were invited to stay with her friend Dave, who lived across the street in another squat, until mid-September 1975. Dave was a very friendly chap who made his money on the edges of society. His very kind girlfriend Grace had been a prostitute but was out of the game now that she was with him.

In late summer of 1975, deciding to take a break from everything, we went to the South of France to pick grapes—Sharon had done this the previous year and had made some surprisingly good money. We traveled from Dover on the car ferry, with all our stuff packed into my little red Italian "Vignale Gamine" convertible Noddy car, that Dave and I had repaired and painted for the trip. The journey south through the countryside of France in our open-topped car was a pure pleasure, as we traveled beautiful back roads all the way down to the Mediterranean.

One extraordinary day in Central France, we entered a small French village at a T-junction, to be greeted by swags of bunting and many rows of flag-waving people standing behind barricades along the main road. As no police or cones blocked the way, I proceeded to turn onto the town's High Street, which was eerily devoid of cars and other vehicles. The spectators in the crowd were screaming and gesticulating at us unintelligibly, so we waved back, naively thinking they enjoyed seeing a silly-looking car as part of some parade or celebration they were expecting.

Some official-looking men with armbands darted out in the road ahead of us with arms flailing like windmills, which made me think I'd better check out what was happening behind me. A quick glance over my shoulder made everything very clear. About 100 yards behind us, a large *peloton* of racing bicyclists was charging fast and unimpeded through the centre of town. Finally realizing why everyone was so agitated, I quickly accelerated the car down the street, pulling into the next side street just as the bikes swept by, barely missing our rear bumper. A few locals who had seen the incident made some heated remarks, but, thankfully, we didn't understand them.

Through an agency, we found jobs at a small private vineyard and winery near the ancient Roman towns of Montpelier and Nimes near the Mediterranean. The work in the fields was hard going, as we toiled in over 90°F heat, alongside Moroccan migrant workers. The harvest was going on during Ramadan, and our fellow workers couldn't drink, even in those energy-sapping conditions, but they gladly accepted an occasional watery head-dousing from us to cool off. At night, exhausted from the hard work, we'd listen to our small transistor radio in our room in the vineyard-keeper's house, lulled to sleep by the exotic folk music from North Africa, and the vibrant pop music from French, Italian, and Spanish stations that floated out on the soft breezes.

After three weeks of grape picking, we were in the best shape of our lives, and happily headed off to Spain with our bulging wage-packets. Spain and Portugal were a mix of back roads, resorts, deserted beaches, farmer's markets, fresh bread from backyard bakeries, and mountain villages. Our stash of money ran very low because of car repairs, so we decided to head back to England. In Madrid, our timing was not good, as security forces were on display all over the city because General Franco was dying, nearing the end of his ghastly forty-year dictatorship.

During the ride back north, along a remote stretch of road in the mountains, without side barriers to prevent vehicles going over the steep cliff, we encountered an armed roadblock. I should mention that these were the years of the most intense ETA Basque Separatist Movement activities, which included attacking and blowing up many targets in Spain and France. We realized this could be a very dangerous situation for us. Were they friends or foes? There were no other vehicles, roads, or buildings visible, and it terrifies me in retrospect to think how easily we could have been plundered and "disappeared." It was very *scary*, on a whole different level than our broadcast raids, but after a detailed but futile search of our car, presumably for drugs and/or weapons, the heavily armed soldiers allowed us to leave.

On our return to London, Sharon and I moved into a spare room in Mick and Rose Lewis' flat in Finsbury Park, and then found a legitimate flat in Tottenham. For a few months in the summer of 1976, we ran a stall in the original Camden Lock Market, which was then located in the courtyard of the Dingwall's Music venue, next to the Grand Union Canal lock. Between selling antiques, junkshop finds, and odd items discovered in our skip scavenging, we earned enough money to live on. My dad even donated a bag full of old barbering equipment he had used in the course of his fifty years' career; it sold the next day. Camden Lock Market was at the center of the new street cultures popping up around London and I remember seeing, in 1975, the first Mohawk haircuts sported by nascent punks, as they slouched through the curious crowds with chains clanking from their jackets.

Sharon and I settled into a regular humdrum home life for a while, and both of us worked steadily on the radio station, recording our shows at our flat and taking part in occasional live broadcasts. This life was interestingly interrupted by a trip to Switzerland in the summer of 1976 to meet Sharon's friends, who lived in a house up an Alpine meadow between Zurich and Basel. I was most impressed by their drawing-table set out on an open flat deck. Heaven! Working, but in such a lovely environment. That scene always stayed with me, and I still like to do my "indoor" work outside. In the autumn of 1976, I began a job through an engineering agency, and was sent to a position at Thorn-Benham, a medium-sized, mechanical contractors in the West End of London.

Crazy Man Broadcast

LIVING AND PIRATING AS WE WERE in such a transient world, sometimes, despite our best intentions, the broadcast itself had an almost secondary role in the proceedings, and adapting to ever-changing conditions on the fly became second nature to us. The mix of eccentric or outright crazed people we encountered at any particular broadcast, coupled with the often-unstable conditions of the buildings from which we transmitted, made for that what's-next? "X" factor whenever we plugged in the equipment.

In the winter of 1975, one such location was Goldie Court, Hazelville Road, Islington, on a decaying estate of 1930s-era five-story council houses. Concord had been invited by a squatter named Paul to broadcast from Flat No. 50 on the second floor of one of the buildings. This lawless housing estate was indeed a wild place, even if one was just squatting; with yells, screams, and loud noises echoing through the dark and dangerous complex at all hours.

As we brought our equipment into the flat, we met a veritable man-mountain, a heavily muscled scary-looking guy named Trevor who lived up the stairs from the broadcast flat. For a while, he hung out and watched us set up, behaving gruffly friendly, seemingly enjoying what we were doing and even sharing his joint with us.

For the antenna installation, we strung the wire easily between the roof of our building and that of another block across the central courtyard. There was a 360° clear view on the roof, so Concord was transmitting very strongly, and all went well for the first hour or two of a quite "normal" broadcast. Then we began hearing loud noises, crashes, and shouts coming from upstairs. Cautiously, I opened the front door, which faced the interior stairwell, just in time to see a TV set falling past our floor to crash onto the tiles below. This was *not* a good omen, and definitely not the sort of fracas to have going on during our clandestine doings. As we continued our broadcast inside the flat, we were now attentively watching and listening at the open door as more crazed yelling came from above. An armchair flew past our landing on its way to meet the same fate as the previously shattered TV set. None of us wanted to go and take a look, but what the hell was going on?

A few minutes later a terrified young man came tumbling wide-eyed down the stairwell; running to our door, he beseeched us for shelter. He said the big guy had taken some drugs, then some more, and had gone stark staring mad, beating up his friends and smashing his place to bits. We let the poor lad in, then closed and locked the door. More crashes and yells erupted from upstairs, and then the incoherent shouts drew nearer. Trevor was banging on all the front doors as he stumbled down the echoing brick-and-concrete stairwell. To minimize our risk, we stopped broadcasting, turned off the lights, and sat quietly in the dark.

Inevitably, the heavy knocking and screaming rained down upon our door. We kept deathly quiet. The scene reminded me of the film *Run Silent, Run Deep*. Trevor continued his rant for about twenty minutes, bashing at the door and screaming that he was going to kill everyone. In this pre-mobile-phone age, there was no way to call the police. The straining door, with all of us holding our shoulders against it, withheld his last assault, and he finally moved on to the next doors. He hammered on them futilely, and ultimately staggered down to the ground floor. Then all went quiet.

Next, we heard a lot of tyre-screeching and loud shouting from the courtyard; the police had arrived in force. Our only clue to what was happening outside our door was from the noises we heard: first, Trevor stumbling back up the stairs, shouting and banging indiscriminately on walls and doors; then, a minute later, a lot of leather-soled footsteps ringing on the concrete stairs. As they climbed, the police were also knocking on all the doors, but we stayed quiet, not exactly wanting to invite them in for tea.

Once the cops had continued up to the next floor, we felt safe enough to start up the transmitter, and we continued our broadcast with a pre-recorded show on a cassette player, but with all of the monitors and radios turned off. After about twenty minutes of silence outside, Jerry, the young man to whom we'd given shelter, decided to venture back up to his flat and see what had happened.

As we sat in the room, with the transmitter silently broadcasting on the floor by the window, we were just beginning to breathe a little easier, when the device took a sudden irrational leap, jumping a couple of feet into the air, then did it again twice more, only higher. The only thing that stopped our precious glowing machine from flying out the window was its electrical power cord, which was plugged into a now-wildly-swaying light socket overhead.

As the transmitter hovered in mid-air, comically poised between the window and the straining socket, Graham grabbed some pliers and cut the wire, which whipped out of the window and slithered upwards, while the transmitter fell back to the (fortunately carpeted) floor. We later found out from Jerry the neighbour, that one of the police officers on the roof had noticed our antenna, thought it suspicious for some reason, and began to tug on it. Luckily, in the dark, the police couldn't see from which window it came, and we escaped further detection.

After that scare, we quickly shut the power down, turned off the lights, and sat tight. The police came by, knocking on all the doors on their trek back down the stairs, demanding entry into the apartments. Even though all of the flats were occupied, no one answered. Eventually, they must have got bored and left with another squeal of tyres. A few minutes later, Jerry from upstairs knocked softly at the door. He told us that the police had chased Trevor up to the roof, and, after quite a tussle, had finally subdued, handcuffed, and arrested him, and taken him down another stairwell to their squad cars.

Discreetly leaving the flat later that morning, we stepped gingerly around the wreckage of the furniture at the bottom of the stairwell. Today in trendy Islington it would be called an art installation.

Seeing Stars!

AS MENTIONED, APART FROM THE HEAVIER political and social stories we covered, another bonus on the cool side of pirating was our contacts with actual stars of the music scene. In addition to playing the latest music and doing interviews with up-and-coming bands, Jeffrey and some of our DJs were wizard at wangling impromptu interviews with celebrities such as Paul McCartney and David Bowie. On my show, I evolved into conducting longer, deeper interviews, one of which featured Loudon Wainwright III, and his then-wife Kate McGarrigle (with their future son Rufus visibly growing in her tummy at the time) in their Kensington hotel bedroom.

Loudon had been a musical hero of mine since I'd seen him for the first time in 1971. Someone had offered me a spare ticket to an Everly Brothers concert at the Royal Albert Hall. (It was hard not sneaking in for free anyway!) The warm-up act was this Loudon Wainwright III person, and I wasn't expecting much when he shuffled on stage. He started playing, and I couldn't believe my ears. Loudon totally captivated me with his Dylanesque music, his unusual voice, and his sharp biting irony and satire. I was smitten, and when he came to London on tour in 1974, I made sure to get an interview with him for my show.

Then there was Lol Coxhall, a great, but mostly unknown soprano sax player. With his shaved head and wire-rimmed glasses, he looked like Alf Garnett, in *Til Death Us Do Part* (the original British TV version of *All in the Family*). In between gigs, Lol would busk for rent and beer money on the streets and subway tunnels of London. His fellow musicians recognized his brilliance and made sure he played with the great British jazz/psychedelic/rock/classical synthesis bands of the time. At the Roundhouse, I first saw him in the Kevin Ayers and the Whole World Band, along with David Bedford, and Mike Oldfield, the creator of *Tubular Bells*.

One day in the Chalk Farm Pub near the Roundhouse, I struck up a conversation with Lol that became a friendship. Although he looked forbidding, he was a warm chap, lived for his music, and was generous to a fault. He was a family man and was always willing to help others in need. When Robert Wyatt, the drummer/singer of Soft Machine, fell out of a window and broke his back. It was Lol who took Robert in while he recovered. Lol passed in 2011, as did his former bandleader Kevin Ayers.

Andre Bell, one of our useful helpers and showbiz contact, was always introducing the Concord crew to well-known rock personalities and promoting the station with music insiders whenever he could. One afternoon he called and said he wanted to take me to see some friends of his. I met him at Ealing Common Tube Station that evening, and we walked to a large terraced home that faced the Common. Outside the door, Andre finally told me "Who" lived here. "Don't panic," he said, "This is Pete Townsend's parents' home, and we're coming to see his brothers Simon and Paul."

I was speechless, and was almost glad that Andre hadn't told me beforehand, as the Who are very dear to my heart. We were greeted at the door by Pete's mother in her apron, and led into the parlour near the kitchen. As we drank tea and munched on biscuits, Andre introduced me to Pete's younger siblings, who were in a band together, doing the club circuit and working up to a record contract. Paul seemed like a clone of Pete, both physically and in his music and guitar playing. Simon was an incredibly talented keyboardist and multi-instrumentalist, and looked, played and sang like a sixteen-year old Stevie Winwood. The lads were eager to get some exposure on Concord, so we made a date to record one of their live performances for later broadcast. As we were chatting, their father Cliff walked into the house carrying saxophone cases and wearing a tuxedo. Still a working musician, he had just finished a wedding gig and was wanting the dinner his wife was preparing. What a domestic "Who" treat for me!

We all make big mistakes in our lives. In the music-broadcasting world, this was mine. Another Concord music benefit was being put together, and I went to the offices of a Soho-based music agency I knew, to see if I could book some acts who were willing to work just for the exposure. Among the groups they offered for the benefit were Graham Parker, and Easy Street, and the agent got the two main members of Easy Street to come in for an interview. Not being keen on either of the choices at the time, (I know, I know!), I passed on them.

Then they gave me a promotional LP of this new American singer they were trying to get launched in the UK. The agents wanted to place him in a few selected gigs to gauge his potential in England. They played some tracks, which seemed interesting, but a tad rock-retro to me. As this newcomer was a complete unknown in England and likely wouldn't pull enough of a crowd for us, I turned their offer down. I mean, who'd ever heard of a bloke called Bruce Springsteen? On my next show I played more of his LP they'd given me, and discovered that I did actually quite like it. At least I have the consolation that I was probably the first DJ to play the Boss on the radio in Britain. And whom did we book for that fundraiser? I don't even remember.

Seasonally Punk

ONE EVENING IN LATE AUTUMN 1976, Jeffrey and I were sitting in Armando's Falafel Café on Lymington Road. It was the usual noisy, packed evening at Armando's, the kind that the two of us had enjoyed, before or after an event or dance, since we were teenagers. Jeffrey had always wanted to become a rock star, and recently was gigging with all-girl groups backing his singing, guitar playing, and original songs.

As we discussed the Punk movement in London—the Sex Pistols, the Clash, and the accompanying clothing, body and hair-style aberrations—we wondered how long the reactive fashion would last. Deciding he needed to do a punk song to cash in on the craze, Jeffrey ruminated on it but wasn't coming up with anything usable. With a flash of inspiration, I suggested that because it was getting towards the end of the year, punk needed a Christmas song! As Christmas-themed seasonal pop-songs always did well in the British pop charts, that idea piqued Jeffrey's imagination. He riffed on some ad-lib lines at the table for a while, but he still wasn't feeling the poetic inspiration.

Out of nowhere, I blurted: "Put your razor in your ear; put your handcuffs on." Jeffrey's eyes gleamed and he smiled and said, "That's it!" He quickly wrote the rest of the song, with some additional input from me, rounded up some musicians and studio time, and "Punky Xmas," with an utterly forgettable piece of pony and trap called "Nightmare" on the B-side, was issued in time for the holiday rush that didn't come. Most of the five hundred singles he'd had pressed went unsold.

A number of years ago, however, Jeffrey told me that "Punky Xmas" was being included on a compilation of punk songs called *White Dopes on Punk*. Subsequently, it was voted by a punk magazine as one of the ten best punk comedy songs of all time! Ironically, the original single is now worth hundreds of dollars on eBay. Nothing ever goes away anymore, so I've become a punk icon! (in my own mind, at least!).

Thank You GPO!

As I've belaboured throughout, as an illegal organization Concord had to be careful with our security at broadcasts, and certainly needed to discover if we had any moles reporting on us, but we also wanted to hear from our fans and listeners on a regular basis. Apart from phone calls during the actual broadcasts, we kept in touch with the help of those kind souls who allowed us to use their mailing addresses. For the real pirate radio aficionados: the first address was at 10 Quex Road, NW6, at a relative of Jeffrey's. Phillip Bendall's home at 89 Sevington Rd, NW4 was the next mail drop, and the first advertised prominently on air. We then moved it to 91 Park Street, Horsham, home-base of SIRA, the Southern Independent Radio Association. Shifting to Don Stevens' home at 52 Oakfield Road, N4 for a while, we finally used 129 Wilshire Close, SW3, home of a strong supporter of pirates. Whether or not the mail was opened or diverted by the authorities before it got to our mail drops, I don't know, but we sure got reams of letters.

Some missives came from ham radio operators in other European countries like Sweden and Germany, or from other British pirates. The hams, usually quite young, would write to let us know the technical aspects of the broadcast—where and how strongly they picked us up. This feedback was invaluable information for us, in tracking our weekly broadcast-reach performance. As with the broadcast from the home-TV antenna that went all the way to East Germany, we were constantly learning about the quirks of broadcasting on MW.

If the writer included a SASE, I would send a reply and a few bumper stickers. A lot of mail was just from typical young radio fans who enjoyed our music and information. Some letters were for specific DJs, wanting them to play a request, and others were from those who wanted to be interviewed or get their organizations publicized. With our varying transmitter size and antenna quality, we had no idea how many people tuned into Radio Concord on a regular basis, but from the phone calls during the broadcasts, and the mail afterward, we were elated and humbled to have such a large, loyal, and geographically wide audience.

Some fans were of a different sort altogether; a creepy letter came from a man who had been dubbed "The Bishop" by the British tabloid newspapers. He was in Pentonville Prison in North London, doing long time for performing all sorts of disgusting acts with minors while posing as (and dressed as) a Catholic bishop. His trial had been extensively covered in the newspapers a few years before, so I knew who he was. In his wordy missive to us, he told us that he listened to our station in his solitary cell, and wanted to record some shows for us on his cassette player, so we could broadcast them and have people write to him. As he had sent the stamps for return mail, I sent him some bumper stickers to put on the wall of his cell and said I'd let him know. Lord Amory wanted the letter for some reason, and I didn't see it again.

With a live broadcast there were always plenty of phone calls during prime times to keep ourselves awake, but to encourage callers in the middle of the night, we would create silly contests. To show the insanity of it, early one morning, broadcasting from a squat near Holloway Prison, I used a burnt-out light bulb from the location as a prize. The phone rang off the hook and I dutifully carefully wrapped the bulb and sent it off to the excited winner. On another show, a draft card given to me by my friend George in America went at record speed at 3 AM. As a regular weekly challenge, I would play the very first note of a song for listeners to identify, and was constantly amazed at the prowess of the music mavens at any time of the night or day.

Of course, with silly contests to get people to call, the coarsest ones always elicited the biggest response. Gleaning from old broadcast logs, a couple we deployed was the "Funny Name," and the "What Noise Was That?" contests. "Keith Hunter farting," and, "a tin of Felix cat food scraping against a plastic boater" were listed in one log. (I don't know if either was the correct answer, or even the question!) Easier to judge perhaps, was the "Disease of the Week" contest, with entries listed on one broadcast log as: Gerry: athlete's foot; Jeremy: broken fingernails; Penny: whooping cough; Bill & Jeff: anal warts; Maxwell: typhoid; Johnny: gonorrhea; and Angela: shingles. Sadly, there was no mention of the "winner."

Rolling Stones Rehearsal

Even during our pirate days, Jeffrey and I were, above all else, still primarily music fans, and luckily for us the 1970s were a vintage era for progressive rock & roll. Going to see noted bands and singer/songwriters at festivals, concerts, clubs, and TV shows was a constant delight; but this next escapade, was quite different.

On a warm August afternoon in 1976, I got a call from Jeffrey: "We're going to Twickenham Film Studios tonight!" he said. It seemed that a film-editing friend of his had got word to him that the Rolling Stones were rehearsing there on a soundstage. This was a few days before their August 21st appearance at the annual Knebworth Festival just north of London. Jeffrey picked me up in his funky Citroen 2CV, and we puttered slowly to the suburbs of southwest London.

Twickenham Studio's heyday had been in the 1940s and 50s, but it was now rented out for whatever anybody wanted to do there. Arriving after dark, we stumbled our way among the many film buildings and hulking sound stages until we heard faint music coming from one of the latter. It turned out to be a heavy-rock band called Lone Star, who were rehearsing for recording an album, but they were able to tell us where the Stones were.

All the doors in the building we sought were closed; no noise or light came from inside. Fortunately, there were no security guards to be seen, and we dragged open a heavy soundproof door just in time to hear the unmistakable piano riff of "Let's Spend the Night Together" from within. Closing the door softly behind us, we tiptoed into a main soundstage area that was set up like a theater, with about 300 cushioned cinema seats. Four other people sat in the middle of a row about a third of the way from the back, so we decided to sit a row in front and to the side of them (safety in numbers). Only then did we dare look closely at the stage.

OMG. On the stage in front of us were the Rolling Stones! Both Jeffrey and I had seen the Stones perform live many times since 1963, but this was a very different, fly-on-the-wall, "Let It Be" moment. Mick Jagger was at the left side of the stage, energetically playing the piano riff. Keith, Bill, and Charlie were scattered haphazardly across the broad stage. What was different, though? Mick Taylor wasn't there! A few days before this rehearsal he had unexpectedly left the group. They'd hurriedly brought in Ron Wood, Keith's old friend from the Small Faces, to fill in for the big show, and Ron was standing on the stage, to the far right of center, near Keith.

Sitting back in the old cushioned seats, we watched rock history. They seemed to be stuck on "Let's Spend the Night Together." Jagger, forcefully controlling the whole rehearsal from the piano, kept starting the song again and again, but it kept breaking down, sometimes after just a few bars, sometimes halfway through. Ron Wood was having a lot of trouble with the rhythm-guitar part, and Jagger was getting more exasperated with every take. Keith would occasionally shamble over to Ron, and facing him, play what was wanted in order to help Ron figure it out on the fly. The show was in two days and this was not looking good. After about an hour's worth of trying, they gave up on repeating the song, in order to run through some other Stones chestnuts before the end of the session.

To give Mick a break on the piano, the group's co-founder Ian Stewart, known as "the Sixth Stone," came onstage for a stretch as the band fiddled with other songs. During the evening Mick would occasionally peer out at the small audience of six with a little quizzical look but never said anything, and the others totally ignored our presence. It was eye-popping to see the guts of this legendary group working right in front of us, hour after hour. Without a doubt, Mick was the taskmaster and leader of the band, always prodding and cajoling everyone to get it right. Keith, incessantly smoking, with his ciggie tucked into the guitar-head when not in use, seemed to be acting as just one of the boys, not contesting Jagger's leadership machismo.

Neither Jeffrey nor I wanted to move and break the spell of the scene before us. The occasional turning of the head to look at each other in disbelief was about all the activity we could muster through the night. I eventually just had to take a loo break, and when I saw that dawn was also breaking, I decided to go home, leaving Jeffrey to watch on. With the Stones' music still ringing in my ears, I walked to the nearest tube station and waited for the morning's first train to arrive.

Swimming in River Near Stonehenge

New Zealand Embassy at Regents Park

Radio Concord Business Card

**Stonehenge Free Festival
1975 poster**

Punky Xmas 1976

**Royal Albert Hall
Crashing the hall**

Stephen Dunifer Free Radio Book

San Francisco Liberation Radio Logo

8

Last Raid &
Return to America

THE WINTER OF 1976-77 WAS MISERABLE, with cold and rainy weather for weeks on end, and the raids (mostly unsuccessful) on the radio station continuing unabated. One evening, Sharon, while walking home from her job at an old people's home, was mugged of her handbag by a young punk. Agency engineering work had me commuting dreary distances across London in the seemingly perpetual dark. My car was giving me mechanical trouble and we had barely enough money to get by.

Then, at the beginning of January 1977, a letter from Sharon's mother arrived at our rental on Mount Pleasant Road, Tottenham. This time, thank goodness, they weren't planning on visiting us the next day! The evening was freezing outside and although we were inside the house, both of us were huddled over our single-bar electric heater in the living room, wearing our thick jackets, hats, gloves, and socks.

Along with the usual pages of family chatter, a newspaper clipping slipped out of the envelope. It showed a front page from the *L.A. Times*, dated the day after Christmas. Above the fold, and dominating the page, was a picture of an L.A. beach packed with people, along with a bold-type headline proclaiming **90° AT THE BEACH!** Looking at this flimsy piece of pulp from America, then at each other muffled up to our ears, we both simultaneously came to the same conclusion. Why not go to California? Since Sharon had been away for over five years and I loved California from my previous visit in 1972, we made the decision that very night.

In the four years since my first visit, the climate in America had changed dramatically with the resignation of Nixon and the end of the Vietnam War. Jimmy Carter seemed to be a populist President-elect who looked at the world realistically. California had a young governor, Jerry Brown, who was prodding the state to lead in environmental changes. We began immediately to make arrangements for the trip; how long we'd be there and what we'd do once there was left open.

Last Bust in 'appy 'ampstead

ALTHOUGH I WAS LEAVING soon, my work with Concord continued, and I was happy that the crew were still eager to keep on with the fight, even with me flying away yet again. For the Easter holiday weekend, just ten days away, we got word of a squat on Templewood Road, at the Vale of Health near Hampstead Heath. A small Concord contingent went to check out the place, that was a walled mansion within a beautifully designed, but overgrown and deteriorating Edwardian-era estate. The house had been squatted by an eclectic mix of artistic characters, and was filled with music, laughs, and politics. Seizing the opportunity of being there early, we strung up the antenna to a tall tree in the dense undergrowth surrounding the house. April 8th, 1977, was the first day of the broadcast, and all was going very well until we got busted—big time.

Taking my turn as a lookout, I was sitting on a garden wall next to my parked car, at the entrance to the mansion's long back access road. Suddenly, without any verbal warning, Concord went abruptly off the air on my car radio. It became obvious that a technical problem was not the issue, as within seconds of that dramatic halt, I saw police and GPO officials running towards me. I, of course, scarpered off in the opposite direction, but since I wasn't wearing running shoes that day, a couple of the police quickly

caught up to me and frog-marched me back to the car. The authorities, most probably recognizing me from my many previous busts,
had obviously scouted out the area well before the raid, and figured
out I was there as a lookout.

At the mansion, the rest of the lookout crew had seen some
unusual activity on the ritzy street near the front of the building,
with men in suits walking around with directional radios perched
on their shoulders. With this forewarning of the inevitable intru-
sion, the crew executed the old pull-out-the-incriminating-wave-
length-crystal maneuver, and fled with the transmitter into the
thick woods surrounding the house. During the ensuing full-scale
police action, the squatting inhabitants of the house played it cool
and claimed innocence when interrogated, saying they "didn't
know it was illegal."

Back at my car, although the GPO officials and police pep-
pered me hard with questions and the usual draconian threats, I
said nothing except to deny everything. The rozzers searched my
vehicle to no avail, and eventually, after much to-ing and fro-ing
on the police radio, took me to Hampstead Police Station in a
Panda car, and left me to cool my heels for a few hours in a small
isolation cell. In an inept attempt to intimidate, they subjected me
to an intense interview of the archetypal good cop-bad cop variety,
but I had trouble knowing which one was which! My skill at par-
rying all their leading questions soon made them realize they'd get
nowhere with me, and the charges to hold me were pretty flimsy
anyway, so they grudgingly let me out to terrorize the decent people of 'ampstead again. No charges were filed.

Going Back to California

FOLLOWING THE HAMPSTEAD BUST, I was less involved with
the Concord broadcasts because of my preparations for leaving
for America with Sharon. As the emerging punk and new-wave
music in London seemed ripe to export, I thought for a while that
I might continue my radio work in the USA by producing a new

British-music show for syndication. Graham Barnes was at college in Plymouth by this time, and I went down there to work with him on the production, and use the Uni's sound studio to make a demo to present. Later, as I waded through listings at the US Embassy library, looking for likely radio stations to carry the show, I realized that, due to the sheer scale of America, I didn't have the time, connections or money to make the syndication scheme work. Reluctantly, I abandoned that idea.

Then one evening, our plans were nearly ruined when our car, stopped behind a previous car accident on the steep gradient of Muswell Hill, was struck at high speed by a drunk driver in a stolen vehicle. The force propelled us across the road, through a brick wall, and nearly into the front window of a house (with horrified people watching inside). We miraculously survived with just a few bruises and cuts.

Wrapping up our lives in England, Sharon and I left for America a few weeks apart in April 1977. We had decided to give the experience of living together in California a try, at least for the length of my visa. After six years of wild adventures, new challenges, much personal growth, great friends made, and so many people encountered, I decided to put pirate radio behind me, and begin the next phase of my life, whatever that might be. A boisterous going-away party with dozens of friends was held at The Flask pub in Highgate, and I bade farewell to my parents at the airport yet again.

After I left, Radio Concord, with Mick Lewis taking the lead, continued regular broadcasting through most of 1977. Their decision to combine with Richard Norris's Radio Celebration from North-West London bolstered the quixotic effort for a while, but there were more and more equipment-seizing raids, and Richard battled the ensuing court cases (and subsequent stiff fines) in vain. In early 1978, after its long valiant run, Radio Concord disbanded and shut down for good.

Back in the USA

SHARON FLEW DIRECTLY TO HER PARENTS IN LA, while I headed to New York with $350 and one travel bag. I was welcomed back by fellow overweight-camp counselor George Deller and Ron Reede, one of my former charges. New York City, then plagued by the infamous "Son of Sam" random street killings, was a strange place to be this time around. No one roamed the streets of Queens at night by car or on foot unless they absolutely had to. *Saturday Night Live* was in its second season and the hottest ticket in town for Ron and his friends. On this trip, I had no personal transportation to get me to California, so I arranged with an agency in Manhattan to convey a drive-away car to LA, where I reunited with Sharon at her parents' home in Woodland Hills.

Soon after her arrival, Sharon had got a job at a hospital in Santa Monica. It didn't pay well, so if we were to make our planned move up to San Francisco, I had to earn some extra money. I put an ad up on a supermarket notice board to the effect that an English housepainter was looking for work, and a day later was hired by a family with a big house up on Mulholland Drive, to paint some of their interior walls and ceilings for $600 plus materials. With that cash in hand, we had enough to buy a dark green VW Bug, and hopefully enough left over for a rental deposit on an apartment. Packing up the car with our few accumulated belongings, we headed north to San Francisco.

Radio Times and Civic Activism in San Francisco

IN 1977, SHARON AND I SETTLED INTO A $105-A-MONTH one-bedroom flat on 16th Avenue in San Francisco's Sunset District, and began our life in a new city. Still hankering for radio involvement, I checked out the community stations in the area and found the Haight-Ashbury Radio Collective. They produced *Out on the Streets*, a monthly show about grass-roots activism and issues, for broadcast on progressive station KPFA-FM. Meeting them was a delight, and I enjoyed the combined seriousness and camaraderie with which they approached their political endeavours. Soon, nevertheless, their methodical approach to radio, with a lot of "process" and criticism/self-criticism elements, had me chafing at the bit. I was more used to the freeform/seat-of-the-pants/pirate radio type of production, and their studied show-making just didn't suit me. Eventually, I did a little work with them, and Sharon became a serious and integral working member of the group.

This productive period saw me obtaining a green card and a job at a small construction-consulting company. In 1979, I started my own business as a construction consultant, with which I carried on until my retirement in 2020. With this new range of experience for me in San Francisco—job, mortgage, wife and child—active radio participation faded out of my life until Sharon and I separated in 1990.

In 1980, I had followed my engineering heart at last, and co-founded a groundbreaking energy management and conservation company with equally passionate business partners Fred Heaton and Jeff Allen. Although we worked on some prestigious projects such as George Lucas' new Skywalker Ranch studios, chronic underfunding, combined with the regressive energy policies of Republican President Ronald Reagan, and California Governor George Deukmejian, squelched that dream five years later. (Forty years later, I feel chagrin when friends and family tell me I was right after all on the whole climate-change and fossil-fuel energy-use thing...)

In 1990, the efforts of American micro-broadcaster and pirate radio pioneer Stephen Dunifer, of Free Radio Berkeley came to my attention. While there were some public and community radio stations functioning in the Bay Area, none of them were the small low-power FM stations that Dunifer advocated. Stephen's efforts rang true for me, echoing my beliefs and my efforts in England. As far as I was concerned, American broadcasting, with its large commercial stations and corporate public-broadcasting network, still provided too narrow a worldview for true free speech.

With some investigating, I discovered that there were already pirate stations scattered around the Bay Area. In San Francisco, Liberation Radio was getting attention, and I could hear their broadcasts quite well, so I got in contact with Richard Edmunson and Jo Swanson of Food Not Bombs, who ran the station from their home near the Cliff House. It was wonderful to find myself once more standing next to a glowing illegal radio transmitter in a makeshift studio, and I became a roving newsman for the station, reporting back from street protests and meetings by phone or with a tape recorder for later broadcast.

After that short but much-needed foray back into pirate radio, my life in San Francisco took me to community activism in other areas: advocating for new parks; renovating existing parks and playgrounds; developing butterfly flyways and butterfly gardens for children; being appointed a member of the SF Parks Department Off-leash Dog Committee, and the City Committee for Redeveloping Treasure Island; then starting community groups to restore historic neighborhood buildings, especially the restoration of the beautiful Sunnyside Conservatory with my co-chair Stacy Garfinkel. During this time, I only showed up on the radio as a guest, or a call-in for one of my particular subjects of civic interest, with nary a thought of having my own radio show again.

In June 2007, after 30 years in San Francisco, I moved with my wife Karen Felker, to the small city of Sebastopol in Sonoma County, California. It's delightful to live in this beautiful area, and receive visits from my family: daughter Rose, a college professor; beloved grandson IssHaq; first-responder son Ronin; and his wife (another) Rose.

And what of my old friend Jeffrey, who sparked that startling pirate-radio episode in my life back in 1971?

Following our radio exploits, Jeffrey's life and career took some interesting twists and turns, to say the least. A short list of his activities includes: being an ITN newsroom gofer; leading a punk band; managing a well-known female rock guitarist; working as a pornographic-chocolate maker; appearing as "the Pigman" in

241

Season 5 of the *Seinfeld* TV show; showing up in a special feature on the *Hard Core* TV-magazine show; allowing his decrepit house-trailer to be featured on the *Blue Collar* TV show; and appearing as a member of the Holocaust Survivors Band; plus some escapades I promised him I'd never allow into print. (Reggie, the pink-butted dog is *not* one of them.)

Some years ago, Jeffrey moved from LA to Florida. And yes, he still calls me up to listen to a new song he's just heard or written. And of course, he's still trying to entice me into wild capers, such as the two of us road-tripping his 1957 pink Cadillac convertible across the country. But it's been a *long* time since he's actually managed to turn me into a fugitive from justice (though not for lack of trying).

California Governator and Jeffrey

Renovated Sunnyside Conservatory

Conservatory Reopening with Mayor Gavin Newsom, Assemblyman Mark Leno, Arnold, and Stacy Garfinkel

Arnold in KOWS Studio

KOWS Bumper Sticker

9

KOWS: Blessed By The FCC!

ONE SUNDAY MORNING IN EARLY 2008, six months after moving north from San Francisco, I was idly perusing the *Sonoma County Gazette*, and spied an ad for a new "Low-Power" (LP) community-radio station that was starting up in Occidental, seven miles to the west of Sebastopol.

LP stations had recently been approved by the Federal Communications Commission (FCC), and KOWS-LP at 107.3 FM (now 92.5 FM) was one of the very first of these to go on the air. The station had begun with recorded programming only, and now they were advertising for local residents to host its live operations. After so many years in the community-activism frays of London and San Francisco, I was feeling the need for another good dose of solid civic involvement. Without any expectations, I theorized that a show on KOWS might help me with my new life decisions, and at the very least, I'd meet some like-minded locals.

I was energized and encouraged by joining other prospective programmers at a crowded KOWS meeting, held upstairs from Occidental's c.1868 Howards Café, next to a tiny radio studio set up in another room. Nestled in the verdantly rugged hills of West Sonoma County, the iconoclastic two-block town of Occidental was nicknamed "The West Pole" by local eccentric Ranger Rick. Whenever I descended into its narrow, wooded valley, it always made me feel as if I were catching sight of a dreamy land-locked Brigadoon. The FM transmitter was located half a mile west at the

Occidental Arts and Ecology Center, a non-profit environmental community, with the antenna eighty feet up a Douglas fir tree. The studio subsequently moved into a church building in Sebastopol, and then to nearby Santa Rosa.)

The discussion at that first KOWS meeting was revelatory, and introduced me to a wide range of delightful local characters inspired by the same ideals. Many were creative types—musicians, actors, comedians, writers—all quite jazzed by this concept, although most had never done a show or even appeared on the radio before. Inducted into the show-host process, I filled out the necessary forms. During the following weeks, inductees received some basic training at the board, and my first two-hour show was scheduled for the next Friday at 7 PM.

So, PICTURE ME NOW, AT 6:59 PM ON MARCH 7TH, 2008, waiting to go on-air. I've got large headphones clamped over my ears, and a boom microphone jutting under my nose. I'm sitting nervously at a supposedly "modest" sound-mixing board with a still-confusing array of control sliders and knobs. The cheap analog clock hanging slightly atilt on the wall is ticking down to seven, and my heart is racing ahead of it in anticipation/trepidation. Should I even be doing this again?

This time around, my intro music is set up on a disc snuggled inside a CD player, not on a balky old turntable. There's no mystically glowing cobbled-together transmitter, no loops of wire to string, no possibility that, at any moment, the door could be splintered by axe-wielding policemen accompanied by snarling dogs; (Sigh!). Reflexively, I fiddle with the sound levels on a board that I could only have dreamed of back in my days at Radio Concord. My first track "Big Shot," by the Bonzo Dog Doo-Dah Band is lined up. The equipment is ready.

Before this debut show, my KOWS trainer had asked me what on-air name I would use. Not having thought about it, I vacillated between using my real name and inventing a really fake one. Splitting the difference, I'm calling myself "Arnoldo." If I'm up to snuff tonight, and approved for a regular show, I'm hoping to share with this new community my experience, knowledge, laughter, and all the music that I love.

I'll play the Beatles, of course, but also George Formby, Peter Sellers, Eddie Cochran, Nick Drake, Noel Coward, Beyond the Fringe, Sparks, Syd Barrett, Moondog, the Clash, and much more of my quirky collection. Some lesser-known British singer/song-writers will also get a spin, plus lots of comedy, and my other deep love, ska. I'll regale my listeners with tales of the performers and the times they lived, along with stories of my own youth and pirate radio exploits in London so many years ago (but now, after writing this, seeming just like yesterday). I've chosen a name for my show that's based on its intro theme song; I'm ready.

The clock's hand ticks up to 7 PM. I press a button, and the zany lyrics of "Tommy's Holiday Camp" bounce gloriously out onto the airwaves once again.

I'm back.

**Concord Crew Having a Pint in 2017
Arnold, Dave Robbie, Simon Newbury and Mick Lewis**

...and the Outro

NEARLY TWENTY YEARS AFTER STARTING this memoir project whilst recovering from a badly broken ankle, I'm finally
writing the "outro" of my experiences with British pirate radio in
the 1970s, and its recent American community radio reprise. Even
now, over six hundred legitimate KOWS shows later, that euphoric
feeling remains the same every time I get behind the mic. This second chance in radio has enabled me to interview some of my own
youth's musical heroes, promote local performing talent, and focus
on important community, county, state, national and world-wide
issues.

Apart from the joy of a radio program that nowadays can be
heard around the world by streaming online, it's also, just like my
pirate days, the happiness of real friends made, events shared, people met, and knowledge gained. And, as I experienced with Radio
Concord, if I'm really lucky, perhaps even lives are changed.

The enduring, and in fact, growing power of broadcast radio
is a continuing marvel around the world. Of course, the delivery
methods have changed since my MW-only days in England. First,
FM provided better quality sound, and then fast computing-power
brought us web-streaming, satellites, podcasts, and apps like
Spotify, Google, YouTube and Facebook. With these access plat-
forms, virtually all audio is now available, at all times, anywhere
in the world, to all who have a connection. (But it didn't come soon
enough to save me from lugging those heavy milk crates filled with

vinyl albums to every pirate broadcast!) With all these new over-whelming choices, radio stations can still help make sense of that cacophony by filtering and curating the information down to a meaningful, personal, or community level.

Certainly, as an awful reminder of terrestrial radio's continu-ing importance, we saw in 2017, 2018, and again in 2019 and 2020, the four most expensive natural disasters in California history, all of which happened to occur in KOWS' own broadcast area. For instance, in 2017, fast-moving wildfires resulted in wide-scale evacuations and power outages that knocked out all cell and wi-fi systems in and around the fire zones, disabling all the digital alerts to cellphones. With few homes having landlines now, inhabitants had no idea what was happening until emergency services person-nel came to evacuate them…or tragically not.

The only communication available from the outside world to those trapped in those fire areas were the few local terrestrial radio stations, both commercial and community, that were still on the air. KOWS stayed on-air, broadcasting information and news on the fires, and interviewing government officials during the onset and aftermath of the conflagrations. Now in 2020, the whole world is dealing with the grave COVID-19 pandemic. In California, TV and radio stations are considered 'vital' and are among the few businesses still able to operate during a complete shutdown. With that remit, we're providing life-saving information from home-show productions, or still going live in the studio if the show host is healthy.

May we learn from those disasters that terrestrial broadcast-ing doesn't have to go the museum-exhibit way of the Morse code and the FAX. For over one hundred years, radio has been such a simple, inexpensive form of communication, available to all, in every country, for good and bad, with the choice to listen or move that dial always ours.

A phone call from a friend in 1971 changed my life forever. From that single divergent point came pirate radio, squatting, sub-lime cultural and music experiences, moving to America, wives, children, a grandchild, lovers, friends and new opportunities. How would my life have unfolded without pirate radio? I have a feeling that it would have been nowhere near as interesting, exciting or impactful.

Thank you for reading about my life and times as a radio pirate and all those that sailed with me. I hope that you too will discover your inner pirate and make a difference in this world.

Arnold Levine
Sebastopol, California
October 25th, 2020
Show website: www.tommysholidaycamp.com
On: www.kowsfm.com every Friday 7-9 PM PST
Book website: www.bannedbythebbc.com
Facebook: www.facebook.com/bannedbythebbc.com

Acknowledgements

So many thanks to all my family and friends who loved and tolerated me during those years, and the years since, and have encouraged me to complete this book.

For her belief in the book, support, and editing help, eternal gratitude and thanks to Amie Hill. Plaudits to publisher Waights Taylor Jr. for his patience with me during my first book project.

Of course, a very special thanks to my friend Jeffrey Schwarz, whose phone call started it all, and with whom I've also shared so many adventures apart from pirate radio. Thanks to all those brave souls who helped with Radio Concord, and made it so special, and of course, to all the other pirates still fighting government control of free speech, and suppression of community voices everywhere. We have nothing without it.

I am indebted to the following for use of their material in this book: the Intro... and ...Outro Chapter titles courtesy of The Bonzo Dog Doo Dah Band; and Banned by the BBC! courtesy of Three Bonzo's and a Piano.

Other pictures, newspaper clippings, and graphics are from the author, friends, and family historical collections.

Glossary of Some British Words and Slang

Belisha beacon	Yellow flashing light on top a black and white pole at pedestrian crossings
Berks	Jerks, idiots
Bikkies	Biscuits (Cookies)
Boffins	Scientists, clever people
Bonnet	Hood of car
Bumper	Bountiful
Bunked in	Got in for free, illegally, or secretly
Butties	Northern England word for bread and butter with filling (sarnie for sandwich)
Cuppa	Cup of tea
Earth	Electrical ground
Estate Agent	Real Estate Company
Knee-trembler	Sex standing up
Lark	Spree, harmless fun, unplanned event
Loo	WC, Toilet, bathroom
Maisonette	British two-story apartment in larger block of flats
Mews	Alley or road to stables between terraced or row houses
Narked	Annoyed
Peardrop	Shaped like an old British boiled sweet that looks like a pear

Plimsoll	Rubber-soled athletic shoe
Puddin' basin haircut	Hair cut the same length all the way around the head
Rozzer, Bobby, Bill	Police
Scarper	Run away, escape
Scouse	Someone from Liverpool
Scuppering	Sinking, sabotaging
Skip	Debris box
Snog	Kiss
Starkers	Naked
Tommy	Name for a generic British soldier
Tonibell	British ice-cream van chain

Printed in Great Britain
by Amazon